JAVA GENESIS

ROGER DUKE
ERIC SALZMAN

Addison Wesley

Addison-Wesley—SprintPrint is an imprint of Pearson Education Australia Pty Ltd. It has been established to provide academics throughout Australia and New Zealand with fast and efficient access to the printing, warehousing and distribution services of Australia's leading educational publisher, ensuring a smooth supply channel to your campus bookseller.

Texts published under the **Addison-Wesley—SprintPrint** banner do not undergo the rigorous editorial and development processes normally afforded to Pearson Education Australia titles. While every effort has been made by the author to ensure the accuracy of the title, Pearson Education Australia does not take responsibility for the editorial quality of SprintPrint titles.

For more information about the **Pearson Education Australia—SprintPrint** service contact the Editorial Department, Pearson Education Australia, Unit 4, Level 2, 14 Aquatic Drive, Frenchs Forest, New South Wales, 2086.
Telephone: 9454 2200.

This material was produced with the assistance of the Learning Resource Development Unit of the Teaching and Educational Development Institute, The University of Queensland.

Acquisitions Editor: Cath Godfrey

Printed in Australia by Ligare Pty Ltd, Riverwood, NSW.

2 3 4 03 02 01 00

ISBN 0-7339-9890-9

Addison Wesley

An imprint of Pearson Education Australia.

Contents

Preface

Why another book on Java? Anyone looking through the shelves of the local bookseller could be forgiven for concluding that the world is already well supplied with Java books.

Java Genesis came about because, although many of the available Java books are excellent in their own way, we were unable to find a text whose approach to Java was in sympathy with the way we felt it should be presented to beginners.

The aim of *Java Genesis* is to explore the art, science and pleasure of programming in Java by taking an experiential approach to learning and using the Java language. Programming can be a tremendously challenging and exciting experience, and programming in Java in particular can be a lot of fun. This book has been designed to be enjoyable and exciting while tackling the challenge of presenting the fundamentals of Java programming.

The approach

Java Genesis adopts a problem-based learning approach to foster self-directed exploration. The reader is encouraged to:

Explore
: Be curious and look for new things to discover. If something is puzzling, explore and try to understand it.

Experiment
: Try new things and see what happens. Form hypotheses about why code works; make changes to code and observe what happens; based on observation, either confirm or change hypotheses and continue to experiment. Use the computer as an experimental instrument.

Experience
: Run code as part of the process of understanding and using it. Try modifying the code in various ways to discover the effect. Programming is a skill based on practical experience.

Extend

Emulate existing code when creating new applications. Discover that code reuse and extension is an invaluable programming skill.

At the core of *Java Genesis* is a collection of over 160 carefully crafted problems. It is obvious that it is only through practice that a computer language, like any languge, can be mastered. Consequently, *Java Genesis* is built around programming problems. These problems are not appended to the end of chapters but are integrated throughout the text. Indeed, we see them as the most important part of the text.

The problems are designed not only to illustrate concepts but to suggest ideas for investigation. Concepts are deliberately introduced first in problems and only later discussed and developed. The aim is to encourage the reader to question, explore and experiment. In *Java Genesis* we want to break away from the dull and dreary approach whereby concepts are introduced and discussed and then exercises are set. We want the reader to discover and be excited by ideas and concepts before reaching the formal treatment in the text.

The problems vary from the quite easy to the moderately difficult. However, in all cases the problems are well within the grasp of any serious reader. This is not to say the reader won't have to carefully mull over ideas and think through issues. We have assumed the reader actually wants to learn Java and fully accepts that this requires dedicated effort. It is our aim to ensure that the reader feels fully rewarded in terms of the knowledge acquired and the pleasure and satisfaction obtained from the creation of interesting programs.

In our view, a problem is incomplete without a solution. Nothing is more unsatisfactory than to receive no feedback after the effort of attempting a problem. It is not just a matter of supplying a solution; the ideas and strategy leading to that solution are just as important. Frequently we want not the whole solution but just a pointer so we can persist in an attempt to solve the problem. With this in mind, the problems in *Java Genesis* come with graded hints leading to full solutions. These hints are designed not only to help the reader who is having difficulties, but to offer alternative suggestions and discuss issues that arise. There are several hundred pages of hints in HTML (hypertext) format on the CD-ROM accompanying the book. *Java Genesis* is ideally suited to the independent learner. Everything the serious student needs for a firm foundation in Java programming is here.

We have adopted the 'inverse curriculum' approach. In the early chapters we make use of existing classes to create relatively sophisticated applications. By making full use of class reuse we can do this without the need to know the details of the classes we use. Instead we need only know the messages that can be sent to a class or object, and the way that class or object will respond. In later chapters, as our understanding of Java develops, we open up these classes and begin to understand and emulate their underlying code.

Graphical applications are emphasised throughout. There is an immense satisfaction and sense of achievement in coding applications that display and animate simple graphical figures. In Java this is relatively straightforward, particularly if the inverse curriculum approach is adopted. Impressive applications can be coded almost from the beginning. Throughout the book all graphics programming is done using Swing.

Intended audience

Java Genesis is aimed at the Java programmer beginner. We assume the reader has some background in secondary school basic science and mathematics, and has some computer literacy in that they can browse a file system and edit text files. No prior exposure to programming is assumed. We successfully use this book as the core of a first-year university introductory Java programming subject.

Although aimed at the beginner, this is not to suggest that the book would be of interest to only a novice programmer. On the contrary, programmers at any level should find the approach invigorating. Nevertheless, it is to the beginner that the book is deliberately addressed, and it is the beginner that we have kept in mind at all times while writing the book.

To be quite clear, *Java Genesis* is not written as a reference book. Of course, if you want to find out about the syntax of a for-loop, or review Java's event-handling mechanism, you will find the material here in what we believe is a clear readable form. But the book is written to enable the Java language to be mastered and used. Hence we have placed the topics in the order in which we believe they should be discovered by a beginner. Throughout the book issues are often revisited in the light of the experience and insight gained.

As much as possible we have resisted the temptation to cover everything. Java is a huge and growing language, and in our experience the beginner is often overwhelmed by the sheer multitude of issues. We have concentrated on what we see as the core concepts. Any reader who seriously tackles the problems in this book will reach a stage where they should be able to successfully absorb other advanced language features as required.

Brief overview

Taking a very wide perspective, *Java Genesis* can be broken into five broad modules.

The first three chapters set the scene and begin the exploration. They introduce the fundamental object-oriented ideas of message passing, class and object, as well as the most basic Java programming constructs such as variables, assignment statements and iteration using the for-loop. Primitive types, arithmetic expressions and strings are also introduced.

Chapters 4 and 5 further explore the basic Java language constructs. Here we meet the while- and do-loops for general iteration, Boolean types and expresions, and the important array data structure.

Chapters 6 to 8 delve deeper into the object-oriented constructs that underpin Java. We explore methods, objects, classes and inheritance. A solid understanding of these core concepts, although more difficult, is absolutely essential if Java's event-handling and graphical user interface model is to be fully appreciated.

Chapters 9 and 10 explore in detail how graphical components and events are handled in Java. Our approach to adding event handlers is non-traditional: from the first we make use of the anonymous inner class construct rather than interfaces. In our opinion, the architecture that results is cleaner and more intuitive. Interfaces are introduced later only for completeness. We use Swing rather than raw AWT. The graphical user interface (GUI) components we consider are action buttons, text fields and labels. This is a deliberate limitation; there are a plethora of Swing components but by concentrating on what we see as core and representative examples we can lay foundations enabling any other GUI component to be mastered if and when the need arises.

Finally, Chapter 11 explores the issue of exception handling and file I/O, and Chapter 12 introduces applets. We have chosen to concentrate on applications rather than applets in the body of the book because we believe Java's future lies in its role as a mainstream programming language. Web programming is an exciting activity, but it is only one aspect of Java. In any case, converting applications into applets is straightforward.

Expected outcomes

On completion of *Java Genesis*, the reader will have:

- thoroughly explored the Java programming language; in particular, will understand the basic syntax and semantics of the language and the basic control structures, and be able to directly apply these concepts to write Java programs;
- a thorough understanding of graphics and event handling, and have explored and applied some basic graphical components such as action buttons and text fields;
- a good working knowledge of the library classes to be found in the Java SDK, and appreciate how these classes are reused when constructing applications;
- explored a few of the software algorithms traditionally used to implement basic procedures, and be able to apply these algorithms;

- a thorough understanding of the object-oriented concepts of message passing, methods, abstraction, information hiding, delegation, polymorphism, class, instantiation, and inheritance, and know how to apply these concepts when programming in Java;
- experienced the crucial role of underlying architectural concepts within software systems, and be able to both recognise common architectural structures within existing software systems and apply them when constructing applications;
- recognised at an introductory level the frequent occurrence in software of basic patterns of code and design, and be able to make use of these patterns in applications;
- appreciated at an introductory level the wider process of software construction, and in particular experienced how informal user requirements are translated first into semi-formal scenarios, and then into implemented code using the Java programming language.

Acknowledgements

Java Genesis would not have been possible without the full support of the first-year programming teaching team within the Department of Computer Science and Electrical Engineering at the University of Queensland. We particularly thank Jay Burmeister, Leesa Murray and Josiah Poon. Our thanks also to the many students who enthusiastically embraced the exploratory problem-based approach and offered invaluable feedback.

We gratefully acknowledge the contribution of Rachel Thrum and the Learning Resources Development Unit at the University of Queensland for the icons used in the margins of the book.

Roger Duke **Eric Salzman**
University of Queensland
January 2000

1 Getting started

Prerequisites

Before starting Chapter 1 you will need to be familiar with the operating system on your computer and understand the way folders and files are organised. You will need to appreciate the difference between folders and files and know how to:

- navigate the file system
- open and close folders and files
- create new folders and files
- do basic text editing
- save files in specific folders
- move folders and files within the file system

Overview

In this short preparatory chapter we will describe how your computer needs to be configured so that our exploration of the Java language can begin in earnest. To be specific, you will need to have Java's Software Development Kit (SDK) and the *Java Genesis* folders and files installed on your computer. You will have the opportunity in this chapter to test your configuration by running a couple of Java applications and compiling some Java code.

1.1 Installing Java

If the Java 2 SDK (or alternatively JDK1.2 as it was previously known) is not installed on your computer, you will need to do so. The latest Java SDK can be obtained directly over the internet from the Sun website (at `java.sun.com`).

We strongly recommend that you install the complete Java system including the documentation and source code. Installation instructions are given on the Sun website.

1.2 Installing the *Java Genesis* files

The complete folders and files needed for the *Java Genesis* problems are on the accompanying CD-ROM. You will need to install these files on your hard-drive. Instructions for this installation are on the CD-ROM.

If *C*, say, is the name of your hard drive, the structure of the *Java Genesis* folders will look like this:

```
C: — genesis ─┬─ Hints
              ├─ packages ─── genesis
              └─ projects ─┬─ Chapter 1
                           ├─ Chapter 2
                           ├─ Chapter 3
                           ├─ ...
                           └─ Chapter 12
```

The folder *C*:*genesis**Hints* contains all the problem hints (see the discussion in Section 1.5). The folder *C*:*genesis**packages**genesis* contains all the files required for the *genesis* package (the role of this package will be explained in later chapters). Inside each 'Chapter' folder are the folders required for the problems in that chapter. For example, the *Chapter 1* folder contains two folders, *Pushing Puzzle* and *Sliding Tile Puzzle*. We will look at the files inside these folders in Section 1.4.

1.3 Using an IDE

Although Java code can be created using a text processor and then compiled and run using the command line, we strongly recommend that you use some appropriate integrated development environment (IDE) to create Java applications. One IDE which we have used very successfully with the material in this book is Kawa. You can install Kawa from the *Java Genesis* CD-ROM. You will be able to use Kawa free for up to 30 days after which a small license fee is payable to Tek-Tools Inc (see `www.tek-tools.com`). For details of installation see the CD-ROM. All the problems in this book can be coded, compiled and run using the Kawa IDE. However, the book is independent of which (or any) IDE you use. If you have your own favourite IDE for developing Java applications, use it by all means.

1.4 Running a Java application

Open the folder *C:\genesis\projects\Chapter 1\Pushing Puzzle.* In this folder there are 8 files, namely:

- three *.java* files:

  PushingPuzzle.java *PushingFrame.java* *PushingPanel.java*

- four *.class* files:

  PushingPuzzle.class *PushingPanel.class* *PushingFrame.class*
  PushingFrame$1.class

- one *.kawa* file:

  PushingPuzzle.kawa

Consider the *.kawa* file first. If you are not using the Kawa IDE you can completely ignore this file. It creates a Kawa project from the files in the folder. If you are using Kawa, see the CD-ROM for information about how to open and use Kawa projects; we shall say no more about it here.

The three *.java* files contain Java program statements. You can examine these files using any text editor although the program statements will most likely mean very little to you at this stage. As we progress through *Java Genesis* the meaning of program statements like this will become clear. Each of these three files define what is known as a Java *class*.

The four *.class* files are generated automatically by the Java compiler. We will use the Java compiler to compile code in Section 1.5. If you look at the contents of these four files using a text editor you will find they cannot be read directly. In fact they contain what is known as byte code. This code is interpreted by the Java 'virtual machine' when the application is run.

The files in the folder *Pushing Puzzle* together create a Java application. We can run this application by running the class `PushingPuzzle`. This is done by executing the *PushingPuzzle.class* file. Ideally, we do this within an IDE such as Kawa (see the CD-ROM for instructions). If you are not using an IDE the file can be run from the command line, e.g. by typing

```
java PushingPuzzle
```

in DOS if you are working in a Windows environment.

[*An aside*: If you are using the command line in Windows rather than an IDE, you must first ensure your CLASSPATH is set appropriately. For example, you will need a statement similar to the following in your autoexec.bat file:

```
SET CLASSPATH=.;C:\JDK1.2\LIB;C:\GENESIS\PACKAGES
```

In the example illustrated here, Java has been installed in the *C:\JDK1.2* folder; on your system this may be different. *End aside*]

PROBLEM 1: pushing boxes

Open the folder *Pushing Puzzle* and run the class `PushingPuzzle`. A window opens containing an arrangement of 4 squares (boxes), 4 crosses and a red arrow. By using the arrow keys on the keyboard, the red arrow can be used to push the boxes. The aim of the puzzle is to push the 4 boxes until they occupy the same positions as the 4 crosses.

See if you can solve this puzzle. To exit the puzzle click on the 'X' in the upper-right corner of the puzzle's window.

□

File-path conventions

Throughout *Java Genesis* you will frequently come across statements of the form "open the folder *Xyz* and run the class `Abc`". The understanding is that if this statement appears in Chapter *n*, say, then the full path-name of the folder *Xyz* is:

C:\genesis\projects\Chapter n\Xyz

Within this folder will be found the file *Abc.java* and the compiled file *Abc.class*.

PROBLEM 2: sliding tiles

Open the folder *Sliding Tile Puzzle* and run the class `SlidingTilePuzzle`. A dialog box opens requesting a 'Number wide'. Supply a positive integer (e.g. 4) and either click with the mouse on the 'OK' button or simply press the 'Enter' key on the keyboard. Next a second dialog box opens requesting a 'Number high'. As before supply a positive integer (e.g. 4 again). A window now opens containing a rectangular grid of numbered tiles similar to the figure below:

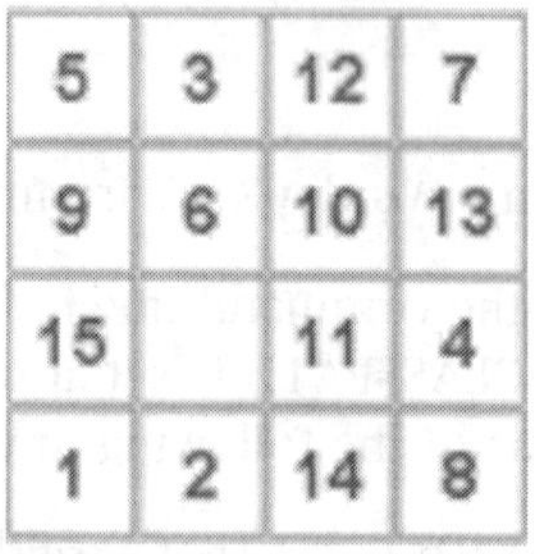

If you click with the mouse on any tile adjacent to the blank position, the selected tile will slide into this blank position.

The aim of the puzzle is to slide the tiles so that they are in number order with tile '1' in the upper-left position and the blank tile in the lower-right position, as illustated in the figure below:

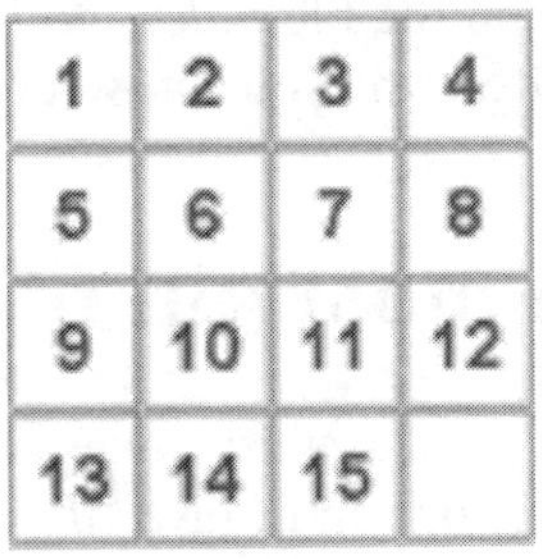

See if you can solve this puzzle. If you press the 'reset' button a new configuration for you to solve will be created.

□

1.5 Compiling Java code

Consider again the files in the *Pushing Puzzle* folder. The code in each of the *.java* files is *compiled* to create the associated *.class* files. Ideally, compilation is done within an IDE such as Kawa (see the CD-ROM for instructions on how to compile code using Kawa). If you are not using an IDE the code can be compiled from the command line. For example, to compile the *PushingPanel.java* file type

```
javac PushingPanel.java
```

in DOS if you are working in a Windows environment.

PROBLEM 3: changing colours

In Problem 1 we saw that if we open the folder *Pushing Puzzle* and run the class `PushingPuzzle`, a window opens containing an arrangement of 4 squares (boxes), 4 crosses and a red arrow.

Try to modify the file *PushingPanel.java* so if this file is then compiled and the class `PushingPuzzle` run as before, the arrow is now coloured blue rather than red. Apart from this the behaviour of the puzzle is unchanged.

Note that although we modify and recompile *PushingPanel.java*, it is still the class `PushingPuzzle` that is run. For help with this problem see Hints.

□

Finding the hints

All problems in *Java Genesis* that require some coding have hints leading to a full solution. These hints can be found in the *C:\genesis\Hints* folder. Open this folder and double click on the file *index.html* to open it within your web-browser. Now simply navigate using your browser to find the hint you require.

1.6 Getting the most out of *Java Genesis*

As explained in the Preface, *Java Genesis* takes a problem-based exploratory approach to leaning how to program in Java. If you want to get the most out of this book we strongly suggest that you:

seriously attempt the problems

We see the problems as the core of this book. The book is intended to be worked through, not just read. Concepts are deliberately introduced into problems before they are fully discussed in the text. Expect to find the problems puzzling at times; rest assured that all will be eventually clarified. We believe that learning a programming language is like learning any other language: jump in the deep end and start using the language right from the beginning. Rules of syntax and semantics then evolve from the practice.

A programmer is really a problem solver. Learning to solve programming problems is a discipline born of a keen desire not to be defeated. When tackling a problem, fight it, think about it, look at it from all aspect, bring what you know to bear, go without sleep and refuse to give in.

use the hints judiciously

If you are to make good use of the hints we have supplied, we strongly urge you to consult them only after seriously attempting a problem. They are there as a last resort, not as an easy way out. Expect most problems to require concerted effort.

Even if you were able to tackle a problem without consulting the hints, we recommend that you look at the hints after completing the problem as they often suggest alternative approaches and discuss related issues.

be curious and explore issues

When creating code you will often find yourself wondering what would happen if you changed the code in various ways. Why not try it and see? Experiment. Enjoy!

Exploring Java 2

Prerequisites

Before beginning Chapter 2 you will need to have installed

- the Java 2 Software Development Kit;
- the *Java Genesis* folders and files.

You will also need to know

- how the *Java Genesis* folders and files are organised;
- how to run a Java program;
- how to compile Java code.

If you are unsure of any of these things, carefully read Chapter 1. Chapter 1 also explains the various organisational and typographical conventions used throughout the book.

Overview

In Chapter 2 we start our study of the Java programming language. We will take a broad look at some Java code and notice what happens when we compile and run the code. For now, we won't examine the code in depth. Like learning any new language, at first you may feel overwhelmed by all the unexplained detail — the code we shall look at is full of special words and constructs whose purpose may well at first appear mysterious. For now, just treat this detail as background noise to be ignored. Be assured that as you progress through *Java Genesis* an appreciation and understanding of the detail will steadily emerge.

2.1 Experiencing Java code

We look at the Java code for a small graphical application, and begin the task of understanding such code, albeit only very informally. The approach is problem based through an experimental process of trial and error; it involves altering the code in various ways to see the effect such alterations have on the application.

Problem:

1 modifying the draw-circle code

2.2 Understanding objects

The idea of an object is introduced and discussed informally with particular reference to objects in everyday life.

2.3 Message-passing in general

Objects communicate by passing messages, and this process is discussed in the general context of everyday objects.

2.4 Message-passing in Java

In object-oriented programming, computation is performed by objects passing messages to each other. The concept of message-passing in Java and the different types of messages and their effects is illustrated through graphical examples.

Problems:

2 sending messages to `SquareFigure`

3 more message-passing

2.5 Classes

The class concept is fundamental in Java and indeed in all object-oriented programming languages. This concept is informally introduced and the general role of a class as a special kind of object discussed.

2.6 Constructing simple classes

The class construct is the basis for programming in Java. Through compiling and running a couple of simple classes, some of the basic constructs of a class are identified and discussed. In the process we look at how information can be sent to the standard Output window or to our purpose-built Transcript window.

Problems:

4 displaying a string in the Output window

5 other strings in the Output window

6 demonstrating the Transcript window

7 other strings in the Transcript window

8 using the class `TextBox` to display strings

2.7 Statement sequences

Code is the name given to the instructions a computer executes. When an application runs, unless otherwise constrained code statements are executed sequentially, working from the first to the last. We look at how simple programs can be constructed using sequential execution.

Problems:

9 sequential print statements

10 sending a sequence of messages

11 constructing a hollow square

Learning outcomes

By the end of Chapter 2 you will have:

- experimented with modifying a given small Java application, recompiled the code after modification, and re-run the application;
- browsed Java code and noticed that information can be gleaned from the code without the need to first have a thorough understanding;
- met the concept of an object at an informal level;
- met the concept of objects passing messages to each other, and the idea that objects can respond in various ways to the messages they receive;
- explored sending messages to some simple Java objects and noticed the effect the messages have upon the objects that receive them;
- met the concept of a class at an informal level;
- constructed a small Java class to perform a simple application;
- made use of the Output and Transcript windows to display output;
- seen how a programming task can be achieved using a sequence of statements.

2.1 Experiencing Java code

In this section we are going to experiment with the code for a particular Java application and so begin the process of understanding and ultimately writing Java programs. Our experiments will involve altering the code in various ways, compiling the altered code, and re-running the application to discover the effects of the alterations.

What we are advocating here is a scientific experiential approach to understanding Java. By altering code on a trial and error basis we can begin to formulate hypotheses about how the code works — hypotheses we can then test by experiment. Furthermore, by studying existing code such as this we can get ideas which we can emulate when writing our own programs. This theme — learning through experiment and emulation — is central to the approach to Java adopted throughout *Java Genesis.*

Let's begin by running the Java application.

- Open the folder *Draw Circle* and run the class `DrawCircle`. A window opens displaying a red circle at its centre.
- To exit the application, close the window containing the circle (by clicking with the mouse on the 'X' in the upper-right corner of the window).

Note: As explained in Chapter 1, each folder associated with Chapter 2 is found in the folder *C:\genesis\projects\Chapter 2.* In particular, the folder *Draw Circle* is found there. The code for the class `DrawCircle` is found in the file *DrawCircle.java* in the folder *Draw Circle.* If you are not sure of the conventions adopted in the book for organsing folders and files see Chapter 1. Details of how to run a Java class are also explained in Chapter 1.

Consider now the code for this application. The folder *Draw Circle* contains three *.java* files:

- *DrawCircle.java* has the code for the class `DrawCircle`
- *DrawCircleFrame.java* has the code for the class `DrawCircleFrame`
- *DrawCirclePanel.java* has the code for the class `DrawCirclePanel`

Here is the code for these three classes:

```
public class DrawCircle {

    /*
    Creates and opens a window of the DrawCircleFrame class.
    */
```

```
    public static void main (String [ ] args) {
        DrawCircleFrame win = new DrawCircleFrame();
        win.setVisible(true);
    }
}
```

```
import genesis.*;

public class DrawCircleFrame extends ExitFrame {

    /*
    Sets the position and size of the window and
    displays an object of the DrawCirclePanel class.
    */

    public DrawCircleFrame ( ) {
        setTitle("A Circle");
        int xWindow = 200;
        int yWindow = 100;
        int width = 400;
        int height = 300;
        setBounds(xWindow, yWindow, width, height);
        setContentPane(new DrawCirclePanel());
    }
}
```

```
import java.awt.*;
import javax.swing.*;

public class DrawCirclePanel extends JPanel {

    /* Paints a solid red circle. */

    public void paintComponent (Graphics g) {
        super.paintComponent(g);
        int xCentre = 196;
        int yCentre = 134;
        int rad = 50;
        g.setColor(Color.red);
        g.fillOval(xCentre-rad, yCentre-rad, 2*rad, 2*rad);
    }
}
```

PROBLEM 1: modifying the draw-circle code

Without concerning yourself with the detail of how the code for the draw-circle application actually works, experiment with altering this code so as to get different effects. For example, see if you can deduce which of the above three classes contains that part of the code responsible for fixing the position and size of the window, and test your choice by attempting to change these aspects. (Don't make too many changes at the one time, or make your changes too big, as you may not be able to deduce what is causing the effects.)

After any modification, before re-running the application you will need to re-compile any *.java* file whose code has been modified. Regardless of which *.java* file has been modified and recompiled, the application is always executed by running the `DrawCircle` class. If your modifications are such that the compiler cannot interpret your code, an error message will be displayed and you will need to correct the code before recompiling. The Java language is quite precise: a program either has a unique meaning or it has no meaning at all. If the compiler cannot fathom what is intended by your code it will indicate via error messages.

Next, try to place the circle somewhere other than at the centre of the window, or draw a larger or smaller circle, or draw a circle of a different colour such as blue or green, etc. Just experiment and have fun.

Try extending the code so that when the application is run two distinct circles are drawn in the window, one red and the other blue.

If you would like a few tips about how to achieve some of the modifications suggested in this problem, see Hints.

□

Note: When you alter a *.java* file the original code is lost as the initial version of the *.java* file is altered to become your new version of the code. If you think you may later want to restore the file to its initial version, copy the original before making any alterations.

The point of Problem 1 is simply to start the process of absorbing some ideas about Java code in an informal way. At this stage you will almost certainly find most of the code unintelligible and will only have vague ideas about how the code does what it does. As we journey into Java and explore more widely you will gain a full understanding of code like this.

The graphic coordinate system

The issue of measuring distances and assigning coordinates to positions in windows arises in Problem 1. In Java, window distances are measured in pixels.

A pixel (from picture element) is the size of the smallest 'dot' that can be displayed on the screen. If your screen has high resolution then a pixel will be smaller (i.e. the dots will be closer together) and consequently a distance measured in pixels will be a smaller absolute distance.

The position of a window on the screen is determined by the coordinates of the window's upper-left corner. These coordinates are measured in pixels from the upper-left corner of the screen. The x-coordinate measures horizontal distance from left to right, while the y-coordinate measures vertical distance from top to bottom.

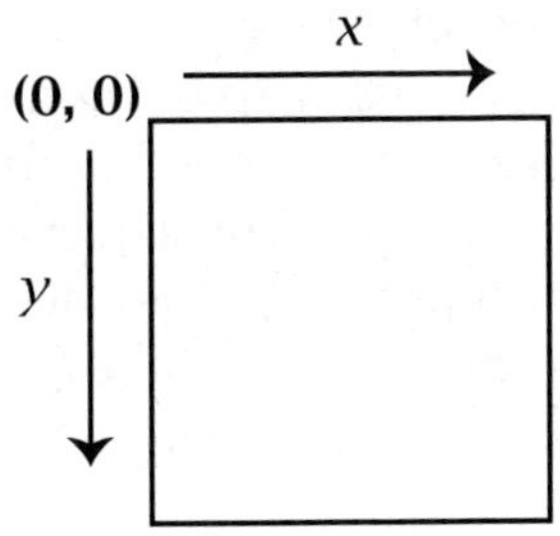

Within a component on the screen (e.g. a window), the coordinates of any given location in that component are measured in pixels from the upper-left corner of the component. Again, the x-coordinate measures horizontal distance from left to right, while the y-coordinate measures vertical distance from top to bottom.

2.2 Understanding objects

Object-oriented programming, as the name suggests, is about working with objects. But what exactly is an object? The simple answer is: everything! We are surrounded by objects — television sets, chairs, trees, people, cars, cats are all objects. Even geometric concepts such as 'square' and 'circle', or abstract entities such as data structures or Java classes stored in a computer, are objects.

The view adopted in object-oriented programming is that an *object* has two essential aspects:

state
: Each object has an associated state which captures information about the current circumstances of the object. For example, a chair may have a position, a colour, and so on; a tree may have a height, an age. An object such as a person may well have a very complicated state, capturing information not just about their name and age, but also their relatives, their financial situation, their educational achievements, and even perhaps whether they are happy, sad, hungry, sleeping, and so on.

methods

Each object has an associated collection of *methods* which enable the object to react with its environment. As a consequence of this reaction, the object may change its state in some way. For example, a television set can change channel, i.e. it has a method such as *change the channel* which when invoked can change the current channel. A complicated object such as a person may well have a large collection of associated methods, e.g. not only methods to move or eat, but also methods for responding with information to requests from the environment.

The fundamental idea behind object-oriented programming is that objects communicate and cooperate by *message-passing*, i.e. they pass messages among themselves. The objects in a system respond to the messages they receive by invoking associated methods and, as a consequence, various tasks can be performed. To give an example, suppose the message *go to bed* is sent to a child object. The child receives the message and in response performs one (or more) of their associated methods. As a consequence, the child will (hopefully) go to bed.

2.3 Message-passing in general

As message-passing is such an important idea in object-oriented programming, it is worth taking time now to look at some aspects of message-passing in more detail. As we will see in the next section when we start looking at message-passing in Java, many aspects of how real-world objects communicate have been captured in Java.

Message arguments

Firstly, messages that convey similar information can often be grouped together. For example, the messages *go to bed* and *go to school* convey information about 'going to'. To capture this commonality we could express these messages in the form *goTo*(*bed*) and *goTo*(*school*). The idea here is that a message consists of its generic name (in this case *goTo*) followed by specific (non-generic) information (in this case *bed* and *school*). The actual values such as *bed* and *school* are called the *arguments* of the message. The advantage of this approach to message construction is that now we can use the same message in many new contexts simply by supplying a different argument. For example, we can now easily construct the messages *goTo*(*home*), *goTo*(*theParty*), and so on.

Receiving a message

When an object receives such a message it can use its generic *goTo* method, together with the argument supplied, to decide how to respond to the message. This point brings up the issue of how an object responds to a message it receives. When a message is received, the object consults its own collection of associated methods to find the one that corresponds to the received message. That method will contain all the information the object needs to know in order to respond appropriately to the message passed to it. So, for example, a child knows how to respond to the generic *goTo*(...) message because it has learnt a method which it has stored internally (i.e. remembered). Of course, children don't always respond to messages as one would expect, but that is another issue. Objects in Java at any rate are always well behaved and respond to a message exactly as their method instructs them.

More than one argument can be sent with a message. If, for example, we wish to move a circle to some new position on the Cartesian coordinate plane, we may send the circle a message such as *moveTo*(3, 5) where 3 is the x-coordinate and 5 is the y-coordinate of the circle's new centre. In this case two arguments (3 and 5), separated by a comma, were supplied with the message.

It may happen that an object receives a message that it does not understand. For example, sending the message *goTo*(*bed*) to a dog would be of no use. In this case, the dog is likely to do nothing but look rather confused. In a Java program, it is a serious matter if an object receives a message that it does not understand as this will usually lead to the Java system stopping the program immediately. The Java compiler is designed to detect such possibilities even before the code is run and to signal an error message.

The receiver object

It is important to observe that we cannot consider a message in isolation: a message must be sent to some object. In other words, a message does not exist except in association with the object that is to receive the message. This object, not surprisingly, is called the *receiver* object. To make this association clear the name of the receiver object is usually bundled together with the message. For example, to tell Mary to go to bed we write *Mary.goTo*(*bed*), with the receiver object (*Mary* in this case) placed first and separated from the message to be sent (*goTo*(*bed*) in this case) by a full stop. Notice that this way of constructing message packages enables us to clearly distinguish the cases of sending the same message to different objects. So to tell both Mary and Tan to go to bed we have *Mary.goTo*(*bed*) and *Tan.goTo*(*bed*) — the same message but sent to distinct objects.

Polymorphism

The last case above raises an important issue. It is possible for distinct objects to receive the same message (for example, Mary and Tan in the case above) but there is no guarantee that the objects will respond to the messages in the same way. For example, Mary may run off to bed immediately, while Tan may be more tardy. The point here is that it is the responsibility of the individual receiver object to decide how to respond to the messages it receives: each object has its own collection of associated methods that it consults. This idea, that the same message can be sent to distinct objects which may respond in distinct ways, is called *polymorphism* and is a crucial concept in object-oriented programming. We will be having quite a lot more to say about polymorphism later (in particular, see Chapter 8).

The sender object

The idea of associating each message with the receiver object can be carried one step further. A message is also associated with the object that sends the message in the first place. This object, again not surprisingly, is called the *sender* object. For example, if Mary's father sends the *goTo(bed)* message, Mary's father is the sender object. In real life, the identity of the sender object is important and may affect the way the object responds. We are likely to respond quite differently to a *moveOn* message if it comes from a police officer than if it comes from a younger sibling.

However, despite the fact that in real life the identity of the sender object may affect the way the receiver object responds to a message, in Java (and indeed other object-oriented languages) the rule is adopted that

> *an object's response to a message depends only on the state when it receives the message, the name of the message, and the values of the arguments passed with the message.*

For this reason the sender object, unlike the receiver object, is not bundled in with the message.

At first sight this rule may appear very restrictive. However this is not the case, for if it is really important that the identity of the sender object be known to the receiver object, this information can be passed as one of the message arguments. For example, if it is important to know who is sending Mary the message to go to bed, we could have constructed the message something like *Mary.goTo(bed, father)*, in which case Mary would be able to interpret the message knowing it was sent by her father and consequently perhaps react quite differently to how she may react if sent the message *Mary.goTo(bed, mother)*, that is, if requested to go to bed by her mother.

Returning information

As observed before, when an object responds to a message it may undergo some change of its state. But in addition, when responding to some messages an object may return some information back to the sender object. For example, if you send the message *whatIsTheTime* to somebody you would expect to receive back some reply. In Java, although the identity of the sender object is not bundled as part of the message, the underlying system always keeps track of which object is sending a message and arranges for any required response to be returned to the sender.

One final point. An object may respond to a message by, in its turn, sending messages to other objects. For example, when a builder person object receives a message like *buildHouse*, she or he will doubtless respond by sending messages to the plumber, brick-layer, and so on. That is, an initial message sent to a single object may lead to a cascade of inter-object communications. Indeed, this is precisely the mechanism which enables an object-oriented Java program to perform complicated computations.

2.4 Message-passing in Java

Now that we have some informal ideas about objects and the passing of messages between objects, we can begin to look at some specific examples of message-passing in Java. The approach adopted in this section is to experiment with sending various messages to objects and observe how the objects respond. In the process we will learn how messages are structured in Java. The examples presented here are structured around sending various messages to the classes `SquareFigure` and `CircleFigure`. These classes have been specifically constructed for *Java Genesis* to illustrate the power of message passing and class reuse.

PROBLEM 2: sending messages to `SquareFigure`

Open the folder *Messages* and run the class `Messages`. A window opens displaying a red square at its centre. In addition, a dialog box opens requesting a message be supplied.

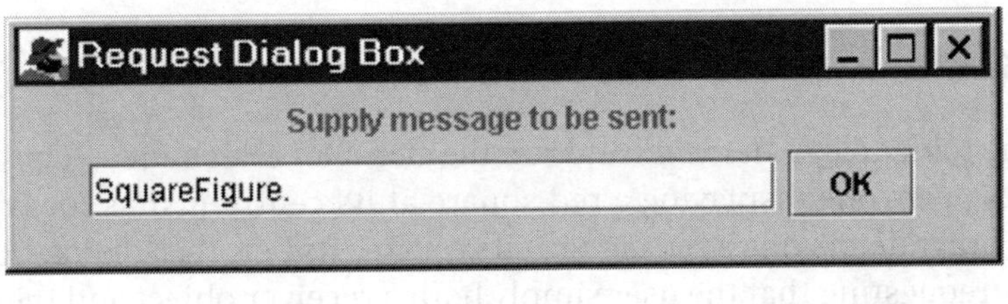

In this case, appending a message to '`SquareFigure.`' by typing directly into this box and then either clicking on OK with the mouse or pressing the 'enter' key, will send that message to the class `SquareFigure` which will then respond in some appropriate way. Some of the messages that the class `SquareFigure`

understands are:

moveRight(*x*)	*moveLeft*(*x*)	*moveUp*(*x*)	*MoveDown*(*x*)
moveTo(*x*, *y*)			
setWidth(*x*)			
setColour(*c*)			
drawHollow()	*drawFilled*()		
getXCorner()	*getYCorner*()		

where the arguments *x* and *y* are integers and the argument *c* is either *Color.red*, *Color.blue* or *Color.green* (note the American spelling). For example, typing `moveRight(50)` into the dialog box and selecting OK will send that message to `SquareFigure`, while typing `setColour(Color.blue)` into the dialog box will send that message to `SquareFigure`. The message named *moveTo* takes two arguments, both integers, separated by a comma. The last four messages take no arguments; Java insists that the argument brackets are still supplied though nothing (except possibly white space) is placed between them.

Try sending various messages with various arguments to `SquareFigure` and observe what effect they have. For each method see if you can deduce by the experimental process of trial and error the effect the message has on the square in the window.

To exit the application, close the window containing the square (by clicking the mouse on the 'X' in the upper-right corner of the window).

If after reflection you are unsure about the effect of any message see Hints.

□

Notice that the two messages *getXCorner*() and *getYCorner*() do not actually change the square in the window in any way. Instead, certain information is output. What information is output when these messages are sent? (See Hints if you are not sure.)

PROBLEM 3: more message-passing

Open the folder *More Messages* and run the class `MoreMessages`. This time two windows open, one displaying a red square at its centre just as for Problem 2, and the other displaying a red circle at its centre. As before, a dialog-box opens, but now requesting that the user supply both a receiver object and the message to be sent to the object.

This time a message can be sent to either the class `SquareFigure` exactly as before, or to the class `CircleFigure`. By typing something of the form `CircleFigure.`*message* directly into the dialog box and then either clicking on OK with the mouse or pressing the 'enter' key, *message* is sent to the class `CircleFigure` which then responds in some appropriate way. Some of the messages that the class `CircleFigure` understands are

moveRight(*x*)	*moveLeft*(*x*)	*moveUp*(*x*)	*MoveDown*(*x*)
moveTo(*x*, *y*)			
setRadius(*x*)			
setColour(*c*)			
drawHollow()	*drawFilled*()		
getXCentre()	*getYCentre*()		

where the arguments take the same values as for the corresponding messages for the class `SquareFigure`. Typing `CircleFigure.moveRight(50)`, for example, in the dialog box and clicking OK will send the message *moveRight*(50) to `CircleFigure`, while typing `SquareFigure.drawHollow()` into the dialog box will send the message *drawHollow*() to `SquareFigure`.

By a process of trial and error, see if you can deduce the effect each message has on the appropriate figure. For help in understanding the effects see Hints.

□

In this case we can see the importance of including the name of the receiver object when sending a message. Without this information it would not be possible for the Java application to know to which object to send the message. As a given message may be understood by many different objects, we cannot in general deduce from the message alone the identity of the receiver object. To resolve any ambiguity the receiver object is included with the message.

2.5 Classes

We have already met several Java classes, e.g. `DrawCircle`, `DrawCircleFrame` and `DrawCirclePanel` in Section 2.1 and `SquareFigure` and `CircleFigure` in Section 2.4. As we shall see as we progress through *Java Genesis*, classes are absolutely central to programming in Java. In the next section we will begin constructing our own classes, but before doing so we take a brief look at classes in general, introducing informally a couple of issues which will be explored more fully in later chapters.

The class as an object

The first class issue to consider is one we have already met, namely, that a class is an object that can be sent messages and will respond appropriately. For example, consider again Problem 2. As this problem illustrates, in order to modify the square in the window in some specified way, all we need to know are the messages that can validly be sent to the class `SquareFigure` and the effect they produce. To use the class `SquareFigure` in this way we don't need to know the details of the code for the class.

But what in fact actually happens at the code level when we send a message to the class `SquareFigure`? The file *SquareFigure.java* contains the code for this class. (If you wish to browse the code online you will find it in the folder *C* : *genesis**packages**genesis*.)

```
package genesis;
import java.awt.*;

public class SquareFigure {

    /* Creates and opens a window frame whose
    associated pane displays a square. */

    // class variable
    private static SquareFigureFrame window;

    public static void create ( ) {
        // creates and opens the window
        window = new SquareFigureFrame();
        window.setVisible(true);
    }

    public static void moveRight (int dx) {
        window.moveRight(dx);
    }

    public static void moveLeft (int dx) {
        window.moveLeft(dx);
    }

    public static void moveUp (int dy) {
        window.moveUp(dy);
    }

    public static void moveDown (int dy) {
        window.moveDown(dy);
    }

    public static void moveTo (int x, int y) {
        window.moveTo(x, y);
    }
```

```
        public static void setWidth (int w) {
            window.setWidth(w);
        }

        public static void setColour (Color c) {
            window.setColour(c);
        }

        public static void drawHollow ( ) {
            window.drawHollow();
        }

        public static void drawFilled ( ) {
            window.drawFilled();
        }

        public static int getXCorner ( ) {
            return window.getXCorner();
        }

        public static int getYCorner ( ) {
            return window.getYCorner();
        }
    }
```

We won't attempt here to explain the detail of this code. Nevertheless we can begin to sense how it works even if much of it at this stage may appear unfathomable.

When the class `SquareFigure` receives the message *moveRight*(50), for example, it looks in its code to find the method `moveRight`, i.e.

```
    public static void moveRight (int dx) {
        window.moveRight(dx);
    }
```

This code is then invoked (i.e. executed) with `dx` set to 50.

[*An aside*: How does invoking the above `moveRight` method with `dx` set to 50 result in the square in the window moving 50 pixels to the right? We must postpone the complete answer to this question until Chapter 9 when we explore how graphical objects can be displayed in a window. Suffice it say that when the statement

```
    window.moveRight(dx)
```

is executed the message `moveRight` is now passed to the object `window`. This object denotes the window in which the square is displayed, and when it receives the message `moveRight` it invokes code that results in the square being redrawn 50 pixels to the right. Notice how each method in the class `SquareFigure` simply passes the received message to the object `window` and this object then has the responsibility to modify the square. *End aside*]

If you look through the code for the class `SquareFigure` you will find a method for each of the messages that this class understands.

The class as a constructor of objects

The second class issue we want to discuss in this section is the role played by classes in defining and constructing objects. To take a real programming example, consider the software for a banking system. Within such a software system we would expect to find a `BankAccount` class that is responsible for constructing and managing customers' individual bank accounts.

Because it is important to clearly distinguish between a class and the objects it constructs, we will preserve the word 'object' to exclusively refer to objects constructed by classes. Despite this convention, it is important to emphasise that a class is nevertheless a perfectly good object in that it has a state and can receive and respond to messages.

In Java the convention is adopted that the name of any class always begins with a capital letter, while the name of any object constructed by a class always begins with a lower-case letter.

Returning to the example of the `BankAccount` class that produces and manages customers' bank accounts, the class will have many methods of its own e.g. for constructing new bank accounts, charging fees, and so on. The variables of the `BankAccount` class will store information common to all bank account, such as the current interest rates, the fixed charges for various services supplied by the bank, and so on.

Class methods

One final observation: notice that the word `static` is used within the declaration of each method in the class `SquareFigure`. This key word is a *modifier* that tells us that the method is a class method. When a class (as distinct from an object of that class) receives a message it looks for a *static* method to invoke in response.

We can illustrate this by considering once more the `BankAccount` class that constructs and manages customers' bank accounts. The *static* variables and methods of this class will describe the state and operations of the class itself, i.e. how it constructs accounts, charges fees, and so on. But each bank account object constructed by the class will have its own state, such as its current balance, and have methods to record depositing money, withdrawing money, and so on. These methods will access variables specific to a particular object, such as the current balance of the account. In Java, the variables and methods associated with the objects constructed by a class are also recorded as part of the code for the class, but this code is distinguished by *not* containing the modifier *static*.

2.6 Constructing simple classes

The classes we've met so far have been relatively complicated. To begin a detailed study of the Java class construct we shall consider at first something much simpler.

PROBLEM 4: displaying a string in the Output window

Open the folder *Gday* and run the class `Gday`. The information "G'day, and welcome!" is output.

□

The file *Gday.java* contains the code for the class `Gday`:

```
public class Gday {

    /*
    A greetings message.
    */

    public static void main (String [ ] args) {
        // prints a greeting in the output window
        System.out.println("G'day, and welcome!");
    }
}
```

Let us look at this class in detail. It begins with the modifier `public` which indicates that the class is visible to and can be accessed by its environment (i.e. it is publicly available), followed by the key word `class`, followed by the name of the class, in this case `Gday`. Notice that in conformance with the convention mentioned in the last section, the class name begins with a capital letter. Notice also that the name of the file containing this class is *Gday.java*. This was no accident: the code for a public class must always be stored in a *.java* file with exactly the same name (including capital letters) as the class name.

Next comes an opening brace '{'. The entire code for the class is placed between this brace and the corresponding closing brace which is the very last thing in the class.

Now follows a class comment. Everything between '/*' and '*/' is ignored by the compiler. A class comment is optional but you are very strongly advised to always start the code for a class with a comment such as this so as to give a clear indication of the purpose of the class.

Finally, there is the code for a method named `main`.

- This method starts with the key word `public` which indicates the method is 'open to the public', i.e. it can be invoked in response to a message sent by a sender object external to the class.
- Then comes the key word `static` which indicates that this is a class method, i.e. it is invoked by sending the appropriate message to the class `Gday` itself.
- This is followed by the key word `void` which indicates that when invoked by a message this method does not return any value to the object sending the message.
- Then comes `main`, the name of the method. This name was used deliberately: when a class is run, the underlying operating system automatically sends the message *main* to the class, i.e. in this case the operating system sends the message *Gday.main*. Consequently the method named `main` will be invoked. If there is no such method in the class selected, an error will be displayed and the application will cease running.
- The method's parameter, `String [ ] args`, enclosed in brackets follow. We shall leave further discussion of this parameter until Chapter 5. For the moment just treat this as extra noise that needs to be inserted.
- Finally, the code to be invoked when the method is executed is placed within braces. This code starts with a comment: anything following '//' on a line is ignored by the compiler. Comments in methods, as with the class comments we saw earlier, are optional, but again you are strongly advised to always add a comment to the code for each method so as to clarify its purpose. Following the comment, the code to be executed is at last found. In this case it consists of just one statement:

```
System.out.println("G'day, and welcome!");
```

The Output window

Consider the statement above in detail. The word `System` refers to a class that is part of the pre-constructed code supplied with Java. Java comes supplied with many classes that can be reused when constructing our own applications, and indeed this is precisely what we will be often doing. In fact, one of the arts to programming in Java is to become familiar with the pre-existing classes so as to be able to reuse them as much as possible. In this case, the class `System` enables the transfer of information to and from the computer user. The details are not important; suffice it to say that `System.out` is an object that represents the standard (default) window for output, and when this object is sent the message `println` it will take the argument supplied with that message and display it in this window. Throughout the book we shall always refer to the standard window for output as the *Output* window.

In our example, the string `"G'day, and welcome!"` is the argument supplied to the message `println`. Strings in Java can be constructed by placing characters within double quotation marks. (Strings are discussed further in Chapter 3.) The argument of the `println` method must be a string or some expression that can be converted into a string.

The code statement ends, as must all code statements in Java, with a semicolon.

PROBLEM 5: other strings in the Output window

Modify the code for the class `Gday` so that a string of your own choice is displayed in the Output window. In other words, experiment with displaying your own information in the Output window. What happens if a number rather than a string is supplied as the argument to the message `println`? Try it and see.

□

The Transcript window

You will have noticed that the Output window displays not just information we have specifically requested but also system information about the state of the program. As this may lead to confusion, we have created a special window, called the *Transcript* window, that enables us to display information output by our program and keep it separate from system information.

PROBLEM 6: demonstrating the Transcript window

Open the folder *Transcript Demo* and run the class `TranscriptDemo`. A new window opens displaying the string "G'day, and welcome!".

□

The file *TranscriptDemo.java* contains the code for the class TranscriptDemo:

```
import genesis.*;

public class TranscriptDemo {

    /*
    Demonstrates the Transcript window.
    */

    public static void main (String [] args) {
        Transcript.println("G'day, and welcome!");
    }
}
```

The import statement

The code for the class TranscriptDemo is very similar to the code for the class Gday but there are a couple of interesting differences. The class starts with an import statement. An import statement enables a class to have access to other classes in the imported package, in this case all the public classes in the *genesis* package.

The *genesis* package

A *package* is simply a collection of classes that play a related role and so are 'packaged' together. The *genesis* package has been specially created for this book and it contains various classes that we will need to help create the examples and problems. In particular, this package contains the class Transcript which is needed whenever we want to use the Transcript window.

[*An aside*: If you are curious and wish to browse the code for the Transcript class, the file *Transcript.java* is in the *C* : *genesis**packages**genesis* folder. Indeed, this folder contains the code for all the classes in the *genesis* package, e.g. the class SquareFigure we met in Section 2.4 is found there. *End aside*]

As with the class Gday, the main method of the class TranscriptDemo contains just one statement, which in this case is:

```
Transcript.println("G'day, and welcome!");
```

Effectively, `System.out` has been replaced by `Transcript`. The `Transcript` class understands the message `println` and responds by displaying the string sent as the argument of the message on a line in the Transcript window.

Throughout *Java Genesis* we make frequent use of both the Output and Transcript windows. The Output window is easy and convenient to use when we have only a small amount of output to display. The Transcript window on the other hand is particularly useful when the output is complicated or lengthy. To use the Transcript window rather than the Output window simply replace the name `System.out` with `Transcript` throughout the code, and ensure that the *genesis* package is imported.

A consequence of using the Transcript window for output is that, unlike the Output window, it must be closed before the current application can cease execution. This can be achieved by closing the window in the usual way by clicking with the mouse on the 'X' in the upper-right corner of Transcript window.

The *java.lang* package

One final point. We have observed the necessity of importing the *genesis* package so that the class `TranscriptDemo` can access the class `Transcript`. Why therefore, is there no import statement in the class `Gday` so that the class `System` can be accessed?

The reason is that the class `System` is in the special *java.lang* package. This package, supplied with the Java Software Development Kit (SDK), is a collection of those classes most frequently accessed by other programs. Because of this the *java.lang* package is automatically imported by every class; there is no need to import it explicitly. All other classes supplied with the Java SDK (i.e. other than those in the *java.lang* package) are within packages that must be imported in order to be accessed. We shall meet many specific examples of this throughout the book; indeed, there is an example in Problem 8 later in this section.

PROBLEM 7: other strings in the Transcript window

Experiment with modifying the class `TranscriptDemo` so that a string of your own choice is printed in the Transcript window. What happens if a number rather than a string is supplied as the argument to the message `println`? Try it and see.

□

To complete this section, here is a problem involving a class `TextBox` that enables us to select the font size and colour of any string we want to display.

PROBLEM 8: using the class `TextBox` to display strings

Open the folder *Display Text* and run the class `DisplayText`. A new window opens displaying the string “G’day, and welcome!”. The displayed text has font size 50 and is coloured red. The window is positioned in the centre of the screen.

The file *DisplayText.java* contains the code for the class `DisplayText`:

```
import genesis.*;
import java.awt.*;

public class DisplayText {

    /*
    Displays a string with given font size and colour.
    */

    public static void main (String [ ] args) {
      TextBox.display("G’day, and Welcome!", 50, Color.red);
    }
}
```

This class is very similar to the classes `Gday` and `TranscriptDemo`. This time the `main` method contains just the statement:

```
TextBox.display("G’day, and Welcome!", 50, Color.red);
```

The message `display` is sent to the class `TextBox` and takes three parameters. The first is the string to be displayed, the second is an integer giving the required font size for the display, and the third is the required colour of the display. Colours in Java are static (i.e. class) variables of the `Color` class (again notice the American spelling). To select a colour we need to extract the required colour from this class in the way illustrated.

Experiment with modifying the class `DisplayText` so as to display different strings with various font sizes and various colours. You will notice that the size of the window changes to fit the size of the message.

□

Discussion

Although the window opened by sending the message `display` to the class `TextBox` enables us to set the size and colour of the text, it is not as generally useful as the Output and Transcript windows. It is included here as a further illustration of the role of message passing in object-oriented programming: the message `display` takes three parameters which determine how the class `TextBox` responds when it receives the message.

The *java.awt* package

The class `DisplayText` starts with two import statements. The first enables the class to have access to the *genesis* package which is where the class `TextBox` is located. The second imports all the public classes in the *java.awt* package. This package is supplied with the Java SDK and contains a collection of classes known as the Abstract Windowing Toolkit (AWT for short)that enables windows to be constructed and manipulated by Java code. This package is imported by the class `DisplayText` as it contains the class `Color` which is needed to set the colour of the displayed text. We shall have more to say about the AWT and the class `Colour` in Chapter 9.

If we hadn't included the two import statements, the classes `TextBox` and `Color` would have been inaccessible to the class `DisplayText` and we would get an error if we tried to compile `DisplayText`.

2.7 Statement sequences

In the examples presented in the last section, the `main` method consisted of only one code statement. If, however, the `main` method had consisted of several code statements (each ending in a semicolon), when the class was run these statements would have been executed sequentially, starting with the first and moving in order to the last.

PROBLEM 9: sequential print statements

What would you expect to see in the Output window if you modify the class `Gday` and replace the code in the method `main` by the following code and then recompile and rerun the application? Try it and see.

```
System.out.println();
System.out.println("G'day.");
System.out.println("Welcome to Java Genesis");
System.out.println();
```

□

Discussion

When the message `println` is received by the `System.out` object, the message's string argument is displayed in the Output window and a new line is started. Any subsequent output will appear on the new line. By sending an empty argument, i.e. by sending the message `println()`, nothing is displayed, but a new line is started. Similar effects occur when the message `println` is received by the `Transcript` class, except that now any output appears in the Transcript window.

PROBLEM 10: sending a sequence of messages

Open the folder *Draw Square* and run the class `DrawSquare`. A window opens with a solid red square drawn in its centre. The code for this class is in the file *DrawSquare.java*:

```
import genesis.*;
import java.awt.*;

public class DrawSquare {

    public static void main (String [ ] args) {
        SquareFigure.create();
    }
}
```

Modify this class by replacing the single code statement in the `main` method by the following sequence of statements:

```
SquareFigure.create();
SquareFigure.moveRight(50);
SquareFigure.setColour(Color.blue);
```

Recompile and re-run the application. Modify this code in various other ways so that when recompiled and re-run the square is drawn in a new position, or with a new colour, and so on.

□

Discussion

Sending the message `create()` to the class `SquareFigure` results in the window containing the square opening. The class `SquareFigure` is in the *genesis* package.

The class `DrawSquare` achieves the same modifications to the square as can be achieved in Problem 2, except that in Problem 2 the window containing the square was automatically opened (i.e. we did not need to explicitly send the message `create()` to the `SquareFigure` class — it was done for us). In Problem 2 we passed messages to the `SquareFigure` class via a purpose-built graphical user interface (GUI). This GUI enabled us to pass each message one at a time and at our own pace. With the class `DrawSquare` the messages are still passed sequentially, but all we see is the final effect.

PROBLEM 11: constructing a hollow square

Construct a class named `DrawHollowSquare` by modifying the class `DrawSquare` so that when the class is compiled and run, a black hollow square with width 100 pixels and with its centre at the position (196, 134) is displayed in a window, i.e. the x-coordinate of the centre of the square is 196 and the y-coordinate is 134, measured in pixels from the upper-left corner of the window's display region.

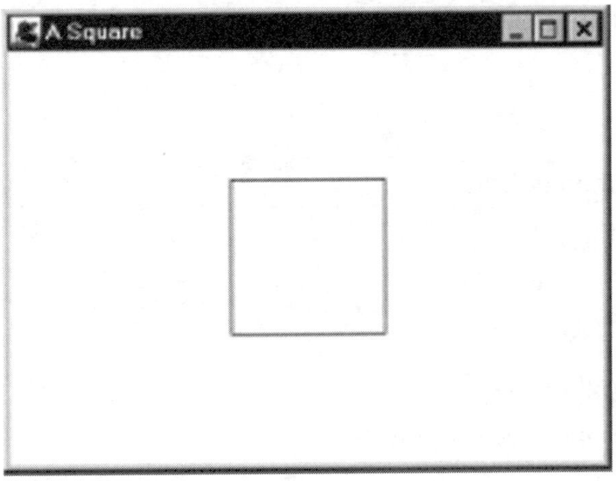

(The values 196 and 134 are chosen so that the displayed square will have its centre at approximately the centre of the display region of the window. This centre is not the same as the centre of the entire window, i.e. (200, 150), because of the title bar at the top of the window and the thin border on the sides and bottom of the window. We will see in Chapter 9 how we can compute the exact centre of the display region.)

For help with this problem see Hints.

□

Discussion

Problems 10 and 11 illustrate an important aspect of class reuse in object-oriented programming. In order to modify the square in the window in some specified way we need only to know

- which messages can validly be sent to the class `SquareFigure`;
- the consequent effect of sending a valid message.

That is, we need to know how the class *behaves*. If we have this information it is then unnecessary to study the actual code of the class in order to make use of it.

This approach to class reuse, where we study the behaviour of an existing class and its objects in terms of the messages they can receive and the way they respond to these messages, is at the heart of object-oriented class reuse. We will repeatedly apply this idea throughout *Java Genesis.*

Chapter 2 self-check

Can you give a brief and informal description of

- an object?
- a class?
- the state of an object?
- object methods?
- messages?
- message-passing?
- message arguments?
- the sender and receiver objects?
- polymorphic message-passing?
- the modifier 'static'?
- a code statement?
- a sequence of code statements?
- how we measure distances in pixels?
- importing a package?

Can you

- modify, compile and run a Java program?
- construct a simple class containing just the single method `main`?
- display a string in the Output window or the Transcript window?
- place comments in Java code?

Basic programming constructs 3

Prerequisites

Before beginning Chapter 3 you will need to understand the structure of a simple Java class containing just the single method `main`, and be familiar with basic object-oriented terminology as introduced in Chapter 2.

Overview

The role of Chapter 3 is to develop some of the core skills needed to construct Java code. These skills will be developed through problems that involve creating code within a class containing a single `main` method. Typically however, this code will make use of existing Java classes, some of which have been written specially for *Java Genesis*, and some of which come with the Java SDK.

Following the pattern established in Chapter 2, the coding details of the pre-existing classes we reuse in this way can be decently hidden from view. All we need to know are the messages that can be sent to these pre-existing classes and what happens as a consequence. By experimenting with code that sends messages to these classes we can develop an understanding of, and techniques for applying, some basic Java programming constructs.

3.1 Working with numbers

We look at how we can construct arithmetic expressions in Java involving integer and floating point numbers. In particular, we look at the various arithmetical operators (addition, multiplication, etc.), and the rules they obey. We introduce the Java class `Math` that can be applied to perform operations on numbers.

Problems:

1 evaluating numerical expressions

2 integer and floating point division

3 using the `Math` class

4 casting numerical expressions

3.2 Local variables, assignment statements

In order to write code to handle arithmetic and other expressions easily it is usually necessary to assign various values to variables and work with these variables rather than directly with the underlying values. We look at how local variables can be declared and given a type. We see how values can be assigned to these variables and how expressions involving variables can be constructed.

Problems:

5 the need for local variables

6 using a local variable

7 local variables of types `int` and `double`

8 local variables storing random integers

3.3 Dialog boxes

In order to perform a computation, a program may require data to be supplied by the user. Furthermore, a program may output information to the user. We consider the use of 'dialog' boxes as a straightforward way to handle this interaction in the case when relatively small amounts of information pass between the user and the program.

Problems:

9 using a dialog box to input an integer

10 using a warning dialog box

11 supplying a floating point number

3.4 Fixed-length iteration

In many situations it is necessary to repeat the execution of a block of code statements a given number of times. We look at a technique, the so-called 'for-loop' control construct, for achieving this.

Problems:

12 sum or product of five numbers

13 moving the square

14 animating the moving square

15 moving the square to the origin

16 summing a series

17 calculating factorials

3.5 Primitive types

Objects in Java are constructed by classes with an object's type given by the class responsible for its construction. However, for efficiency Java has a few primitive types (e.g. numbers) that can be constructed and manipulated directly without the need for an underlying class. We briefly summarise these primitive types.

3.6 Characters and strings

We complete this chapter by looking at how characters and strings can be declared and manipulated in Java.

Problems:

18 printing a triangle of stars

19 printing name and age

20 tossing a die

21 string manipulation

22 reversing a string

Learning outcomes

By the end of Chapter 3 you will have:

- met Java integer and floating point numbers;
- used the arithmetic operators +, -, *, /, and % to construct arithmetic expressions;
- used methods in the Java `Math` class to perform various operations on numbers and to generate random numbers;
- seen how to cast a number of one type into another type;
- met the number types `int` and `double`;

- declared variables whose values can be a given number type;
- written code to assign values to variables;
- used dialog boxes to input data or output simple messages;
- met the assignment operators = and ++ ;
- applied the 'for-loop' construct to execute statements iteratively;
- met all eight primitive Java types;
- looked at the way characters and strings can be used in Java;
- used methods in the Java `String` class to perform various operations on string objects.

3.1 Working with numbers

When constructing expressions involving numbers, the operators addition (+), subtraction (–) and multiplication (*) behave much as they do in traditional mathematical expressions. So, for example:

`3 + 4`	evaluates to	`7`
`3 - 4 * 2`	evaluates to	`-5`
`7.2 - 3.1`	evaluates to	`4.1`

Precedence

Notice that multiplication has a higher precedence than addition or subtraction, i.e. it is performed first. If in the second expression above we wanted the subtraction to be performed before the multiplication we would need to insert brackets. That is

`(3 - 4) * 2` evaluates to `-2`.

PROBLEM 1: evaluating numerical expressions

Open the folder *Numerical Expressions.* The class `EvalNumExp` whose code is given on the next page is in the file *EvalNumExp.java.*

When executed, the result of evaluating the expression `3 - 4 * 2` is printed in the Output window.

Replace this expression in turn with each of the expressions below, recompile and rerun the class. The Java value of each expression will be output. In addition, formulate some expressions of your own and evaluate them using this Java class.

```
7 + 3.6
3 - (4 - 1) * 2
3 * 2.0 + 4
7.6345 * 2.23
0.0001 * 1
999999999       (i.e. 9 nines)
9999999999      (i.e. 10 nines)
9999999999.0    (i.e. 10 nines followed by .0)
999999999 * 999999999    (i.e. 9 nines multiplied by 9 nines)
```

```
public class EvalNumExp {

    /*
    Evaluating numerical expressions.
    */

    public static void main (String [ ] args) {
        // prints the value of a numerical expression
        // in the Output window
        System.out.println(3 - 4 * 2);
    }
}
```

□

Discussion

In Java, integers (whole numbers such as 3, 7, −1, etc.) are treated differently from floating point numbers (3.4, 7.0, and so on) that include a decimal point and digits after the decimal point. The general rule is that if all the numbers in a numerical expression are integers then the value of the expression will be an integer. However, if one or more numbers in the expression is a floating point number, the value of the expression will also be expressed as a floating point number, i.e. with a decimal point and digits after the decimal point.

Working with integers

Notice that integer arithmetic can give some strange results when the integer becomes large as the space allocated to store the integer may not be sufficient to store it accurately. For example, the statement

```
System.out.println(9999999999);
```

involving 10 nines will not compile because, as we shall see later in this section, the compiler expects the integer to be of Java type `int` and within the range

-2,147,483,648 to 2,147,483,647.

However, the statement

```
System.out.println(999999999 * 999999999);
```

involving 9 nines multiplied by 9 nines does compile and will run without any error being indicated. But the output produced consists of only 9 digits and is clearly incorrect. Because the result of multiplying these two integers is too large to be stored in the space allocated, information is lost. **Be warned!!**

The rule that integer expressions evaluate to integers has a pronounced and somewhat suprising effect when we consider integer division (/).

PROBLEM 2: integer and floating point division

By modifying the class `EvalNumExp` as appropriate, evaluate in turn each of the following 12 expressions and print the result in the Output window.

```
3 / 2          3 + 2 / 3        (3 + 2) / 3
3.0 / 2        3 / 2.0          3 + 2.0 / 3
3 % 2          7 % 4            4 % 2
4.0 % 2        4.3 % 2.1        (3/2*2)+3%2
```

Can you guess what the operators '/' and '%' are doing? Experiment with more expressions for yourself until you have the hang of what's going on here (but see the discussion below if you are in need of some clarification).

□

Discussion

- Division (i.e. '/') has a higher precedence than addition (in fact, it has the same precedence as multiplication) so if we want to do the addition first we need to use brackets.
- As 3 and 2 are integers, 3/2 evaluates to an *integer*, with the result this expression in Java evaluates to 1, *not* 1.5. **Be warned!!** Essentially, division of integers discards the remainder. If we want to get the value 1.5 we need to ensure at least one of the numbers is floating point.
- The symbol '%' denotes modular division, i.e. it evaluates to the *remainder* after division. This symbol works for floating point as well as integer division, but notice that approximations may be used when doing floating point division.

The class `Math`

More complicated arithmetic expressions can be evaluated using the Java class `Math` included with the *java.lang* package. As we mentioned in Chapter 2, the *java.lang* package contains classes that are frequently needed by Java programs, and so it is automatically imported by every Java class; it does not need to be explicitly imported. The following messages are just some that the `Math` class understands; they each have the effect of returning a value:

- *abs*(x) returns the positive value of the number x; the value returned is an integer if and only if x is an integer
- *max*(x, y) returns the maximum of the numbers x and y; the value returned is an integer if and only if both x and y are integers
- *min*(x, y) returns the minimum of the numbers x and y; the value returned is an integer if and only if both x and y are integers
- *pow*(x, y) returns a floating point number whose value is the number x raised to the power of the number y
- *sqrt*(x) returns a floating point number whose value is the square root of the number x
- *random*() has no argument and returns a floating point number randomly selected and lying strictly between 0.0 and 1.0 (i.e. a number $0.0 < x < 1.0$)

The `Math` class also enables the trigonometric and other functions to be evaluated. We will introduce these and other messages as the need arises.

PROBLEM 3: using the `Math` class

Open the folder *Using Math.* The class `UsingMath` whose code is given below is in the file *UsingMath.java*:

```
public class UsingMath {

    /* Evaluating numerical expressions using Math. */

    public static void main (String [ ] args) {
        // prints the value of a numerical expression
        // in the output window
        System.out.println(Math.max(3, 4));
    }
}
```

When executed, the result of evaluating the expression `Math.max(3, 4)` is printed in the Output window.

Replace this expression in turn with each of the following expressions, recompile and run to evaluate the expressions in Java:

```
Math.abs(-23.4)

Math.pow(4, 2)

3 + Math.sqrt(4)

Math.random()
```

Try some expressions for yourself until you are familiar both with the messages that can be sent to the class `Math` and the way the class `Math` responds.

□

Casting numbers

When working with numbers it may happen that we wish to convert a number from one type to another. To give two examples, the expression `(int)4.7` converts the number 4.7 to the integer 4 and the digits after the decimal point are discarded, while the expression `(double)4` converts the integer 4 to the floating point number 4.0 which now contains digits after the decimal point. This process of converting one numerical type into another is an example of what is known as *casting*.

The types `int` and `double`

The key word `int` denotes the default Java integer number type, while `double` denotes the default Java floating point number type. In every arithmetic expression we have met so far, Java has assigned the type `int` to each integer and the type `double` to each floating point number. (In Section 3.5 we will discover Java has other integer and floating point number types.) The Java type associated with a number indicates, among other things, how much space in memory is allocated for storing the number. For example, the word `double` indicates that the floating point number is allocated 'double' storage by the Java compiler so as to increase its accuracy. A floating point number of type `double` is in the approximate range

$$\pm 1.79769313486231570 \times 10^{308} \quad \text{(15 significant figures)}.$$

When casting, the appropriate key word is placed in parentheses at the beginning of the expression to which it refers and becomes part of the expression, as illustrated in the following problem.

PROBLEM 4: casting numerical expressions

Replace the expression given as the argument to the `println` message in the class `UsingMath` with each of the following expressions in turn. Recompile and run the class to evaluate each expressions.

```
(int)4.7

(int)(6 * Math.random()) + 1

(double)4

3 / (double)2
```

Again, experiment with different expressions to get an understanding of casting numbers. For more information see the discussion below.

□

Discussion

The second expression in Problem 4 above is a good example of how casting can be used effectively. The expression `Math.random()` returns some floating point number randomly chosen between 0.0 and 1.0. If we then multiply by 6 we get a random number strictly between 0.0 and 6.0. By now casting this as an integer we effectively discard that part of the number after the decimal point to get an integer randomly chosen from the integers 0, 1, 2, 3, 4 and 5. Adding 1 gives an integer randomly chosen from the integers 1, 2, 3, 4, 5 and 6. Hence the overall expression models the tossing of a die as it returns a random integer in the range 1 to 6.

3.2 Local variables, assignment statements

Suppose we wish to write some simple code to generate a random integer in the range 1 to 6 and then display in the Output window this number followed by its square root. A first attempt at achieving this may look something like:

```
System.out.println((int)(6 * Math.random()) + 1);
System.out.println(Math.sqrt((int)(6 * Math.random()) + 1));
```

PROBLEM 5: the need for local variables

Modify the class `UsingMath` by replacing the code for the `main` method with the two lines of code above. What do you get as output if you recompile and run this code? Experiment and run the code several times.

The problem here is that each time the expression

```
(int)(6 * Math.random()) + 1
```

is evaluated it generates a *new* random integer in the range 1 to 6. What we want is to output the number and then output the square root of the *same* number. How do you think we might achieve this?

□

Local variables

We can solve this problem by creating a *local variable* and then *assigning* to this variable the value of the random integer when it is generated. The complete code to do this is given in the class `LocalVarDemo`:

```
public class LocalVarDemo {

    /*
    Demonstrates the use of a local variable.
    */

    public static void main (String [ ] args) {
        // prints out a random integer in the
        // range 1 to 6 and its square root
        int randomInteger;
        randomInteger = (int)(6 * Math.random()) + 1;
        System.out.println(randomInteger);
        System.out.println(Math.sqrt(randomInteger));
    }
}
```

PROBLEM 6: using a local variable

Open the folder *Local Variables* and run the class `LocalVarDemo`. In fact, run it several times until you are convinced it is working as specified.

Try replacing the expressions that are within the argument of the `println` message with other expressions that use the local variable `randomInteger`.

□

Discussion

In the class `LocalVarDemo`, the statement

```
int randomInteger;
```

declares a variable named `randomInteger` of type `int`, where `int` is the Java key word denoting the integer type. This variable is an example of a *local* variable: it is declared within a method and has a meaning only within that method, i.e. it cannot be referred to outside the method. A name such as `randomInteger` is known as an *identifier*.

Identifiers

An identifier

- is any sequence of characters, each of which is either an upper- or lower-case letter, or a digit, or the underscore character '_', or the dollar character '$';
- cannot be a reserved word (`static`, `private`, `int`, `double`, `class`, and so on) which in Java are reserved for special purposes;
- cannot have a number as its first character.

It is convention to let the first character of a variable name be a lower-case letter, and to capitalise the first letter of any subsequent sub-word (as illustrated by the identifier `randomInteger`). Identifiers are case-sensitive, so the identifier `randomInteger` is distinct from the identifier `randominteger`. You are strongly advised to select meaningful names when declaring a variable. The name should give some indication of the role the variable plays within the code. A judicious choice of variable names can greatly enhance the readability of code.

Variable typing

In the above declaration, the key word `int` indicates that the value of the variable `randomInteger` must be an integer of type `int`. We say that `int` is the *type* of the variable. Java is what is known as a strongly typed language which means that every variable must be given a type when it is declared and can only be assigned values of that type.

The assignment statement

A value is assigned to a variable by an *assignment statement*. The statement in the class `LocalVarDemo` assigning a value to the variable `randomInteger` is:

```
randomInteger = (int)(6 * Math.random()) + 1;
```

That is, an integer in the range 1 to 6 is assigned to this variable. As this example illustrates, the variable that is to be assigned a value is placed on the left and is separated by '=' from the expression on the right whose value is assigned to the variable. You should read the character '=' in this context as 'is assigned to be': it does not represent equality in the traditional mathematical sense.

Once a value has been assigned to a variable, the variable takes that value in any expression, which is precisely what happens in the class `LocalVarDemo`.

Within a method there can be any number of variable declarations, and they can occur at any place in the code. Of course, a variable must be declared before it can be assigned a value, and it must be assigned a value before it can be used in an expression.

Summary

The general structure (known as the *syntax*) of a variable declaration is

type identifier ;

For example, in the declaration in the class `LocalVarDemo`, *type* was `int` and *identifier* was `randomInteger`. A variable of type other than `int` can be declared (e.g. see the next problem where a variable of type `double` is declared).

The general syntax of an assignment statement is

variable = *expression* ;

where the variable is already declared and where the expression must evaluate to a value whose type is the same as the type given to the variable in its declaration.

PROBLEM 7: local variables of types `int` and `double`

If the code for the `main` method in the class `LocalVarDemo` is replaced in turn by the code fragments below and the class recompiled and run, what result is printed in the Output window? In each case run the program to test your answer.

(a)
```
int width;
int height;
width = 4;
height = width * 2;
int area = width * height;
System.out.println(area);
```

(b)
```
double aNumber = 4.2;
aNumber = aNumber + 1;
aNumber = aNumber + 1;
int anInteger = (int)aNumber;
System.out.println(anInteger);
```

Try various examples of your own to get a feel for how variable declaration and assignment works. For help with this problem see Hints.

□

Discussion

- Notice that in Problem 7 an initial value is assigned to a variable as part of that variable's declaration statement. This is illustrated in the fifth statement in part (a) and the first and fourth statements in part (b). This shows we have an alternative syntax for a variable declaration, namely

  type identifier = *expression* ;

  where the expression must return a value whose type is *type*.

- A variable that is assigned a value can nevertheless be assigned another value (and the old value is lost), as happens in the second and third statements in part (b). At first `aNumber` is assigned the value 4.2. Then in the second statement it is assigned the value 4.2 + 1 (i.e. 5.2). Finally, in the third statement it is assigned the value 5.2 + 1 (i.e. 6.2).

- The variable `aNumber` in part (b) is declared to have the type `double`. Consequently the value of this variable will always be some floating point number of type `double`. Hence casting is needed when assigning the value of `aNumber` to the variable `anInteger` of type `int` in the fourth statement. The rule is this: if a variable has the type `double`, then any numerical expression involving that variable will evaluate to a floating point number of type `double`. Casting will be needed if we want the expression to evaluate to an integer.

PROBLEM 8: local variables storing random integers

Construct a class `ThreeNumbers` that assigns the values of three distinct random integers in the range 1 to 10 to three distinct variables, prints the three numbers in the Output window, then prints their (floating point) average, and finally prints the sum of their squares expressed as an integer.

For help with this problem see Hints.

□

3.3 Dialog boxes

The following code takes two integers and displays their sum in the Transcript window:

```
int num1 = 3;
int num2 = 4;
Transcript.println(num1 + num2);
```

But suppose we want a program where the values of the two numbers are not pre-determined as in this case, but are supplied by the user when requested by the program? This would enable the program to be more general (and hence more useful) as any two numbers could be supplied by the user.

The class DialogDemo achieves this by making use of 'request' dialog boxes:

```
import genesis.*;

public class DialogDemo {

    /* Demonstrates the use of dialog boxes. */

    public static void main (String [ ] args) {
        // requests two integers and prints their sum
        int num1 = DialogBox.requestInt("First integer:");
        int num2 = DialogBox.requestInt("Second integer:");
        Transcript.println(num1 + num2);
    }
}
```

PROBLEM 9: using a dialog box to input an integer

The code for the class DialogDemo is in the folder *Dialog Demo*. Run this class. A dialog box opens requesting the first integer. After typing an integer into the space provided in the dialog box you will need to click on the OK button in the dialog box (or press the 'enter' key) to send the integer to the application. Then another dialog box opens requesting the second integer. When this integer is supplied the sum of the two integers is displayed in the Transcript window.

(After running the code you will need to terminate the application by closing the Transcript window.)

What happens if you supply data that is not an integer? Try it and see!

□

Discussion

The class DialogBox is in the *genesis* package. (Hence the statement

```
import genesis.*;
```

is placed at the top of the DialogDemo class so that the class DialogBox can be accessed.) When the statement

```
int num1 = DialogBox.requestInt("First integer:");
```

is executed, a dialog box opens displaying the string First integer:. If an integer is then typed into the dialog box and the OK button (or the 'enter' key) pressed, that integer value is assigned to the variable num1. In other words, when the message requestInt is sent to the class DialogBox, the class responds by

- opening a dialog box;
- returning an integer value of type int, where the value returned is the integer typed into the dialog box by the user.

Notice that the running application pauses until the user supplies a number.

If something other than an integer is supplied a warning dialog box opens asking you to try again.

The warning dialog box

A warning dialog box contains only information: it has no field where data can be inserted. In fact, we can add warning dialog boxes to code by sending the message warn to the class DialogBox and supplying the message we want to display as a (string) argument to the message.

PROBLEM 10: using a warning dialog box

Modify the code for the class DialogDemo by adding the statement

```
DialogBox.warn("Thank you for supplying the two integers.");
```

immediately after the statement declaring the variable num2. Recompile and run the application.

□

Notice that a warning dialog box does not return a value to the program — it simply opens a dialog box window. When a warning dialog box appears the running application pauses until the OK button has been clicked.

Beware! When using dialog boxes, the underlying application does not necessarily terminate even though the dialog boxes are no longer displayed on the screen. If the application is still active it will need to be terminated manually. Failure to do this will result in the running process remaining active and that may interfere with other Window applications you run later. In the above example we can terminate the application by closing the Transcript window.

Other dialog boxes

There are two other types of request dialog boxes available. Sending the message `requestDouble` to the class `DialogBox` will return a floating point number value of type `double`, while sending the simple message `request` will return a value of type `String`. In both cases a string is supplied as the argument to the message and that string is displayed in the dialog box. (Strings will be discussed in more detail in Section 3.6.)

PROBLEM 11: supplying a floating point number

Construct a class `MoreDialogs` that uses dialog boxes so that two (floating point) numbers can be supplied by the user. The Transcript window then displays the average of these two numbers on one line and the larger of the two on the next line.

Experiment with constructing your own classes making use of dialog boxes to request data from the user and to supply information to the user.

For help with this problem see Hints.

□

3.4 Fixed-length iteration

In Problem 9 we looked at code to find the sum of two numbers supplied by the user. The code was quite simple, but suppose we want to sum 5, 10 or even more numbers? In order to avoid having to write a lot of similar code statements we need a way to repeatedly execute statements a given number of times. The ‘for-loop’ control construct enables us to do this.

The for-loop

The following code takes 5 numbers supplied by the user and displays their sum in the Transcript window:

```
double nextNum;
double sum = 0.0;
for (int i = 1; i <= 5; i = i + 1) {
    nextNum = DialogBox.requestDouble("Supply a number:");
    sum = sum + nextNum;
}
Transcript.println(sum);
```

PROBLEM 12: sum or product of five numbers

The above code is in the class `ForDemo` and can be found in the folder *For Demo*. Run this class, supplying numbers as requested.

Modify the code to display instead the product of the five numbers.

For help with this problem see Hints.

☐

Let us look at the for-loop construct in detail. The syntax (i.e. the structure) of the for-loop in the class `ForDemo` is

`for (` *start* `;` *check* `;` *update* `) {` *statement_sequence* `}`

where *start* initialises a variable that is used as a 'counter'; *check* specifies a condition that is to be satisfied before permitting the execution of the sequence of statements; *update* indicates what change we require to the counter variable before re-evaluating *check* and possibly repeating the execution of the sequence of statements; and *statement_sequence* is the sequence of statements (each ending with a semicolon as always) that is to be repeatedly executed—this sequence is placed within braces and is called a *block*.

Consider the for-loop in the above code, namely:

```
for (int i = 1; i <= 5; i = i + 1) {
    nextNum = DialogBox.requestDouble("Supply a number:");
    sum = sum + nextNum;
}
```

The counter variable is `i` and is declared to be of type `int` with initial value 1. Almost always the counter variable of a for-loop will be an integer. The check condition is `i <= 5` (where '<=' denotes 'is less than or equal to') and so the statements in the block are executed again if and only if the value of `i` is less than or equal to 5. Clearly, as the initial value of `i` is 1 and 1 <= 5, the block will be executed at least once. The update

```
i = i + 1
```

increases the value of i by 1 each time the statements in the block have been executed. Hence the effect is that the block will be executed 5 times, for i equal to 1, 2, 3, 4 and 5. When i becomes 6 the check fails and the loop is finished, the statements in the block are no longer executed, and the program continues by executing the statements that follow the for-loop construct.

When constructing a for-loop it is important to ensure that the loop is executed exactly the required number of times. Care must be taken in setting the correct start value for the counter and in ensuring the check condition captures the correct finishing value.

The '++' abbreviation

Because we often want to increase the value of a variable by 1, Java introduces special notation: the assignment statement:

`i = i + 1` can be abbreviated to `i++`

Hence the for-loop above could have been expressed equivalently as:

```
for (int i = 1; i <= 5; i++) {...}
```

Also, the counter variable could have been declared before the for-loop, so

```
int i;
for (i = 1; i <= 5; i = i + 1) {...}
```

would have been an alternative way of constructing this for-loop.

One final comment on the code for the ForDemo class. The local variable sum essentially captures the 'sum so far'. It is initialised to zero, and with each execution of the loop has nextNum added to it. Using a local variable in this way to act as an accumulator of results so far is a common programming trick.

Example: simple animation

We saw in Problem 10 of Chapter 2 that if we run the code

```
SquareFigure.create();
SquareFigure.moveRight(50);
```

first a window opens with a square placed in its centre, and then the square is moved 50 pixels right. Rather than moving 50 pixels right in one go, we could get the same end result if we move by 5 pixels 10 times, as given by the following code:

```
SquareFigure.create();
for (int i = 1; i <= 10; i++) SquareFigure.moveRight(5);
```

Notice here that the statement-sequence part of the for-loop contains only one statement. In this case there is no need to place it within braces (although it is often a good idea to do so, nevertheless, so as to make clear exactly what is being repeatedly executed as part of the loop).

PROBLEM 13: moving the square

The above code is in the class `MoveSquare` and can be found in the folder *Move Square*. Run this class.

Modify the code so that instead of moving right 5 pixels 10 times, the square moves right 1 pixel 50 times.

□

An aesthetic problem with this last example is that we don't see the square moving, as the window is not drawn until all the computations are complete. Consequently, the window opens with the square shown in its final position. But all is not lost! In the *genesis* package there is a class `Delay` which enables us to delay execution of an application. If we send this class the message `milliseconds` and supply an integer as argument, the execution will halt for that number of milliseconds (one second is a thousand milliseconds).

PROBLEM 14: animating the moving square

Modify the class `MoveSquare` so that the `main` method now contains the code:

```
SquareFigure.create();
for (int i = 1; i <= 10; i++) {
    Delay.milliseconds(500);
    SquareFigure.moveRight(5);
}
```

Recompile and run the application. You will see the square move right by 10 jumps each of 5 pixels, with each jump occurring after half a second.

Further modify the code so that the square now makes 50 jumps each of 1 pixel, with each jump occurring every 100 milliseconds (i.e. 1/10th of a second).

Experiment with other animations of the square using the for-loop construct and the `Delay` class. For example, write code so that the square changes colour as it moves, or moves in a diagonal direction, or toggles now and then between hollow and filled. Enjoy!

(See Section 2.4 for a list of those messages that can be sent to the class `SquareFigure`.)

□

PROBLEM 15: moving the square to the origin

Construct a class `SquareToOrigin` that uses the messages `moveLeft(..)` and `moveUp(..)`, the for-loop construct, and the `Delay` class to move the square by jumps of 1 pixel every 50 milliseconds to the origin. The idea is to move the square left until it reaches the left border of the window and then move it up until it reaches the top.

(If you run the class `SquareToOriginDemo` in the folder *Square To Origin Demo* you will see what is meant to happen. File *SquareToOriginDemo.java*, however, is currently empty: it has been compiled and then the code deleted from the file. It still runs because the compiled *.class* file has been left in the folder. Your task is to construct a class `SquareToOrigin` which when compiled and run has the same effect.)

Note: We can calculate how many 1 pixel moves to the left are needed to reach the left border of the window by making use of the `getXCorner()` message. When this message is sent to the class `SquareFigure` the class responds by returning an integer giving the x-coordinate of the upper-left corner of the square. This tells us how far the corner is from the left border. For further help see Hints.

□

Using the loop counter within the statement block

The value of the loop counter itself can be used within a loop's associated block of statements. For example, consider the code:

```
for (int i = 10; i <= 21; i = i + 2) System.out.println(i*i);
```

The counter `i` takes the values 10, 12, 14, 16, 18 and 20 before it exceeds the check value of 21. As this counter appears in the expression `i*i`, when the code is executed the square of each even number between 10 and 20 will be displayed in the Output window.

In this example we could have coded the for-loop as

```
for (int i = 20; i > 9; i = i - 2) System.out.println(i*i);
```

in order to display the square of each even number between 10 and 20 in reverse order. There is no reason to do it this way in this example; nevertheless, it illustrates that the loop counter can run down as well as up, and this is often very useful.

PROBLEM 16: summing a series

Construct a class SumSeries that computes the sum

$$1 + 1/(2^2) + 1/(3^2) + 1/(4^2) + 1/(5^2) + \ldots + 1/(20^2)$$

and displays the sum in the Output window.

(This series is the first 20 terms of an infinite series that converges to $\pi^2/6$. How close to are we to $\pi^2/6$ after just 20 terms?)

For help with this problem see Hints.

□

PROBLEM 17: calculating factorials

Construct a class `Factorial` which when compiled and run opens a dialog box requesting the user supply a positive integer, and when that integer is supplied displays its factorial in the Transcript window. That is, if the positive integer n is supplied by the user the number obtained by calculating

$$n * (n-1) * (n-2) * (n-3) * \ldots * 2 * 1$$

is displayed. For example, factorial 5 is $5 * 4 * 3 * 2 * 1 = 120$.

As the factorial of a number can be very large, do the calculations using floating point arithmetic, i.e. declare the variable used to store the factorial to be of type `double`.

For help with this problem see Hints.

□

3.5 Primitive types

The number types `int` and `double` are known as *primitive* types because in Java these numbers are not objects created by some class. Java has 8 primitive types:

`int`, `byte`, `short` and `long`	(for integer numbers)
`double` and `float`	(for floating point numbers)
`boolean`	(for values *true* or *false*)
`char`	(for characters)

The integer types byte and short enable the handling of small integers; less storage is allocated to them than for the type int. These types are useful if we are working with a large collection of relatively small numbers as the total storage needed will be minimised and arithmetic operations can be handled efficiently. A byte integer is in the range -128 to 127; a short integer is in the range -32,768 to 32,767.

The type long enables the handling of large integers and more storage is allocated than for the type int. This type is useful if we are working with large integers and accuracy is important, but they require more storage and the arithmetic operations take longer. A long integer is in the range

$$-9,223,372,036,854,775,808 \text{ to } 9,223,372,036,854,775,807$$

The type float enables the handling of small floating point numbers and less storage is allocated than for the type double. Again, this type is useful if we are working with a large collection of floating point numbers and we require less accuracy. A float number is in the approximate range $\pm 3.40282347 \times 10^{38}$ (6 or 7 significant digits).

Throughout *Java Genesis* we will almost always work with the type int for integers and double for floating point numbers.

The primitive type boolean can take only the values *true* or *false*. We consider this type in detail in Chapter 4.

Finally, the primitive type char is one of the topics of the next section.

3.6 Characters and strings

Characters

The primitive type char encompasses all the single characters that appear on the typical keyboard, e.g. the upper- and lower-case letters, the numbers, and the other characters such as !, @, and #. A character is represented in a Java program by placing it within single quotation marks. For example, the statement

```
char myChar = 'b';
```

declares a variable myChar of type char and assigns it the character b . Special keyboard characters are denoted by using the '\' character combined with some other character. For example, the statements

```
char myTab = '\t';
char myEnter = '\n';
```

assigns the tab character to the variable `myTab` and the 'enter' character to the variable `myEnter`.

Strings

Characters by themselves are not all that interesting, but become important when placed in sequences to form strings. A *string* in Java is denoted by a sequence of characters within double quotation marks. Hence the statement

```
String myString = "G'day, and welcome!";
```

declares the variable `myString` of type `String` and assigns to that variable the value `G'day, and welcome!`.

The value of a string variable such as `myString` is an object of the class `String`. This class is in the *java.lang* package supplied with the Java SDK. Unlike a character, the type of a string is not a primitive type, but like all objects takes as its type the class responsible for constructing it.

[*An aside*:Actually, the fact that the variable `myString` is constructed by using the class `String` is not obvious; the Java code above simply shows the literal representation of the string as a sequence of characters within double quotation marks. Nevertheless, the class `String` contains the methods that are invoked when a string object is constructed. (We will have more to say about the construction of objects in Chapter 7.) The class `String` also contains the code that dictates how a string object is to respond when sent a message. (As these methods are invoked in response to a string *object* receiving a message, they do not start with the modifier `static` and are known as *instance* (i.e. object) methods; see Chapter 7). *End aside*]

String concatenation

There are various useful operations in Java that can be performed with strings. One of the most useful is string concatenation, denoted by '+'. For example, the code

```
String myString = "this is good";
myString = myString + "bye";
```

assigns the string `this is goodbye` to the variable `myString`.

PROBLEM 18: printing a triangle of stars

Make use of the for-loop construct and string concatenation to write a class `StarTriangle` which, when compiled and run, displays in the Output window the following triangle of stars:

```
*
**
***
****
*****
```

For help with this problem see Hints.

The string concatenation operation will append non-string objects onto a string by first converting them to strings. For example, the code

```
String myString = "my number is ";
int myInteger = 34;
myString = myString + myInteger;
```

assigns the string `my number is 34` to the variable `myString`. This is very convenient as it enables us to create a string from various types of objects. Every object has a string representation, and it is this string representation that is appended when we use the concatenation '+' operator. In the case of a number, for example, the string representation is just the usual text string denoting the number.

Operator overloading

Notice that in Java the operator '+' plays two quite distinct roles. When applied to numbers it denotes the usual numerical addition; but when applied to strings it denotes string concatenation. The Java compiler is able to deduce which role is intended from the context. Using a symbol to play distinct roles in this way and distinguishing between these roles simply from the context is known as *operator overloading.*

PROBLEM 19: printing name and age

Construct a class `NameAndAge` which when compiled and run opens a dialog box requesting the user's name, and then opens another dialog box requesting the user's age in years. It then displays the string

```
Hello xxx. You are yyy years old.
```

in the Transcript window, where `xxx` is the name and `yyy` the age supplied by the user.

For help with this problem see Hints.

More on output

So far, whenever we wanted to output something we have sent the message `println(..)` to the `System.out` object or the Transcript class. There is however, another message, `print(..)`, that these objects understand. With this message a new line is not started after the output has been displayed, so the next string to be output follows on the same line. For example, the statements

```
System.out.print("aa");
System.out.println("bb");
```

would display the string aabb in the Output window.

PROBLEM 20: tossing a die

Construct a class `DieTosses` which simulates the tossing of a die. When it is run it displays in the Transcript window 10 random integers in the range 1 to 6, with a space between each integer. For example, a typical output would be:

```
5 3 4 6 6 2 1 3 4 2
```

Modify the program so that it prints out 1000 integers rather than just 10.

For help with this problem see Hints.

□

Sending messages to strings

There are several messages that can be sent to a string object. They include:

- `charAt(..)` which takes an integer argument and returns the character in the receiver string that is at that position in the string. For example,

  ```
  "this is a string".charAt(3);
  ```

  returns the character 's'. Note that the first character in a string is at index position 0, the second at position 1, and so on. **Be warned!!**

- `equals(..)` which takes a string as argument and returns *true* if and only if the argument string is identical to the receiver string. For example,

`"aabb".equals("aabb");`	returns	`true`
`"aabb".equals("aa bb");`	returns	`false`
`"aAbb".equals("aabb");`	returns	`false`

- `toLowerCase()` which takes no argument and returns a new string identical to the receiver string but with each letter lower-case. For example,

  ```
  "This is IT".toLowerCase();
  ```

returns the string `this is it`.

- `toUpperCase()` is defined similarly; it takes no argument and returns a new string identical to the receiving string but with each letter upper-case.
- `length()` which takes no argument and returns the integer giving the number of characters in the receiver string. For example,

  ```
  "aa bb ".length();
  ```

  returns 6 (blank characters are part of a string).

Notice that because the first character of a string is in index position 0, the last character will be in index position `length()-1`.

The instance methods that are invoked when a string object receives any message are in the class `String`. Browse the Java documentation for the class `String` if you would like to study all the messages that a string object can receive.

PROBLEM 21: string manipulation

Construct a class `SpaceOut` which when compiled and run opens a dialog box requesting the user supply a string, and then displays in the Transcript window the string but with all the characters in capitals and with an extra space inserted after each character.

For help with this problem see Hints.

□

PROBLEM 22: reversing a string

Construct a class `ReverseName` which when compiled and run opens a dialog box requesting the user supply their name, and then displays in the Transcript window the name but in reverse order, i.e. with the last character of the name first and the first character of the name last. For example, if the name `Mary Christmas` is supplied by the user, then the string

```
samtsirhC yraM
```

will be displayed in the Transcript window.

For help with this problem see Hints.

□

Chapter 3 self-check

Can you give an informal description of

- the difference between integer and floating point numbers in Java?
- the number types `int` and `double`?
- casting one number type into another number type?
- the character type `char`?
- the primitive types in Java?
- variable declaration?
- assignment of a value to a variable?
- the structure and meaning of the for-loop construct?
- a block of statements?
- the type `String` in Java?

Can you write Java code that

- uses the arithmetic operators +, -, *, /, and % to construct arithmetic expressions?
- performs arithmetic operations by sending messages to the class `Math`?
- generates random floating point numbers?
- generates random integers within some range?
- declares a variable of a given type?
- assigns a value to a variable?
- casts one number type into another number type?
- uses the assignment operators = and ++ ?
- opens a dialog box to request data from the user?
- opens a dialog box to pass information to the user?
- uses a for-loop to repeatedly execute a block of statements a given number of times?
- constructs and uses strings to output information using the messages `println` and `print`?
- uses the string concatenation operator + ?
- performs operations with strings by sending messages to string objects?

Control constructs 4

Prerequisites

Before commencing Chapter 4 you will need to be familiar with

- the declaration and use of integer variables of type `int` and floating point variables of type `double`;
- basic Java constructs involving expressions and assignments;
- the for-loop construct.

We shall also occasionally

- make use of dialog boxes;
- construct and display string expressions in the Output or Transcript windows.

Consult Chapter 3 if you are unsure of any of these.

Overview

Control constructs are statements providing control over how execution proceeds. In Chapter 2 we met the simplest type of control, executing statements sequentially. In Chapter 3 we met our first iterative control construct, the for-loop. In this chapter we will look at most of the other Java constructs for controlling execution. These involve selecting between alternatives as well as iteration and repetition. We will see how to execute statements optionally, how to select between the execution of distinct blocks of statements, and how to generalise the for-loop construct to repeatedly execute a block of statements. We will also look at the primitive type `boolean` and the various Boolean operators.

4.1 Conditional control constructs

At times we may wish to execute a block of statements only if certain conditions apply or, more generally, to choose between statement blocks on the basis of some condition. We look at statement constructs which give us this control.

Problems:

1 winning the toss

2 a strange modification to integers

3 randomly colouring the circle

4 selecting which tennis player serves first

4.2 The while-loop

In Chapter 3 we met the for-loop construct that makes use of a 'counter' variable to enable a block of statements to be executed a fixed number of times. A frequent requirement however, is for the execution of a block of statements to be repeated for as long as some specified condition remains true. Although the for-loop can be adapted to handle this case, we study a construct, the while-loop, that specifically allows a block of statements to be executed repeatedly.

Problems:

5 tossing a die for consecutive sixes

6 tossing two dice for a pair of sixes

7 average tosses for a pair of sixes

8 moving the square again

9 a strange sequence of integers

4.3 Case study: greatest common divisor

As an application of the for-loop construct, we consider the problem of developing and coding an algorithm to find the greatest common divisor (gcd) of two positive integers. In the process we discuss some of the general issues that arise when developing algorithms.

Problems:

10 computing the gcd

11 an improved gcd program

4.4 Case study: approximating square roots

As another application of the for-loop construct, we consider the problem of developing and coding an algorithm to find an approximation to the square root of a number.

Problem:

12 computing approximate square roots

4.5 The do-loop

The while-loop construct enables us to repeatedly execute a block of statements for as long as some specified condition remains true. The condition is checked each time *before* the block of statements is executed. In this section we look at the do-loop which is essentially a variant of the while-loop construct, except that the associated condition is checked *after* each execution of the block of statements rather than before.

Problem:

13 circles with random radii

4.6 Boolean type

To this point we've considered the primitive types `int` and `double` for numbers and `char` for characters. We now consider values and variables of the primitive type `boolean`, looking at how they can be defined and used. We also consider the operators that can be applied to expressions of `boolean` type.

Problems:

14 the Fibonacci sequence

15 a wandering square

4.7 The switch-statement

The if-statement provides a neat way of programming a choice between two alternative actions. At times however, we may need to consider a choice between more than two actions. We look at the switch-statement which provides clean features to assist in cases where the choice of which action to perform depends on an integer or character value.

Problem:

16 flashing colours

Learning outcomes

At the conclusion of Chapter 4 you will understand:

- how the if-statement provides us with two forms, one which allows a block of statements to be optionally executed, another which allows a choice to be made between executing two distinct blocks of statements;
- how and when to use the three forms of iteration, the for-loop, the while-loop and the do-loop, and appreciate their differences;
- some issues to consider when designing an algorithm;
- the primitive type `boolean`, and the various operators that can be applied to Boolean expressions;
- how and when to use the switch-statement to select between several alternatives.

4.1 Conditional control constructs

The simplest view of a program is that it consists of an ordered sequence of statements. The meaning is that we expect these statements to be executed one after the other in the order of appearance. This feature is called statement *sequencing*.

For example, suppose we have an amount `balance` in our savings account at a local bank. At certain times the bank will add interest to the balance. In the following code fragment we compute the interest, add it to the balance, then print out the new balance:

```
interest = balance * interestRate;
balance = balance + interest;
System.out.println("New balance is: " + balance);
```

When we execute this code we require these statements to be executed one after the other, in the given order.

Sequencing gives us only limited control. For example, our complete week starting with Monday may look like:

go to work;
go to work;
go to work;
go to work;
go to work;
go to tennis;
read a book;

Such simple sequencing is somewhat unrealistic; we don't live life that way. Suppose we go to the bank on Mondays if we don't have enough cash to survive the week. In this case we can organise our life to look like:

go to work; if money-short go to the bank;
go to work;
go to work;
go to work;
go to work;
go to tennis;
read a book;

The if-else statement

The use of *if* in this example allows us to perform something optionally. However, frequently we wish to make a choice between alternatives. To illustrate this, suppose on Saturday there is no point in going to tennis if it is raining; rather, we will go to the football instead:

go to work; if money-short go to the bank;
go to work;
go to work;
go to work;
go to work ; // TGIF
if fine go to tennis; else go to football;
read a book;

This idea of choosing which statements are to be executed based on some condition is of fundamental importance, and Java, like all similar programming languages, includes specific constructs that enable such choices to be made. Referring to our earlier banking example, suppose the interest rate depends on the balance of the account. Specifically, if the balance of the account exceeds `limit`, interest is paid at `interestRate1`, otherwise it is paid at `interestRate2`. Let's code this in Java:

```
if (balance > limit)
    interest = balance * interestRate1;
else
    interest = balance * interestRate2;
balance = balance + interest;
System.out.println("New balance is: " + balance);
```

Note the syntax for the if-else statement:

```
if (expression)
        statement1 ;
else
        statement2 ;
```

The meaning is that if *expression* evaluates to *true*, then $statement_1$ is executed; otherwise (i.e. if *expression* evaluates to *false*) $statement_2$ is executed.

The else-statement part of the if-statement is optional, i.e. the if-statement can be just:

```
if (expression)
        statement ;
```

In this case, *statement* is executed if and only if *expression* evaluates to *true*.

Code indenting

In specifying the syntax in this way we are implying a style of code writing. Here we indent the code in the statements. By doing this we can visually pick up where the if-statement begins and ends, which statement belongs to the first part to be executed if the condition is true, and so on. You have perhaps already noticed that we have been indenting the code presented in this book.

However, the indenting is only for our benefit to help us read and understand the code; the compiler works out the unique meaning implied by the code it reads ignoring indenting or extra white space. Note that we cannot have white space in identifiers, numbers, reserved words etc. Hence the string

```
56    789
```

in our program would be interpreted as two integers, not as the integer 56789. (Indeed, because no Java syntax permits two integers in succession, this would cause an error message to be generated by the compiler.)

Example: the larger number

As an illustration of how we can use the if-else statement, consider the following problem. Suppose we have three variables `num1`, `num2` and `num3` each of type `int` and we want the value of `num3` to be the larger of the values of `num1` and `num2`. Of course, to achieve this we can use the class `Math` and the message `max` in the following way:

```
num3 = Math.max(num1, num2);
```

But consider how we can achieve the same thing using the if-else statement instead:

```
int num1 = ..; // assign some value to num1
int num2 = ..; // assign some value to num2
int num3;
if (num1 > num2)
    num3 = num1;
else
    num3 = num2;
```

PROBLEM 1: winning the toss

Construct a class `WinToss` which generates two random integers in the range 1 to 6. If the first random integer is greater than the second the string 'first player wins' is displayed in the Output window; otherwise 'second player wins' is displayed.

For help with this problem see Hints.

□

Boolean expressions

Central to the execution of an if-statement such as

`if` (*expression*)
    statement ;

is *expression* which must evaluate to *true* or *false*. Such an expression is called a *Boolean* expression.

Comparison operators

Typically, Boolean expressions make use of the following comparison operators to compare numerical expressions:

==	equal to
!=	not equal to
>	greater than
>=	greater than or equal to
<	less than
<=	less than or equal to

For example, the expression

`3 == 4`	evaluates to *false*;
`3 != 4`	evaluates to *true*;
`3 > 4`	evaluates to *false*;
`3 >= 4`	evaluates to *false*;
`3 < 4`	evaluates to *true*;
`3 <= 4`	evaluates to *true*.

Notice in particular that '==' is used to test for equality. **Be warned!!** The usual mathematical symbol '=' is not used here because that symbol is reserved in Java for the assignment operator (see Section 3.2).

In the examples above we compare actual numbers; in general we can use the comparison operators to compare any numerical expressions. For example,

```
balance > limit
```

was the Boolean expression in the earlier banking example. Indeed, we met Boolean expressions when we studied the for-loop in Chapter 3. The first example in Section 3.4 was

```
for (int i = 1; i <= 5; i = i + 1) {...}
```

where the check-part of the loop is the Boolean expression `i <= 5`. Indeed, this is no accident: the check part of a for-loop will always be a Boolean expression, and the loop continues only if this expression evaluates to *true*.

PROBLEM 2: a strange modification to integers

Construct a class `ModifyInteger` which when compiled and run requests a positive integer from the user and then modifies the supplied integer in the following way. If the supplied integer is even, it is divided by 2; otherwise (if it is odd) it is multiplied by 3, then 1 is added, and then the result is divided by 2. That is, if the supplied integer is n, say,

if n is even compute $n/2$;
otherwise compute $(3 * n + 1)/2$.

The program displays first the supplied integer and then its modified value in the Transcript window.

For help with this problem see Hints.

□

PROBLEM 3: randomly colouring the circle

Analogous to Problem 13 of Chapter 3, the expression

```
CircleFigure.create();
```

will open a window with a circle drawn at its (approximate) centre, provided the *genesis* package is imported. If in addition the *java.awt* package is imported, the expressions

```
CircleFigure.setColour(Color.red);
CircleFigure.setColour(Color.blue);
CircleFigure.setColour(Color.green);
```

will respectively turn the circle red, blue and green (see Section 2.4 for a description of the messages that can be sent to the class `CircleFigure`). Using this information, construct a class `RandomColourCircle` which will display a circle that is either red, blue or green with each colour having a probability of 1/3.

For help with this problem see Hints. The Hints also suggest alternative ways of coding this problem.

□

Discussion

In Problem 3 we have a situation similar to the following. Suppose `num` is a variable of type `int` whose value is either 1, 2 or 3, say, and suppose:

- if the value of `num` is 1 then we want to execute *statement*$_1$;
- if the value of `num` is 2 then we want to execute *statement*$_2$;
- if the value of `num` is 3 then we want to execute *statement*$_3$.

We can code this situation by using three if-statements in the following way:

```
if (num == 1)
      statement1;
if (num == 2)
      statement2;
if (num == 3)
      statement3;
```

In this special case where exactly one of the three bracketed if-expressions evaluates to *true*, the procedure can be coded in the following alternative way:

```
if (num == 1)
      statement1;
else
   if (num == 2)
      statement2;
   else
      statement3;
```

This alternative coding is preferable as it clearly captures the fact that exactly one of the three bracketed if-expressions evaluates to *true*. Notice that the statement associated with an `if` or `else` can itself be an if-else statement. Because this situation arises frequently, we adopt the convention of not indenting the embedded if-else statement but rather aligning the code in the following way:

```
if (num == 1)
      statement1;
else if (num == 2)
      statement2;
else
      statement3;
```

We emphasise that this alternative coding is equivalent to the original coding only when exactly one of the original three bracketed if-expressions evaluates to true. The codings are not equivalent if it is possible for none of the three expressions to evaluate to true, of if more than one can evaluate to true. **Be warned!!**

Statement blocks

Consider now the problem that if a certain condition is satisfied we want to execute several statements and not just one. For example, returning to the earlier banking example, suppose that if the balance in the account exceeds `limit`, interest is paid at `interestRate1` and in addition a `bonus` is also paid. To compute this we may be tempted to write (erroneous) code such as:

incorrect

```
if (balance > limit)
    interest = balance * interestRate1;
    interest = interest + bonus;
else
    interest = balance * interestRate2;
balance = balance + interest;
System.out.println("New balance is: " + balance);
```

Code such as this would not compile. The compiler would tell us that the `else` token is wrong. In fact, the message from the compiler would tell us we are using an `else` but there is no corresponding `if`. The problem here is that when the compiler reaches the semicolon after `interestRate1` it concludes that the if-statement has finished because it is not immediately followed by a corresponding else-option. **Be warned!!** The indenting we employ may be excellent for us to determine the intended structure, but it is only worthwhile if it corresponds to the structure the compiler would infer.

What we need to do here is place the indented sequence of statements (following the if-statement) within braces so as to make it a *block* of statements. As we saw when considering the for-loop in Chapter 3, a statement block is any sequence of statements (with each statement ending with a semicolon as always) enclosed in braces. In fact, this sequence can even be empty, i.e. it is valid to have the braces enclose nothing (except possibly white space). If the block consists of just one statement, the braces are not actually needed. Nevertheless, even in this case the braces are often included so as to help clarify to any reader the intention of the code.

The general rule is this: *any place a statement is required, a statement block can be inserted instead.*

With this in mind, let's correct the program above:

```
if (balance > limit)  {
    interest = balance * interestRate1;
    interest = interest + bonus;
} else
    interest = balance * interestRate2;
balance = balance + interest;
System.out.println("New blance is: " + balance);
```

Again we have illustrated a preferred code-writing style, indenting in a similar way the if-block of statements and the else-block of statement. The reader is in no doubt as to what belongs to which part and where each begins and ends. Our indenting corresponds to the structure the compiler would infer and all is well! What if we want a block of statements rather just a single statement to follow the else-part? No problem! We can insert a block of statements here by enclosing the statements in braces. In full generality, the syntax of the if-else statement is:

`if` (*expression*) {
    $statement\_sequence_1$
`} else {`
    $statement\_sequence_2$
}

where *expression* is a Boolean expression and where *statement_sequence*$_1$ is executed if *expression* evaluates to *true*, while *statement_sequence*$_2$ is executed if *expression* evaluates to *false*.

Some programmers always use braces to enclose the statements associated with an if-else statement even if there is only one such statement, claiming this enhances readability. The point we would make is this: when you have decided upon a style, use it consistently throughout your program so that someone else reading the code can quickly adapt to your approach.

Example: swapping values

As another illustration of how we can use the if-statement, consider the following problem. Suppose we have two integer values that are assigned to the variables num1 and num2 both of type int, and suppose we want to ensure that the value assigned to num1 is the larger of the two values. Hence if the value of num1 is less than the value of num2 we want to swap these values so that num1 has num2's original value and num2 has num1's original value. Here is code to achieve this:

```
int num1 = ..; // assign some value to num1
int num2 = ..; // assign some value to num2
if (num1 < num2) {
    int temp = num1;
    num1 = num2;
    num2 = temp;
}
```

Notice what we need to do here to swap the values of the variables. Simply coding

```
num1 = num2;
num2 = num1;
```

would not work. It would result in num1 having the same value as num2 (from the first assignment) but with num2 unchanged (for in the second assignment num1 now has the same value as num2). Hence num1 and num2 would both end up with the same value, namely, the original value of num2. **Be warned!!**

PROBLEM 4: selecting which tennis player serves first

This example is a simulation for deciding which of two tennis players is to begin serving. First, a player is selected at the toss of a coin (i.e. with probability

1/2). Then the selected player chooses whether or not to serve first. Suppose we know that 72% of players winning the toss elect to serve.

Construct a class `TennisServer` which simulates this process and displays in the Output window the result of the simulation, e.g. 'first player wins toss and serves', or 'second player loses toss and serves', or whatever.

It may help you to recall that the class `Math` returns a random floating point number between 0 and 1 when sent the message `random()`. For more help see Hints.

□

4.2 The while-loop

The for-loop we met in Chapter 3 uses a counter variable to enable us to repeatedly execute a block of statements a fixed number of times. But suppose we want to repeatedly execute a block of statements an indefinite number of times so long as a certain condition holds. The while-loop construct allows us to do this conveniently.

As an illustration, consider our earlier example involving the week's activities:

```
go to work;
go to work;
go to work;
go to work;
go to work;
go to tennis;
read a book;
```

We can write this more compactly as:

```
day = Monday;
while (day is not Saturday) {
    go to work;
    day = the next day; // the day after
}
go to tennis;
read a book;
```

The above 'while' construct allows a block of statements to be repeatedly executed so long as an associated condition remains true. In Java, we provide a similar construct called the *while-loop*. It has the syntax:

while (*expression*) {
    statement_sequence
}

Here *expression* must be a Boolean expression, i.e. it must evaluate to *true* or *false*. Also, if *statement_sequence* consists of only one statement, the braces can, as is usual, be omitted.

When we start the execution of a while-loop, *statement_sequence* is executed only if *expression* evaluates to *true*. After *statement_sequence* has been executed, we return to evaluate *expression* again. If it still evaluates to *true*, *statement_sequence* is executed again. This process of evaluating *expression* and executing *statement_sequence* repeats for as long as *expression* evaluates to *true*.

Hopefully, *statement_sequence* will change the values of the program variables in some way so that the value of *expression* can eventually become *false*, otherwise the while-loop will execute indefinitely and we'll be here for a very long time! Constructing while-loops that do not terminate but loop forever (known as *infinite* loops) can be a very serious programming error and must be carefully guarded against. **Be warned!!** We will be saying something about how you can guard against such an error later in this chapter.

PROBLEM 5: tossing a die for consecutive sixes

Open the folder *Toss 6* and run the class Toss6 whose code is given below:

```
import genesis.*;

public class Toss6 {

    /*
    Toss a die until a 6 appears */

    public static void main (String [ ] args) {
        int nextToss = (int)(6* Math.random()) + 1;
        Transcript.print(nextToss);
        while (nextToss != 6) {
            nextToss = (int)(6* Math.random()) + 1;
            Transcript.print(" "+nextToss);
        }
    }
}
```

When executed, this class simulates the tossing of a die until the first 6 is tossed. It displays in the Transcript window the sequence of integers generated until the first 6 appears.

Modify this code to construct a class `Toss6Consec` that simulates the tossing of a die until two consecutive sixes are tossed, displaying in the Transcript window the sequence of integers generated until the first consecutive pair of sixes appear.

For help with this problem see Hints.

□

Notice that in Problem 5 the number of repetitions of the loop in the class `Toss6` (and also in the class `Toss6Consec`) cannot be calculated in advance; the number of repetitions will depend on the particular sequence of random numbers that is generated. On different executions different length sequences of numbers will be generated.

PROBLEM 6: tossing two dice for a pair of sixes

Construct the class `Toss6Pair` which simulates the tossing of a pair of dice. Both dice are tossed together and this tossing together continues until a pair of sixes is tossed, i.e. until a 6 appears on both dice at the same time. When executed the class displays in the Output window the number of times the pair of dice is tossed before the required pair of sixes appears.

For help with this problem see Hints.

□

The dice-tossing computer simulation in Problem 6 enables us to make estimates of various statistics. For example, on average how many tosses of two dice are needed until a pair of sixes is obtained?

PROBLEM 7: average tosses for a pair of sixes

Construct a class `Average6Pair` which, like the class `Toss6Pair`, simulates the tossing of two dice until a pair of sixes is obtained, but instead of performing the simulation once only, repeats the simulation 1000 times displaying in the Output window the average number of tosses required.

For help with this problem see Hints.

□

The next problem revisits the class SquareToOrigin introduced in Problem 15 of Chapter 3. In that problem for-loops were used to move a square from the centre of a window to the upper-left corner of the window. The idea adopted in that class was to send SquareFigure the messages getXCorner() and getYCorner() that return the x- and y-coordinates respectively of the upper-left corner of the square. With this information for-loops can be constructed that first move the square left to the edge of the window, and then move the square up to the top of the window. The square moves one pixel every 50 milliseconds. Here is the code:

```
import genesis.*;

public class SquareToOrigin {

    public static void main (String [ ] args) {
        SquareFigure.create();
        int distanceLeft = SquareFigure.getXCorner();
        int distanceUp = SquareFigure.getYCorner();
        int i;
        for (i = 1; i <= distanceLeft; i++) {
            Delay.milliseconds(50);
            SquareFigure.moveLeft(1);
        }
        for (i = 1; i <= distanceUp; i++) {
            Delay.milliseconds(50);
            SquareFigure.moveUp(1);
        }
    }
}
```

PROBLEM 8: moving the square again

Construct a class WhileSquareToOrigin that, like the class SquareToOrigin, moves the square to the origin one pixel every 50 milliseconds by first moving it left to the left edge of the window and then moving it up to the top of the window. This time however, use while-loops rather than for-loops. For example, to move the square left to the left border of the window construct a while-loop whose associated expression returns *true* if and only if the square is not yet at the left border of the window.

For help with this problem see Hints.

□

PROBLEM 9: a strange sequence of integers

Look again at the class `ModifyInteger` introduced in Problem 2. When run, first a positive integer is requested from the user, and then the supplied integer is modified in the following way: if the supplied integer is even, it is divided by 2; otherwise (if it is odd) it is multiplied by 3, then 1 is added, and then the result is divided by 2. That is, if the supplied integer is n, say,

if n is even compute $n/2$;
otherwise compute $(3 * n + 1)/2$.

Consider the following question: if we continue this process (i.e. at each stage we take the integer produced by the previous stage, and if it is even divide by 2, otherwise multiply by 3, add 1, and then divide by 2) will we eventually get the number 1? For example, suppose we start with 3. Then we get:

3
5 (because 3 is odd and 5 = (3*3 + 1)/2)
8 (because 5 is odd and 8 = (3*5 + 1)/2)
4 (because 8 is even and 4 = 8/2)
2 (because 4 is even and 2 = 4/2)
1 (because 2 is even and 1 = 2/2)

It turns out that for every initial positive integer anyone has ever tried, this process has always reached the number 1, but a proof that this is the case for all integers has yet to be found.

Construct a class `StrangeSequence` which when run first requests the user to supply a positive integer, and then displays in the Transcript window the sequence of integers produced by the above process, stopping when finally the number 1 is reached. The program then displays in the Transcript window the length of the sequence produced. For example, if the integer 3 is supplied by the user, the output should be something like

```
3 5 8 4 2 1
The length of the sequence is 6.
```

(Note: Because nobody has been able to prove that the number 1 is always reached, we cannot be certain our program will always terminate!)

For help with this problem see Hints.

□

4.3 Case study: greatest common divisor

To illustrate how we can develop a program to undertake a particular task, consider the problem of finding the greatest common divisor (gcd) of two positive integers. We shall progressively refine and code in Java an algorithm to compute the gcd.

An obvious scenario for finding the gcd is to first find the prime factors of the two integers and then extract those factors that are common. For example, to find the gcd of 270 and 360:

- the prime factorisation of 270 is 2 * 3 * 3 * 3 * 5;
- the prime factorisation of 360 is 2 * 2 * 2 * 3 * 3 * 5;
- thus the largest common factor is 2 * 3 * 3 * 5 which gives 90 as the gcd.

But there is a much simpler algorithm due to Euclid. This is one of the oldest algorithms dating from about 300 B.C. and can be described by the following informal scenario:

- start with two positive integers;
- check to see if the two integers are equal;
- if so, then this common value is obviously the gcd;
- if not, then replace the pair of integers by a pair calculated as follows:
  - the smaller of the two integers remains unchanged, but
  - the larger of the two integers is replaced by the difference between the larger (i.e. itself) and the smaller;
- repeat this process until the two integers are equal; this common value is then the gcd.

For example, applying this algorithm to the numbers 270 and 360:

- we start with 270 and 360;
- replacing the larger with the difference between it and the smaller, but leaving the smaller unchanged, gives us 270 and 90;
- repeating this gives 180 and 90;
- repeating this once more gives 90 and 90;
- at this point the two numbers are equal, so we conclude the gcd is 90.

Verifying the algorithm

While it worked for this pair of numbers, does it work for any pair? Let's investigate! Consider a and b and suppose $a > b$. Let $d = a-b$ and suppose f is a common factor of both a and b. Then

$$d = f * a_1 - f * b_1 \quad \text{where } f * a_1 = a \text{ and } f * b_1 = b.$$

Clearly, this tells us that f is also a factor of d , since we can rewrite this last line as

$$d = f * (a_1 - b_1).$$

That is, any common factor of the integers a and b is also a common factor of the integers d and b, where $d = a-b$.

Conversely, suppose that d and b have a common factor g. Then

$$a = b + d$$
$$a = g * b_2 + g * d_2 \quad \text{where } g * b_2 = b \text{ and } g * d_2 = d$$

This implies

$$a = g * (b_2 + d_2)$$

and so a also has g as a factor. That is, any common factor of the integers d and b, where $d = a-b$, is also a common factor of the integers a and b.

To summarise, if we take a pair of positive integers and replace the larger by the difference between it and the smaller while leaving the smaller unchanged, the new pair of numbers so obtained has exactly the same common factors as the original pair of numbers. In particular, and this is the crucial observation here, the gcd of the new pair of numbers will be the same as the gcd of the original pair. Consequently, if the new pair of numbers are equal, then this common value must be the gcd of the original pair of numbers because it is clearly the gcd of the new pair.

Termination

There is one more issue that we need to consider. How do we know that Euclid's algorithm will always terminate? Perhaps it is possible to find a pair of numbers such that when Euclid's algorithm is applied we never reach the stage where both the numbers become equal?

The subtle point to observe here is that every time we apply a stage in Euclid's algorithm we get a pair of numbers whose maximum is *strictly* smaller (because we have replaced the larger number by a number that is strictly smaller). But the numbers are always positive, so their maximum will also be positive. So, this maximum is a positive number that at each stage gets strictly smaller. Clearly this cannot go on forever. Hence we can be sure the algorithm must eventually terminate, i.e. the stage must be reached when the two numbers are equal. This argument assures us that if we use a while-loop to implement Euclid's algorithm it will not loop indefinitely.

Code development

Let's now develop the program. Here we take our time to illustrate how we might incrementally develop and improve a computer program. We start by declaring a couple of variables to store the numbers whose gcd we require:

```
int num1 = ..;
int num2 = ..;
```

As we need to repeat the computation, we propose a program like

```
while (num1 != num2) {
    ...
}
```

Now we apply the next stage of Euclid's algorithm: the smaller of the two numbers is unchanged but the larger is replaced by the difference between it and the smaller:

```
if (num1 > num2)
    num1 = num1 - num2;
else
    num2 = num2 - num1;
```

Putting it all together:

```
int num1 = ..; // assign some value to num1
int num2 = ..; // assign some value to num2
while (num1 != num2) {
    if (num1 > num2)
        num1 = num1 - num2;
    else
        num2 = num2 - num1;
}
```

PROBLEM 10: computing the gcd

Construct a class Gcd that requests two positive integers from the user via dialog boxes and displays in the Transcript window the gcd of these two numbers. Your class should use the coding of Euclid's algorithm developed above.

Test the class by using it to find the gcd of various pairs of positive integers.

For help with this problem see Hints.

□

Improving the algorithm

Although Euclid's algorithm as described above efficiently finds the gcd of two positive integers, the question still arises as to whether it can be further improved. The key step in the above algorithm is the replacement of the larger of the two numbers by the difference between it and the smaller, i.e. the smaller number is subtracted from the larger.

But why stop there? Why not subtract the smaller number from the larger as often as possible, subject to the restriction that the resulting number must not become negative? In fact, we already have a Java operator, the modulus operator '%', that does precisely this. So the suggestion is that the key step in the algorithm be modified so that we replace the larger of the two numbers by the number *larger % smaller*.

Verification

Will this new version of the algorithm still give us the gcd of the two original positive integers? It will, but we need to also modify the terminating condition. Let's investigate!

First, observe that replacing the larger number by *larger % smaller* and leaving the smaller number unchanged will, just as with the previous algorithm, give us a new pair of numbers whose gcd is the same as the original pair. (The proof of this is essentially the same as before.)

Termination

Now consider the issue of termination. The original algorithm terminates when the two numbers become equal, at which stage this common value is the gcd we seek. But this stage is only reached if at the previous stage in the algorithm the larger number is a multiple of the smaller. In this case, considering the new algorithm, the value of *larger % smaller* would become 0. Hence the new algorithm terminates not when the two numbers become equal but when the smaller of the two numbers becomes 0, at which stage the other (larger) number is the gcd we seek.

Finally, notice that if a and b are two positive integers with $a > b$, then it follows $(a \% b) < b$. That is, if a is the larger number, replacing a by $a \% b$ and leaving b unchanged ensures that b now becomes the larger number.

Code development

Let us now refine this new algorithm into Java code. First, declare two variables of type `int` and assign to them the positive integer values whose gcd we wish to find:

```
int num1 = ..;
int num2 = ..;
```

Next, by swapping the values of these variables if necessary, ensure that `num1` is the larger of the two:

```
int temp;
if (num1 < num2) {
    temp = num1;
    num1 = num2;
    num2 = temp;
}
```

Finally, repeatedly apply the modulus operation to reduce the larger number by the smaller:

```
while (num2 != 0) {
    temp = num2;
    num2 = num1 % num2;
    num1 = temp;
}
```

Notice that in this code we assign the value of `num1 % num2` to `num2`, and assign the previous value of `num2` to `num1`, ensuring that afterwards `num1` remains the larger and `num2` the smaller of the two numbers.

Summary

What this example illustrates is the way we approach the development and coding of an algorithm to solve a particular problem. The above details are not in themselves important; what is important is the procedure. First we develop an algorithm informally and verify that it solves the problem at hand (part of the verification will be to show that the algorithm terminates). Then we code the algorithm (in Java in our case). Finally, we revise the algorithm to see if it can be improved.

PROBLEM 11: an improved gcd program

Construct a class `ImprovedGcd` that requests two positive integers from the user via dialog boxes and displays in the Transcript window the gcd of these two numbers. Your code should use the improved coding of Euclid's algorithm developed above.

Test the class by using it to find the gcd of various pairs of positive integers.

For help with this problem see Hints.

□

4.4 Case study: approximating square roots

A positive integer that is not a perfect square has an irrational square root. Such a square root cannot be expressed exactly using a finite decimal representation. Consequently, we are often forced to approximate when evaluating square roots.

The class `Math`, when sent a message of the form `sqrt(`*n*`)` where *n* is some positive number, will return an approximation to the square root of *n*. In this section, however, we want to ignore the `Math` class and instead look at how the while-loop construct, combined with an observation first made by Newton, can be applied to compute an approximation to the square root of a positive number.

Newton's approximation

Newton observed that if *s* is an approximation to the square root of a number *n*, then

$$(s + (n/s))/2$$

is a better approximation. We won't attempt to justify this assertion here, but simply take it as true and apply it to calculate approximations to square roots.

Here is an informal scenario for calculating an approximation to the square root of some positive number *n*, say, based on Newton's method:

- start with some approximation *approx*, say, to the square root of *n*;
- if *approx* is not sufficiently close to the square root of *n* replace *approx* by

  $$(approx + (n/approx))/2;$$

- continue until *approx* is sufficiently close to the square root of *n*.

Code development

Let's now refine this scenario into Java code. First, declare a variable num, say, of type double and assign to it the positive number whose square root we want to evaluate:

```
double num = ..;
```

Next, find an initial approximation to the square root of num. We can take num/2 as the initial approximation. Admittedly this is not a very good approximation, but it won't matter because the approximations will become increasingly accurate as the algorithm progresses:

```
double approx = num/2;
```

Now create a while-loop to compute the next value of approx using Newton's method. The while-loop will terminate only when approx is sufficiently close to the square root of num. In our case, we shall accept approx as sufficiently close if $\mathtt{approx}^2$ is within 10^{-6} of num:

```
while (Math.abs(approx*approx - num) > 0.000001)
    approx = (approx + (num / approx)) / 2;
```

PROBLEM 12: computing approximate square roots

Construct a class SquareRoot that requests a positive floating point number from the user and calculates an approximation to its square root using Newton's method as coded above. The approximate square root is displayed in the Transcript window.

Test your class by using it to find the square root of various positive numbers.

For help with this problem see Hints.

□

4.5 The do-loop

The do-loop is essentially a variant of the while-loop. It has the following syntax:

```
do {
    statement_sequence
} while (expression) ;
```

Here *expression* must be a Boolean expression (i.e. it must evaluate to *true* or *false*) and unlike the while-loop, this terminating conditional comes *after* the do-loop's *statement_sequence*. The result is that *statement_sequence* is always executed before the test is (re)applied and so the do-statement will always execute the body *statement_sequence* at least once. After the execution of *statement_sequence*, it will be executed again only if *expression* evaluates to *true*.

Notice that any do-loop can be rewritten as a while-loop, e.g. the above general form is equivalent to

```
{ statement_sequence }
while (expression) {
    statement_sequence
}
```

where *expression* and *statement_sequence* on each occasion are the identical constructs as for the do-loop.

To illustrate the do-loop, consider the class Toss9 (you will find this class in the file *Toss9.java* in the folder *Toss 9*):

```
import genesis.*;

public class Toss9 {

    /*
    Repeatedly generate a random integer every 1/5th of
    a second in the range 1 to 50 until a 9 is generated.
    */

    public static void main (String [] args) {
        int randInt;
        do {
            randInt = (int)(50*Math.random()) + 1;
            Transcript.print(randInt+" ");
            Delay.milliseconds(200);
        } while (randInt != 9);
    }
}
```

When run, this code randomly generates an integer in the range 1 to 50 every 1/5th of a second until a 9 is generated. Notice the way the do-loop is used here: because we have to generate at least one random number, it is best to delay the test for the integer 9 until after the number has been generated. Hence the do-loop is the natural construct to choose.

PROBLEM 13: circles with random radii

Construct a class `RandomRadius` that, by sending the message `create()` followed by the message `setRadius(..)` to the class `CircleFigure` (see Section 2.4) opens a window containing at its (approximate) centre a circle whose radius is an integer randomly selected in the range 10 to 120 pixels. Then every half a second the circle's radius is randomly changed to between 10 and 120 pixels. The process stops when the circle's radius becomes greater than 115 pixels.

For help with this problem see Hints.

4.6 Boolean type

We have already seen Boolean expressions that evaluate to one of two possible values, *true* or *false*, and we have seen the need for these Boolean values in controlling execution associated with an if-statement or with iterative constructs such as the while- and do-statements. However, we can also declare variables to be of `boolean` type. For example, the statement

```
boolean wonToss = false;
```

declares a variable `wonToss` of type `boolean` and initialises its value to *false*. This follows the pattern we have already seen for the declaration of number and string variables. Note that the only values of `boolean` type are *true* and *false*.

Boolean operators

There are three Boolean operators which correspond closely to the logical connectives we use in common everyday English conversation. For example, consider the sentence: *If I am **not** well, I'll stay in bed.* The English word **not** negates the meaning of the following word or phrase. (Notice it doesn't indicate what I'll do if I am well.)

Similarly, we might say: *I will go if and only if it is fine **and** the trains are running.* The connective **and** joins conditions and means that if both are true then the overall condition is true and I will go. However, if either one of the conditions is false (or indeed if both are false) then the result is false and I won't go.

And finally, look at the sentence: *We will go swimming if Dad is home **or** my sister is visiting.* The intent here is that if one or other condition is true then the overall assertion is true and we will go swimming. Both conditions do not need to be satisfied: one is enough. (If both are true, well and good: it gives us a choice about how to fulfil the assertion.)

In Java there are three Boolean operators that mirror these logical connectives. They are '!' (for logical *not*), '&&' (for logical *and*) and '||' (for logical *or*) (here '||' is the character '|' repeated) and they each construct a new Boolean expression. For example, if *a* and *b* are Boolean expressions, then

!*a*
a && *b*
a || *b*

are also Boolean expressions (i.e. evaluate to *true* or *false*). The following table gives their meanings (in this table *a* and *b* stand for arbitrary Boolean expressions):

operator	informal name	example	meaning
!	not	!*a*	*true* if *a* is *false* *false* if *a* is *true*
&&	and	*a* && *b*	*true* if and only if both *a* and *b* are *true*
||	or	*a* || *b*	*false* if and only if both *a* and *b* are *false*

Precedence

Just as the arithmetic operators of addition, multiplication etc. are ordered according to precedence (see Section 3.1), so too are the Boolean operators. The operator '!' has highest precedence followed by '&&' then '||'. As an example, consider the Boolean expression

!*a* || *b* && *c* || *d*

where *a*, *b*, *c* and *d* are arbitrary Boolean expressions. Parenthesising to display the equivalent inferred precedence we would have:

(!*a*) || (*b* && *c*) || *d*

This expression evaluates to *true* when at least one of !*a*, (*b* && *c*) or *d* evaluates to *true*, i.e. when *a* is *false*, or when both *b* and *c* are *true*, or when *d* is *true*.

Just to reiterate this point, in Java we can declare a variable `condition`, say, of type `boolean` by the statement

```
boolean condition = !a || b && c || d;
```

where a, b, c and d are Boolean expressions defined earlier in the code. While this logical expression has a unique interpretation, often such logic expressions are not all that readable. It is usual to include parentheses to make the code easier to understand, especially as precedence rules vary from language to language — unfortunately.

As an example, consider again the class Toss6Consec that was constructed in Problem 5. In this class the while-loop terminated only when consecutive tosses were sixes. The main method of that class (see Hints for Problem 5) contained the following code:

```
int lastToss = 0;
int nextToss = (int)(6* Math.random()) + 1;
Transcript.print(nextToss);
while (lastToss + nextToss != 12) {
    lastToss = nextToss;
    nextToss = (int)(6* Math.random()) + 1;
    Transcript.print(" "+nextToss);
}
```

The while-loop condition used in this class to test that the last two tosses were not both sixes is the somewhat artificial:

```
lastToss + nextToss != 12
```

Using the Boolean operators this condition can now be coded as the logically equivalent:

```
lastToss != 6 || nextToss != 6
```

This expression more closely captures the informal intention, hence enhancing the readability of the code.

Example: the Fibonacci sequence

The code for the class Toss6Consec made use of an interesting and common programming strategy. In that program we needed to keep track of not just the latest toss of the die (variable nextToss) but also the previous toss (variable lastToss). After each toss and before the next toss the value of lastToss had to be reset to be the latest toss value:

```
lastToss = nextToss;
```

As another example of this strategy, consider the Fibonacci sequence

1, 1, 2, 3, 5, 8, 13, ...

where each integer in this sequence (except for the first two) is the sum of the previous two integers. For example,

the third integer is 1+1 = 2;
the fourth integer is 1+2 = 3;
the fifth integer is 2+3 = 5; and so on.

Suppose we want to write a program to generate the integers in this sequence. At each stage we will need to keep track of the last two integers in the sequence so far so as to calculate the next integer in the sequence.

PROBLEM 14: the Fibonacci sequence

Construct the class `Fibonacci` that when run outputs to the Transcript window the integers in the Fibonacci sequence in order, ending when the first integer greater than one million and divisible by 5 is output.

For help with this problem see Hints.

□

To end this section, here is a challenge problem that makes use of Boolean expressions as well as while-loops, for-loops and if-statements. This exercise is not in itself difficult, but it will require great care to ensure all the loops are correctly constructed. You will find careful indenting of the code will greatly help you keep track of what is happening.

PROBLEM 15: a wandering square

Construct a class `WanderingSquare` that when run starts by sending the class `SquareFigure` (see Section 2.4) the message `create()`, and then repeatedly moves the square 20 pixels randomly either left, right, up or down. The square moves at a speed of 1 pixel every 10 milliseconds. The motion stops when the upper-left corner of the square has x-coordinate 0 or 342, or y-coordinate 0 or 218. (These values are chosen as they will be the coordinate values of the upper-left corner of the square when the square is (approximately) at either the left, right, top or bottom edge of the display region of the window, i.e. the square stops moving when an edge of the window is reached. In Chapter 9 we will see how these values can be precisely determined.)

To give you some idea of what is required, open the folder *Wandering Square Demo* and run the class `WanderingSquareDemo`. The *.java* file for this class is empty; the code that was in it was compiled and then deleted, but the compiled *.class* file remains in the folder.

For help with this problem see Hints.

□

4.7 The switch-statement

The if-statement is awkward if we are confronted with multiple selections with many alternatives. Consider code which determines the number of days in a month when given the month as an integer in the range 1 to 12 (in the code below we suppose `month` is a variable of type `int` whose value is in the range 1 to 12):

```
int daysInMonth;
if (month == 1) daysInMonth = 31;       // for January
else if (month == 2) daysInMonth =28;   // for February
else if (month == 3) daysInMonth =31;   // for March
else if (month == 4) daysInMonth =30;   // for April
else if (month == 5) daysInMonth =31;   // for May
else if (month == 6) daysInMonth =30;   // for June
else if (month == 7) daysInMonth =31;   // for July
else if (month == 8) daysInMonth =31;   // for August
else if (month == 9) daysInMonth =30;   // for September
else if (month == 10) daysInMonth =31;  // for October
else if (month == 11) daysInMonth =30;  // for November
else daysInMonth = 31;                  // for December
```

Notice that this code is *very* cumbersome!

Java provides another alternation statement which is useful in situations where the decision is based on an integer value (`byte`, `short`, `int`, `long`) or upon a character value (`char`). It is called the *switch-statement*. The syntax of the switch-statement is:

```
switch (expression) {
    case value1 : statement_sequence1 ;
    case value2 : statement_sequence2 ;
    case value3 : statement_sequence3 ;
    ...
   default : statement_sequencen;   // the default is optional
}
```

First, *expression* is evaluated. Unlike the expression associated with the if-statement or the for-, while- and do-loops, the type of *expression* is not `boolean`. Rather, its value must be an integer or a character. The option whose `case` *value* matches the value of *expression* is selected and the *statement_sequence* following it is executed. If no match occurs and the `default` tag is present, that option is selected.

The break-statement

In executing the *statement_sequence* following, the labels (i.e. the '`case` *value*' part) are effectively invisible and each *statement_sequence* from this point to the conclusion of the switch-statement is in line for execution. This is not what we generally want. We usually want the *statement_sequence* corresponding to the case in point to be executed and then execution to resume at the statement following the complete switch-statement. This is achieved by a break-statement which has the simple syntax

```
break;
```

Thus the most common usage of the switch-statement is like the following:

```
switch (expression) {
   case value1 : statement_sequence1 ; break;
   case value2 : statement_sequence2 ; break;
   case value3 : statement_sequence3 ; break;
   ...
   default : statement_sequencen ;   // optional
}
```

Now let's rewrite the code to determine the number of days in a month:

```
int daysInMonth;
switch (month) {
    case 4:
    case 6:
    case 9:
    case 11: daysInMonth = 30; break;
    case 2: daysInMonth = 28; break;   // non leap year
    default : daysInMonth = 31;
}
```

There are interesting aspects of this code so take time to read it carefully. Notice in particular, that if the value of `month` is 4, 6 or 9, the result is the same as if this value was 11. This is because there is no break-statement after the (empty) statement-sequences associated with these cases, so execution continues to a break-statement, and this occurs only after the assignment `daysInMonth = 30`.

PROBLEM 16: flashing colours

Open the folder *Flashing Colours* and run the class `FlashingColours`. A window opens containing a circle whose colour changes frequently. To stop the

execution of this program close the window containing the circle. The code for the class `FlashingColours` is as follows:

```
import genesis.*;
import java.awt.*;

public class FlashingColours {

    /*
    Flashing the colours of a circle.
    */

    public static void main (String [] args) {
        CircleFigure.create();
        CircleFigure.setRadius(100);
        int rand;
        while (true) {
            Delay.milliseconds(250);
            rand = (int)(5*Math.random());
            if (rand == 0) CircleFigure.setColour(Color.red);
            else if (rand == 1)
                CircleFigure.setColour(Color.blue);
            else if (rand == 2)
                CircleFigure.setColour(Color.green);
            else if (rand == 3)
                CircleFigure.setColour(Color.magenta);
            else CircleFigure.setColour(Color.yellow);
        }
    }
}
```

Modify the code for this class so as to use a switch-statement rather than the nested if-statements.

For help with this problem see Hints.

□

Chapter 4 self-check

Can you describe

- a Boolean expression?
- the Boolean comparison operators ==, !=, >, >=, < and <= ?

- the distinction between the operators = and ==?
- statement blocks?
- the distinction between the for-loop, the while-loop and the do-loop?
- the Java `boolean` type?
- the Boolean operators `!`, &&, and `||`?

Can you describe the syntax of the following Java constructs:

- the if-statement?
- the if-else statement?
- statement blocks?
- the while-loop?
- the do-loop?
- the switch-statement?

Can you write Java code that

- uses an if-else statement to select between statement blocks for execution?
- uses a while-loop or a do-loop for iteratively executing a block of statements?
- declares and uses variables of `boolean` type?
- uses Boolean expressions and applies Boolean operators?
- uses the switch-statement to select between several code options?

Arrays 5

Prerequisites

Before beginning Chapter 5 you will need to be familiar with the contents of all previous chapters in *Java Genesis*. In particular, you should have a good understanding of:

- the primitive types `int` and `double`;
- how to construct and display strings in the Output or Transcript windows;
- how to code a class containing a `main` method;
- how to use conditional-statements to select between code options;
- the for-loop and the while-loop constructs.

Overview

It frequently happens that we need to work with a collection of similar data. For example, a bank may manage several thousand accounts for its customers and from time to time may need to pay interest to these accounts. Similarly, in order to give a final grade to students taking some course it is necessary to record and process the marks obtained by each student.

To handle such situations we create and use special coding constructs known as *data structures*. In this chapter we introduce a particularly useful and straightforward Java data structure, the *array*.

An array data structure is especially useful when we want to record and manipulate an assembly of elements of identical type. In an array the individual data items are recorded sequentially, and this simple structure makes the processing of data held in the array straightforward. In particular, the for-loop is ideally suited for working with arrays.

5.1 The array data structure

We consider how we can create arrays to handle items of data of the same type which need to be processed in an identical way. We look at how we can store and access the individual data items in an array.

Problems:

1 square roots of 10 integers

2 an array of die tosses

3 array-variable assignment

4 number of students awarded each grade

5 gathering statistics on die tossing

6 below average

7 desperately seeking 6

5.2 Case study: sorting an array

Sorting names into alphabetical order and sorting students' results in order of decreasing grades are but two situations where ordering individual data items in a collection is important. In this section we introduce two methods of sorting: selection sort and bubble sort.

Problems:

8 exploring sorting an array

9 selection sort demo

10 coding selection sort

11 bubble sort demo

12 coding bubble sort

5.3 Literal arrays

When we declare a variable we can at the same time directly assign a value to that variable. For example, the statement

```
int anInteger = 34;
```

declares the variable `anInteger` to be of type `int` and directly assigns to it the integer value 34. In this section we see how we can declare an array variable and at the same time directly assign to it a literal array value in a similar way.

5.4 Multi-dimensional arrays

We extend the array data structure to arrays of arrays. The techniques introduced can be generalised to arrays of 3 or more dimensions, but our discussion will be limited to 2-dimensional arrays.

Problems:

13 processing marks

14 corner store

Learning outcomes

At the conclusion of Chapter 5 you will understand:

- the need for data structures to collect elements of some common type;
- the array data structure, and how to
  - declare an array;
  - assign values to the elements of an array;
  - access specific array elements;
- the close association between the for-loop and the array;
- how to search an array;
- elementary sorting techniques, and in particular
  - the selection sort algorithm;
  - the bubble sort algorithm;
- the use of two-dimensional arrays, and how to
  - declare them;
  - process them using nested for-loops.

5.1 The array data structure

Let us look at an example to see why arrays are a necessary addition to Java (or any similar programming language).

Sorting integers

Suppose we have two variables `num1` and `num2`, say, of type `int` and require `num1` and `num2` together to store the values originally assigned to them, but with `num1` holding the smaller:

```
int num1 = ..; // assign some value to num1
int num2 = ..; // assign some value to num2
int temp;
if (num1 > num2) {
    temp = num1;
    num1 = num2;
    num2 = temp;
}
```

Now suppose we have three variables `num1`, `num2` and `num3` of type `int` and want a permutation of the original values such that `num1 <= num2 <= num3`:

```
int num1 = ..; // assign some value to num1
int num2 = ..; // assign some value to num2
int num3 = ..; // assign some value to num3
int temp;

// first ensure that num2 is not smaller than num1
if (num1 > num2) {
    temp = num1;
    num1 = num2;
    num2 = temp;
}
// next ensure that num3 is also not smaller than num1
if (num1 > num3) {
    temp = num1;
    num1 = num3;
    num3 = temp;
}
// finally ensure num3 is not smaller than num2
if (num2 > num3) {
    temp = num2;
    num2 = num3;
    num3 = temp;
}
// now they are ranked in non-decreasing order
```

What now if we have 4 variables to sort? Then, when you think you've resolved that problem, what about 5? And so on? Our above program would grow and grow. Imagine looking for an error in a program like the one above which sorted hundreds of integer variables into ascending sequence! Consider the problem of inventing variable names just to store the hundreds of integers!

What we need is some construct that enables us to work with a collection of similar entities without the need to assign a distinct variable name to each entity. Hopefully we can then use such a construct to solve the general problem of arranging a set of numbers in ascending order without the need to be specific about how many numbers are being sorted. We want a program that will sort 2, 20, or 200,000 numbers without modification.

Sequences

There is a mathematical notation which we modify for our use: the idea of a *sequence* of values. For example, we can write a sequence mathematically as:

$$s = \langle 12, 56, 48, 12, 17 \rangle$$

and refer to any particular element in the sequence using subscript notation, e.g.

$$s_1 = 12, s_2 = 56, \text{ and so on.}$$

The idea of a sequence is captured in Java by the *array* construct. To illustrate how this is done, consider the following situation. Suppose we have the mathematical sequence

$$s = \langle 1, 4, 9, 16, 25, 36 \rangle$$

consisting of the first 6 non-zero perfect squares. That is, the length of the sequence s is 6 and for any integer k such that $1 \leqslant k \leqslant 6$, the element s_k in position k in the sequence is the integer k^2.

The array construct

Let's capture this in Java using the array construct. In Java, we declare an array variable using the syntax:

type `[]` *arrayname* ;

For *type* we can substitute any data type the compiler knows about. This type is called the *base type* of the array. For example, we could write

```
int [] perfectSquares;
```

(read 'an array of type `int` called `perfectSquares`'), which specifies we have a variable `perfectSquares` which can only reference an array of elements all of type `int`. At this point of declaration the array is given a name, but the array itself does not yet exist. We create the array with an *array allocation* expression that declares the length of the array and indicates its base type. In our case we have the first 6 non-zero perfect squares and we want to establish an array to let us store these 6 integer values. We perform this feat by:

```
perfectSquares = new int [6];
```

The general syntax for an array allocation declaration is

arrayname = `new` *type* [*expression*] ;

where *arrayname* is the previously declared variable name for the array, *type* is the base type of the array, and *expression* is an expression of type `int` that evaluates to some positive integer denoting the length (i.e. the number of positions) of the sequence.

[*An aside*: You will see in Chapter 7 that the right-hand side of this declaration is the syntax for creating an object, i.e. an instance of a class. This suggests that arrays are really instances of a class. This is indeed true, but the Java language has special syntax for arrays. `String` is an another example of a class for which Java has special syntactic concessions. These concessions are permitted because these types are so commonly used. It can be argued, however, that these special cases destroy the 'purity' of the Java language. *End aside*]

We can combine the array declaration with the array allocation, e.g.

```
int [] perfectSquares = new int [6];
```

We have now created the array `perfectSquares` of length 6, but we have yet to assign any values to the 6 positions in this array. To do this we need to know how can we access individual elements in the array.

Accessing array elements

The notation we use to access an element in an array is similar to the mathematical one we saw above, but of course we cannot use subscripts. Instead, we enclose the index expression in square brackets, which enables the index expression not only to be presented in-line, but also quickly discerned visually. For instance,

```
perfectSquares[4]
```

denotes the integer at index position 4 in the array `perfectSquares`.

Some aspects, however, need close attention. The indexing of an array always starts from 0, not 1. **Be warned!!** So in our case above, `perfectSquares[0]` at index position 0 denotes the *first* integer in the array, and `perfectSquares[5]` at index position 5 denotes the *last* (i.e. the *sixth*) integer in the array.

The general syntax for accessing an element in an array is

arrayname[*expression*]

where *arrayname* is the previously declared variable name for the array and *expression* is an expression of type `int` that evaluates to some positive integer between 0 and one less than the length of the array.

Assigning values to array elements

Now that we know how to access an element in an array, let's apply this to assign values to the 6 positions in our array. Remembering our for-loop, we can see it is ideal for working with the array data structure. We can access each and every element in turn by a for-loop like:

```
for (int i = 0; i < 6; i++) {
.. perfectSquares[i]  .. // as needed
}
```

You can see that `perfectSquares[i]`, i.e. the one expression, permits access to each and every array value merely by changing the index value `i`, which in this case is also the loop control variable. As the for-loop does this changing, it is ideally suited to this style of processing. Effectively we can give a unique name to each element of the collection by varying the value of the index.

So here then is the code that will create the array `perfectSquares` and populate it with the first 6 non-zero perfect squares:

```
int [] perfectSquares = new int [6];
for (int i=0; i<6; i++) perfectSquares[i] = (i+1)*(i+1);
```

When executed, `perfectSquares` becomes the array $\langle 1, 4, 9, 16, 25, 36 \rangle$ as required. Notice that the element `perfectSquares[i]` at index position `i` in the array is assigned the value `(i+1)*(i+1)`, *not* `i*i`, because the first index of an array is 0, *not* 1.

The attribute `length`

One other neat feature of arrays in Java is the attribute `length`. To find the length of the array `perfectSquares`, say, we use the expression

```
perfectSquares.length
```

In our case, this will evaluate to 6, of course. Using the attribute length gives us an alternative, and preferable, way to code the above for-loop:

```
for (int i=0; i<perfectSquares.length; i++)
    perfectSquares[i] = (i+1)*(i+1);
```

At the risk of boring repetition please note: in the case above the expression `perfectSquares.length` evaluates to 6, and yet the highest valid index is 5! Because the first index of an array is 0, not 1, the number of elements in the array, i.e. the value returned by `perfectSquares.length`, is one more than the maximum permitted index used to access an array element.

To complete this example, here is the code for a class `PerfectSquares` that when run creates an array consisting of the first 6 non-zero perfect squares, and then displays the elements of the array on a line in the Transcript window:

```
import genesis.*;

public class PerfectSquares {

    public static void main (String [ ] args) {
        int [] perfectSquares = new int [6];
        for (int i=0; i<perfectSquares.length; i++)
            perfectSquares[i] = (i+1)*(i+1);
        for (int i=0; i<perfectSquares.length; i++)
            Transcript.print(perfectSquares[i]+"  ");
    }
}
```

Notice the way a for-loop can be used to write code to output the elements in an array. (In this case we could have combined the allocation of elements to the array and their display in the Transcript window into one for-loop.)

PROBLEM 1: square roots of 10 integers

Taking the class `PerfectSquares` as a guide, construct a class `SquareRoots` which creates an array `squareRoots` of length 10 and fills this array with the square roots of the integers from 1 to 10. It then prints in the Transcript window the contents of the array.

As a square root is in general not an integer, the base type of array `squareRoots` will need to be `double`. Make use of the class `Math` and the message `sqrt` to evaluate the square roots. For further help with this problem see Hints.

□

PROBLEM 2: an array of die tosses

Construct a class `TossArray` which creates an array of length 12 and fills the array with 12 random integers in the range 1 to 6. It then displays in the Transcript window the average of these 12 numbers followed by the numbers themselves.

For help with this problem see Hints.

□

A point of special note: array-variable assignment

Consider the following:

```
int i = 78;
int j = 65;
```

If we now execute

```
i = j;
```

the right-hand side evaluates to the integer 65, and this value is then associated with the identifier `i`. The value of `j` stays the same, but the value associated with `i` has altered. Now `i` and `j` are the names of distinct entities having an integer value. Even when the values are identical as in this case (they are both 65), we have two distinct copies, one known as `i`, the other as `j`. If we now execute the statement

```
i = i + 1;
```

the value of `i` becomes 66, but the value of `j` remains unchanged at 65.

Assignment of array variables (and, indeed, any object variable) has a completely different semantics. Consider the following code:

```
int [] array1 = new int [4];
... //suppose array1 is assigned values
... //i.e. 4 int's make up array1
int [] array2;
array2 = array1;
```

As a result of the assignment in the last line above, `array1` and `array2` both denote, or reference, the *same* array of values. Putting this another way, the array which is the value of `array1` is not duplicated (cloned) and copied to `array2`, as would be the case with simple types. Without getting too technical, object variables are really references to, or if you like, names of, some underlying object. When we perform assignment, we *duplicate the reference* and not the set of values. We say that the result of the assignment

```
array2 = array1;
```

is that `array1` and `array2` are *aliases*, or common names, for the structure initially associated with the name `array1`. We can now access the structure via either name.

PROBLEM 3: array-variable assignment

This problem explores array-variable assignment. What is displayed in the Output window if we execute the following code?

```
int [] intArray = new int[4];
for (int i=0; i<4; i++) intArray[i] = i+1;
int [] temp = intArray;
temp[1] = 6;
for (int i=0; i<4; i++) System.out.print(intArray[i] + " ");
```

Try this by hand, and if you are unsure write a program to check your answer.

□

Discussion

The declaration and assignment

```
int [] temp = intArray;
```

ensures that `intArray` and `temp` are just alternative names for the same array. Hence the assignment `temp[1] = 6` means that `intArray[1]` also becomes 6. Consequently, the output will be

```
1 6 3 4
```

To summarise the main points:

assignment to a variable of primitive type involves assigning the *value* of the right-hand side to the variable;

assignment to an object instance (including array variables and `String` variables) involves evaluating the right-hand side reference, and assigning this *reference*. Consequently, the assigned-to variable becomes an alias of the object referenced on the right-hand side.

Returning now to the issue of processing the elements in an array, consider the following examples and problems.

Example: student grades

Each student in a class is given a mark between 0 and 100, and from this mark a grade can be calculated, as specified in the following table:

mark range	grade
85 .. 100	7
75 .. 84	6
65 .. 74	5
50 .. 64	4
45 .. 49	3
20 .. 44	2
0 .. 19	1

We want to write code that will read in a sequence of numbers representing student marks, and then output to the Transcript window the number of students awarded each of the grades.

The first problem is how many student marks to expect. Let's design the program so that it first requests from the user the number of students whose marks will be processed:

```
int classSize = DialogBox.requestInt("Class size?");
```

Next, a repository is needed to store for each grade the number of times that grade is awarded. We'll declare an array of type `int` and length 7 to store these numbers. Each element of this array will be zero initially, indicating we haven't yet input any student's mark that has been awarded that grade:

```
int [] numGrades = new int [7];  // for the seven grades
for (int i=0; i < numGrades.length; i++)
    numGrades[i] = 0;
```

Now we can read in each mark, determine the grade represented by the mark, and increment the relevant value in the array. Remember that the array indices are offset by one, so a grade of 7, for example, is recorded by incrementing by 1 the value `numGrades[6]`, and similarly for the other grades:

```
int mark, grade;
for (int i=0; i < classSize; i++) {
    mark = DialogBox.requestInt("next student's mark:");
    if (mark > 84) grade = 7;
    else if (mark > 74) grade = 6;
    else if (mark > 64) grade = 5;
    else if (mark > 49) grade = 4;
    else if (mark > 44) grade = 3;
    else if (mark > 19) grade = 2;
    else grade = 1;
    numGrades[grade-1]++;
}
```

Finally, we need to print out the result of the processing. We do that with a little bit of flair to create a tidy, easily read report.

```
Transcript.println("Number of various grades awarded");
Transcript.println("================================");
for (int i = numGrades.length-1; i >= 0; i--)
  Transcript.println("\t" + (i+1) + "\t|\t" + numGrades[i]);
Transcript.println("________________________________\n\n");
```

(In this code the statement `i--` is a shorthand for the assignment statement `i=i-1`.)

PROBLEM 4: number of students awarded each grade

The completed code above is in the class `Grade` in the folder *Grade*. Test out the code by running the class and supplying various values for the class size and for the students' marks.

What happens if the user supplies a mark greater than 100 or less than 0? Modify the code so as to detect this case and request that the mark be re-entered.

Challenge question: is it possible to code this class without using the deeply nested if-statement?

For help with this problem see Hints.

PROBLEM 5: gathering statistics on die tossing

The aim of this problem is to write code to simulate the tossing of a die so as to gather some statistics about die tossing.

Construct a class `TossStatistics` which when compiled and run opens a dialog box requesting the user supply the number of times a die is to be tossed. It then simulates the tossing of a die this number of times and prints in the Transcript window a table indicating the number of times each digit between 1 and 6 was tossed, and gives the average for each digit (i.e. the number of times the digit was tossed divided by the total number of tosses) expressed as a floating point number correct to 4 decimal places.

For example, if the user requests that the die is tossed 143 times, say, the output will be something like:

```
Toss statistics
================================
1   19  0.1329
2   31  0.2168
3   23  0.1608
4   20  0.1399
5   20  0.1399
6   30  0.2098
________________________________
```

Note: a floating point number `x`, say, of type `double` can be expressed correct to 4 decimal places by the expression

```
Math.round(10000*x) / 10000.0
```

That is, multiply `x` by 10^4, round to the nearest integer by sending the message `round` to the class `Math`, and finally divide by 10^4 expressed as a floating point number (to ensure we have floating point and not integer division).

For further help with this problem see Hints.

□

PROBLEM 6: below average

Suppose we have a sequence of marks and want to print out all those marks in the sequence that fall below the average.

A first approach to this problem, following the sequential way we think, might be:

1. read in each mark and store it in an array;
2. find the sum of the marks;
3. find the average;
4. now print out those marks which are below the average.

Step 1 requires a loop. So does step 2. Step 3 is determined by dividing the result of step 2 by the total number of marks. Finally, step 4 also requires a loop and can be computed only after the result from step 3 has been produced.

Notice that we can combine steps 1 and 2 into the one loop. The importance of this is not major, but it does mean we can remove the baggage of one loop from our program and this means it will run quicker. As we read in the numbers, we can at the same time find their sum by adding each new number to a `sum` variable!

Construct a class `BelowAverage` which when compiled and run solves this problem.

For help with this problem see Hints.

□

Example: searching an array

Suppose we want to search through an array to find the smallest index of the array at which a particular element occurs. For example, if the array is $\langle 3, 5, 4, 5 \rangle$ and we search for 5, then 1 is the index position at which 5 first occurs (recall that an array starts at index position 0). Here is an attempt to write code to do such a search (in the code assume `intArray` is some array of integers):

```
int target = ..;      // the number we're seeking
int foundAt = -1;     // some index value not in the array
for (int i=0; i<intArray.length; i++)
    if (target == array[i]) foundAt = i;
System.out.println ("Found "+target+" at index "+foundAt);
```

Does this achieve what we want

- if the number we seek is not present?
- if the number we seek is present more than once?

Clearly it is essential to ensure our program works as required in each circumstance. Although there is a close tie between the for-loop and the processing of arrays, is the for-loop always our best option? The issues raised by the above code will help us clarify this.

When we write a for-loop we are essentially committing ourselves to processing all the elements in the array. For the searching problem we really want to stop the processing as soon as we've found what we're seeking. Here is improved code using a while-loop rather than a for-loop (again assume `intArray` is some array of integers):

```
int target = ..    // the number we're seeking;
int foundAt = 0;
boolean found = false;
while ((foundAt < intArray.length) && !found) {
    if (intArray[foundAt] == target) found = true;
    else foundAt++;
}
if (found)
  System.out.println("Found "+target+" at index "+foundAt);
else
  System.out.println(target+" not found");
```

This code now deals with the case when there may be more than one occurrence of the number we seek: the while-loop exits as soon as the first occurrence is found. It also deals with the case when the number we seek is not in the array. In this case the Boolean `found` will have the value *false* when the while-loop exits.

PROBLEM 7: desperately seeking 6

Construct a class `Seeking6` which, to simulate the tossing of a die ten times, creates an array of length 10 and fills the array with 10 random integers in the range 1 to 6. This array is then searched to determine the toss (if any) at which the first 6 occurred. This information is displayed in the Output window.

For help with this problem see Hints.

□

5.2 Case study: sorting an array

In the last section we motivated the need for the array construct by considering the general issue of sorting a collection of items. We return to that issue now.

PROBLEM 8: exploring sorting an array

The aim of this problem is to discover some scenario (informal algorithm) that describes how to go about sorting a collection of items. Open the folder *Sort Circles* and run the class `SortCircles`. A window opens containing 8 circles in a line, where the radius of each circle is randomly selected between 10 and 29.

The position of any pair of circles can be swapped by clicking on both circles with the mouse and then clicking with the mouse on the 'swap' button at the bottom of the window. The idea is to arrange the circles in ascending order of size from left to right by repeatedly swapping selected pairs of circles. When the circles are successfully sorted in this way the message `SORTED!!` is displayed at the top of the window and no more pairs of circles can be swapped.

Experiment until you can describe a logical and specifiable algorithm to arrange the circles in ascending order. For example, one possible (very inefficient) algorithm might be *keep swapping any pair at random until the array is sorted.* See if you can come up with a more efficient algorithm than this.

□

Searching for a sorting algorithm

Clearly, coming up with a well described algorithm is a necessary first step if we want to create a program to perform sorting. What we want is a clear and precise description that can be converted into Java code.

If you just randomly exchange pairs of circles until all the circles just happened to fall in ascending order, the method may work sometimes but it could possibly loop forever. You would also have to test after each exchange to see if the circles were sorted, and this testing would in general require considerable resources. While we might not wait too long for 8 circles, if we had a few thousand we may have to wait a day or two!

If you only randomly exchange pairs of circles which are out of order, that would be a definite improvement, but again you would need to do quite a bit of testing.

Did you do any better than either of these two ideas? We will now demonstrate two possible approaches to sorting the circles, *selection sort* and *bubble sort*.

Selection sort

To get some idea of how the selection-sort algorithm works, try the following simulation.

PROBLEM 9: selection sort demo

Open the folder *Selection Sort Demo* and run the class `SelectionSortDemo`. Can you describe the algorithm that is being used to sort the circles? Run the program several times until you understand this approach to sorting.

□

Discussion

Here is the way it works.

- First, by looking at the whole line of circles, find a circle for which there is none smaller. (This will be the smallest circle, unless there is more than one circle equally small in which case it will be any one of these circles.) Exchange this circle with the circle in the first position.
- Next, look at the line of circles ignoring the first circle and repeat the approach, i.e. find a circle in the rest of the line for which there is none smaller and exchange it with the circle in the second position.
- Next, look at the remainder of the line ignoring the first two, find a circle in this remainder for which there is none smaller and exchange it with the circle in the third position, and so on.
- Proceed in this way until the only circle left unchecked is the one in the last position.

This is the so-called *selection sort* algorithm.

Does the algorithm work? Clearly the first circle has to be in the correct position because there is none smaller. Similarly, the second circle has to be in the correct position because there is none smaller ignoring the first circle. Continuing in this way, each circle is in the correct position because, ignoring those circles before it in the line, there is none smaller. This is a good argument for saying that the approach must sort the circles into ascending order.

Code development

To illustrate how we can translate the selection sort algorithm into Java code, consider the problem of creating code that applies the selection sort algorithm to sort into ascending order an array of integers. For example, if the array is $\langle 4, 1, 5, 4 \rangle$, the program will converted it to $\langle 1, 4, 4, 5 \rangle$.

Suppose we have an array `intArray` of type `int` and length `size`:

```
int [] intArray = new int[size];

//
//   some values are assigned to intArray
//
```

Here are the steps in the selection sort algorithm applied to `intArray`:

- let index `i` start at 0;
- for each value of index `i`
  - let `minValue` be the smallest integer in the array between `i` and the end of the array, i.e. in the range `i` to `size-1`;
  - let `minPosn` be the index position of this smallest integer;
- if `minPosn` is not the same as `i` (i.e. if the smallest integer in the rest of the array is not already at index position `i`) swap the element at `i` with the element at `minPosn`; the result will be that `minValue` will now be in index position `i`;
- increase `i` by 1 and repeat the above for all `i<size-1`.

PROBLEM 10: coding selection sort

Code implementing the above selection sort algorithm is given at the top of the next page. Make use of this code to construct a class `SelectionSort` which when run begins by opens a dialog box requesting the number of integers to be supplied. It then successively opens dialog boxes so that this number of integers can be supplied.

The integers are first displayed in the Transcript window in the order in which they were supplied, then sorted into ascending order, and finally displayed in sorted order in the Transcript window.

```
int minValue, minPosn;
for (int i = 0; i<size-1; i++) {
    minPosn = i;
    minValue = intArray[i];
    for (int j=i+1; j<size; j++)
        if (intArray[j] < minValue) {
            minValue = intArray[j];
            minPosn = j;
        }
    if (minPosn > i) {
        int temp = intArray[i];
        intArray[i] = intArray[minPosn];
        intArray[minPosn] = temp;
    }
}
```

For help with this problem see Hints.

□

Bubble sort

To get some idea of how the bubble-sort algorithm works, try the following simulation.

PROBLEM 11: bubble sort demo

Open the folder *Bubble Sort Demo* and run the class `BubbleSortDemo`. Can you describe the algorithm that is being used to sort the circles this time? Run the program several times until you understand this approach to sorting.

□

Discussion

Here is the way it works.

- Make a sweep through the circles starting at the first circle and comparing each pair of adjacent circles, i.e. compare each circle with the circle immediately to its right.
- If a pair of adjacent circles is out of order, swap that pair. That is, swap a pair of adjacent circles only if the circle on the right is smaller than the circle on the left.

- Repeat this process until a complete sweep can be made through the array without any adjacent pair of circles being swapped (when all adjacent pairs are in order).

This is the so-called *bubble sort* algorithm.

Clearly, if all adjacent pairs of circles are in order, the entire line of circles must be in order.

PROBLEM 12: coding bubble sort

This problem is like Problem 10, only this time the aim is to use bubble sort rather than selection sort.

Make use of the bubble sort algorithm to construct a class `BubbleSort` which when run begins by opening a dialog box requesting the number of integers to be supplied. It then successively opens dialog boxes so that this number of integers can be supplied. The integers are first displayed in the Transcript window in the order in which they were supplied, then sorted into ascending order, and finally displayed in sorted order in the Transcript window.

For help with this problem see Hints.

□

Comparing selection sort with bubble sort

Which algorithm is the better, selection sort or bubble sort? An answer to this question depends on circumstances and on what we mean by 'better'. Selection sort generally involves fewer swaps than bubble sort. But at each stage in the selection sort algorithm the remaining array needs to be searched in order to find the next smallest element. This searching takes resources and can greatly slow the algorithm. The bubble sort algorithm, on the other hand, may only involve checking adjacent elements but in general requires more swaps. To sort large data collections there exist more efficient sorting algorithms than either of these too.

5.3 Literal arrays

In Section 5.1 we met the following code for declaring `numGrades` to be an integer array of length 7 and setting each element of the array to be 0:

```
int [] numGrades = new int [7];
for (int i=0; i < numGrades.length; i++)
    numGrades[i] = 0;
```

We can, however, accomplish this declaration and assignment with the following statement:

```
int [] numGrades = {0, 0, 0, 0, 0, 0, 0};
```

This statement has exactly the same effect: it declares `numGrades` to be an integer array of length 7 with each element having the value 0. The expression

```
{0, 0, 0, 0, 0, 0, 0}
```

is known as a *literal array*. It creates an array with precisely the elements shown. In general, a literal array declaration will have the syntax

type [] *arrayName* = { $expression_0, expression_1, .., expression_{n-1}$ };

where each $expression_i$ is an expression of type *type*. This declares *arrayName* to be an array of type *type* and of length n, whose element at index position i is the value of $expression_i$.

To give another example, in Section 5.1 we met the following code to create the array $\langle 1, 4, 9, 16, 25, 36 \rangle$ consisting of the first 6 non-zero perfect squares:

```
int [] perfectSquares = new int [6];
for (int i=0; i<6; i++) perfectSquares[i] = (i+1)*(i+1);
```

An equivalent way of doing this using a literal array declaration would be:

```
int [] perfectSquares = {1*1, 2*2, 3*3, 4*4, 5*5, 6*6};
```

Notice Java's syntax for a literal array: the elements are placed within curly braces and separated by commas. You may find this syntax unexpected as curly braces are usually used mathematically to specify a set, not a sequence. However, as Java has no primitive set type, it uses the curly braces to define literal arrays, as illustrated in the cases above. To be consistent, throughout the remainder of this book we, too, will use curly braces when listing the elements of an array.

It is important to appreciate that a literal array can be assigned to an array variable only as part of the declaration statement for that variable. In the case of the array `numGrades` above, for example, it would be an error to write

```
int [] numGrades;
numGrades = {0, 0, 0, 0, 0, 0, 0};
```

Such statements will not compile. **Be warned!!**

5.4 Multi-dimensional arrays

Suppose we have a class of students and we need to record their marks on each of four separate assignment tasks. We can do this in Java by creating an array whose length is the class size and where each element of this array is itself an array of length 4 of the individual marks obtained by that student.

Here is the Java statements that declare such an array of arrays. First we declare a variable whose value is the class size:

```
int classSize = ...;  \\ number of students in the class
```

We then declare the array of arrays as follows:

```
int [][] assessmentMarks = new int [classSize][4];
```

Looking at this last declaration closely, consider first the left-hand side:

```
int [][] assessmentMarks
```

We read this as declaring "an array variable called `assessmentMarks` each of whose elements is an array of integers of type `int`".

Consider now the right-hand side of the declaration:

```
new int [classSize][4]
```

We read this as telling us that the array `assessmentMarks` is "an array of length `classSize` (from the first pair of square brackets) where each element is an array of length 4 (from the second pair of square brackets) of integers of type `int`".

Notice carefully the order in which the square brackets appear in this declaration. The first pair of square brackets tells us that the array itself (the 'outer' array) will be an array of length `classSize`, while the second square brackets tells us that each element in the outer array will itself be an array (the 'inner' array) of length 4.

Accessing elements of a 2-dimensional array

Given code that contains the above declaration of the 2-dimensional array `assessmentMarks`, in any subsequent code a statement such as, say,

```
assessmentMarks[6]
```

evaluates to the entire integer array of length 4 containing the assessment marks for the 7th student in the class (i.e. the student whose marks are recorded at index position 6). A statement such as, say,

```
assessmentMarks[6][2]
```

evaluates to the 3rd assessment mark for the 7th student (i.e. the integer at index position 2 in the array `assessmentMarks[6]`).

To give an example of how such expressions are used, the following code sums the marks for each student in the class and prints out the result:

```
for (int i=0; i<classSize; i++) {
    int sum = 0;
    for (int j=0; j<4; j++)
        sum = sum + assessmentMarks[i][j];
    System.out.println("total for student "+i+" is "+sum);
}
```

Notice the use of embedded for-loops to process a 2-dimensional array. In this case the outer loop index `i` references a particular student, while the inner loop index `j` references a specific mark of that student.

As another example, here is the code for a class `ProcessingMarks` to record the 4 assessment marks for each student in a class of 8 students. Each assessment mark for each student is calculated as a random integer in the range 0 to 25 (not perhaps a very fair way of grading students!). The 4 assessment marks for each student are displayed on a separate line in the Transcript window.

```
import genesis.*;

public class ProcessingMarks {
    /* Processes students' assessment marks. */

    public static void main (String [] args) {
        int classSize = 8;
        int [][] assessmentMarks = new int [classSize][4];
        // for each student
        for (int i=0; i<classSize; i++) {
          // for each assessment
          for (int j=0; j<4; j++) {
            assessmentMarks[i][j] = (int)(26*Math.random());
            Transcript.print(assessmentMarks[i][j]+"\t");
          }
          Transcript.println();
        }
    }
}
```

In this code the outer loop runs through the 8 students selecting each in turn. For each student selected the inner loop runs through the 4 assessment marks for that student.

PROBLEM 13: processing marks

The class `ProcessingMarks` above is in the folder *Processing Marks.* Extend this class so that the average mark (taken over all students in the class) of each of the 4 assessments is displayed, truncated to 2 decimal places, on a line in the Transcript window.

For help with this problem see Hints.

□

Case study: a corner store

A small corner store owner allows her customers weekly accounts on specific items purchased through the week. These items are :

butter, milk, papers, bread.

The numbers are tallied through the week as purchases are made. At the end of a week, one array of purchases by one customer might be

2, 4, 9, 5

indicating that in that week this customer purchased 2 kilos of butter, 4 litres of milk, 9 papers and 5 loaves of bread. There are 50 customers stored on the computer identified by the numbers 0 to 49.

The price of a single unit of each item is as follows: butter is \$2.30 a kilo, milk is \$1.60 a litre, newspapers are \$0.90 each and bread is \$1.60 a loaf.

It is our task to write the part of the system that produces the bills at the end of the week. The information about customers and purchases can be summarised in a table:

customer	**butter**	**milk**	**paper**	**bread**
0	4	2	3	2
1	1	3	7	3
2	2	3	8	0
...	...	...	...	...

Clearly we need a two-dimensional array to store the purchase details. Let's call it

```
int [][] purchases = new int [50][4];
```

indicating 50 rows (one per customer) and 4 columns (one column per product) of values of type `int`.

We also need a one-dimensional array to store the prices of each item:

butter	milk	paper	bread
230	160	90	160

Here we have stored item cost in cents. Let's define it fully:

```
int [] costPerItem = {230, 160, 90, 160};
```

Billing one customer

How can we determine the amount owed by a customer, say the *i*th?

```
int debt = 0;
for (int j = 0; j < purchases[i].length; j++)
    debt = debt + purchases[i][j] * costPerItem[j];
String debtAsString;
if (debt%100 < 10)
    debtAsString = "$"+debt/100+".0"+debt%100;
else debtAsString = "$"+debt/100+"."+debt%100;
Transcript.println("Customer "+i+" owes "+debtAsString);
```

Notice that the expression `purchases[i]` evaluates to the array of purchases of the *i*th customer , hence the expression `purchases[i].length` used in the for-loop evaluates to the integer 4 in each case.

Formatting output

Did you work out what the variable `debtAsString` was all about? The idea is to convert the amount owing by the customer into a string for output to the Transcript window. The debt is at first calculated in cents, but we wish to display it in the usual way as dollars and cents with 2 figures after the decimal point. Indeed, we want to have two figures after the decimal point in all cases, even if these figures are zero. Simply dividing by 100 in floating point arithmetic does not completely solve the problem as, for example, 160 cents would print out as 1.6. Here we calculate the dollar and cent values using integer arithmetic. But a problem still arises with the cents display if the number of cents is less than 10. In this case we need to insert an extra zero, e.g. 306 cents needs to be displayed as 3.06.

Billing all customers

What we need to do is embed the code above for the *i*th customer in another for-loop that runs through all customers:

```
for (int i = 0; i < purchases.length; i++) {
    int debt = 0;
    // code as above
}
```

The expression `purchases.length` evaluates to the length of the outer array, i.e. to number of customers. Putting all this together, here is the code for a class `CornerStore` that processes the accounts of the store's customers. To keep it manageable we have supposed there are only 5 customers rather than 50:

```
import genesis.*;

public class CornerStore {
    /* Processing customer accounts. */

    public static void main (String [] args) {
        int [] [] purchases = { {3, 4, 6, 2},
                                {1, 3, 7, 3},
                                {2, 3, 8, 0},
                                {1, 4, 3, 1},
                                {0, 0, 7, 0}
                              };
        int  [] costPerItem = {230, 160, 90, 160};
        // for each customer
        for (int i = 0; i < purchases.length; i++) {
          int debt = 0;
          // for each grocery item
          for (int j = 0; j < purchases[i].length; j++)
             debt = debt + purchases[i][j] * costPerItem[j];
          String debtAsString;
          if (debt%100 < 10)
                debtAsString = "$"+debt/100+".0"+debt%100;
          else debtAsString = "$"+debt/100+"."+debt%100;
          Transcript.println
                    ("Customer "+i+" owes "+debtAsString);
        }
    }
}
```

Notice that we have used the literal array

```
{   {3, 4, 6, 2},
    {1, 3, 7, 3},
    {2, 3, 8, 0},
    {1, 4, 3, 1},
    {0, 0, 7, 0}
}
```

to assign the values to the 2-dimensional array `purchases`. This is an example of a 2-dimensional literal array; inside the curly braces we have 5 literal arrays (one for each customer) each of length 4 (for the purchases of each item).

PROBLEM 14: corner store

The class `CornerStore` above is in the folder *Corner Store*. Modify the code for this class so as to print out an itemised account for each customer in the style:

```
CUSTOMER:   2
2 units of butter at $2.30  $4.60
3 units of milk at $1.60    $4.80
8 units of paper at $0.90   $7.20
Total                       $16.60
```

Only items for which some quantity was purchased by the customer are output.

For help with this problem see Hints.

□

Chapter 5 self-check

Can you give an informal description of:

- the circumstances under which you would consider using an array structure?
- the expression for declaring an array of elements of a given type and with a specified number of elements?
- how to refer to the element at a particular position in an array?
- why the for-loop marries so well with array processing?
- how to print out each element of an array in turn?
- the selection-sort algorithm?

- the bubble-sort algorithm?
- the syntax for a literal array?
- when to use a literal array?
- the expression for declaring a 2-dimensional array with a specified number of rows and columns?
- how to process the elements of a 2-dimensional array using nested for-loops?

Methods 6

Prerequisites

Before beginning Chapter 6, you will need to have a good understanding of the basic features of the Java language as covered in the earlier chapters of *Java Genesis*. In particular, you will need to be familiar with

- primitive types such as `int` and `double`;
- basic Java constructs such as assignment-statements and Boolean expressions;
- if-statements, for-loops and while-loops;
- the array data structure.

Overview

Throughout the earlier chapters of *Java Genesis* we met many examples that involved sending some message to some class. For example, to generate a random number we sent the message `random` to the class `Math`, or to move a square we sent the messages `moveRight` to the class `SquareFigure`. When a class or an object receives a message it responds by invoking one of its methods. Up to this point we have concentrated on how to write code to send messages. In this chapter we look at the other side of the issue: how to construct the methods that are invoked in response.

Essentially, a method is a message handler. It is general purpose code associated with a class that is invoked only when an appropriate message is received by the class or an object of the class. Some methods require various pieces of data as input while others require none. Some methods return a value to the sender of the message, while others do not. Each of these aspects is discussed in this chapter.

Some methods are invoked when a message is received by the class, while others are invoked when a message is received by an object of the class. In this chapter we concentrate on constructing *static* or *class* methods, i.e. methods that are invoked when a message is received by a class. Non-static or *instance* methods, invoked when a message is received by an object of a class, are discussed in more detail in Chapter 7.

6.1 Constructing and invoking methods

We begin by looking at the basic structure of a method and observe that when constructing a method we need to decide

- if the method is to be publicly available,
- if it is to be a class or instance method,
- what type of value, if any, it returns,
- what name to give the method, and
- the number and type of its parameters.

We see that this information is needed not just to construct the method but also to construct any message invoking the method.

Problems:

1 converting Centigrade to Fahrenheit

2 gcd revisited

3 a method to toss a die

6.2 Methods and arrays

We often want to process different arrays in a similar way, e.g. print out the contents of any array of integers. We see how methods with parameters of array type can help us in these situations.

Problems:

4 summing an array

5 chasing the tail

6 extracting data

7 gcd of an array of integers

8 arrays without duplications

9 tossing four dice

6.3 Recursion

Functions in mathematics are often defined recursively. For example, the factorial of an integer greater than 1 (see Problem 17 of Chapter 3) satisfies the recursive relationship

$$\begin{aligned} factorial(0) &= 1 \\ factorial(n) &= n * factorial(n-1) \quad \text{for } n \geqslant 1. \end{aligned}$$

In this section we see how such recursive relationships can be translated directly into code to create recursive methods.

Problem:

10 computing factorials recursively

6.4 passing arguments to parameters

We look at the various issues that arise when passing an argument of a message to the corresponding method's parameter. In particular, if the message argument is a variable v, say, of primitive type, then the value of v is copied to the corresponding parameter and any subsequent changes to the parameter's value within the method's code will have no affect on the value of v. However, if a message argument is a variable *ob*, say, of object type (e.g. an array) the corresponding parameter in the method becomes an alias for *ob* and any changes to the object within the method will be reflected as changes to *ob* itself.

Problem:

11 rounding off

Learning outcomes

At the conclusion of Chapter 6 you will understand:

- how to construct and use static methods;
- the role played by method parameters;
- how to make use of the arguments of a message in order to pass data when invoking a method;
- the effect of passing a primitive value to a method, the effect of passing an object value to a method, and the difference between them;
- how to declare a return type for a method;
- how to return a value from a method;
- the scope of variables declared within a method.

6.1 Constructing and invoking methods

Whenever a message is sent to a class or an object of that class, some method in the class is invoked in response. Up to this point in *Java Genesis* we have frequently sent messages to classes in order to invoke methods, but we haven't concerned ourselves with the structure or code of the invoked methods; we have been quite happy to ignore such details. Indeed, as we have mentioned before, this is one of the great advantages of object-oriented programming: in order to make use of a class (or an object of that class) all we need to know are the messages that can be sent to the class (or object) and what happens as a consequence.

In this chapter we will look at methods in general, but with particular emphasis on the so-called static methods that are invoked in response to a class (as distinct from an object of that class) receiving a message. (We will consider objects of classes and instance (i.e. non-static) methods in more detail in Chapter 7.)

The `main` method

To begin, recall that `main` is itself a method. It is specified as:

```
public static void main (String [] args) {

    ...  // some sequence of statements

}
```

[*An aside*: Now that we have studied arrays we can at last understand what is intended by the parameter declaration

```
String [] args
```

It is nothing more than a declaration of an array called `args` of type `String`. In fact, we have never actually supplied such a parameter when invoking the `main` method! Rather, a default null array of strings has been automatically supplied by the Java system when the class containing the `main` method is run. We could supply our own array of strings as parameter if we wished, but as we shall never need to do so we shan't go into details here. *End aside*]

The `main` method of a class is invoked automatically by the Java system when we run the class. Other class methods, however, can only be invoked by sending an appropriate message to the class. To illustrate how such methods can be constructed, and the role they can play, consider the following example.

Sums of square roots

Suppose we wish to write a Java program to calculate

$$\sqrt{a} + \sqrt{b} + \sqrt{c}$$

where a, b and c are given floating point numbers, and suppose we know nothing about the `sqrt` method of the class `Math`. All is not lost, as in Section 4.4 we developed some code to implement Newton's method to calculate square roots:

```
double num = ...;
double approx = num/2;
while (Math.abs(approx*approx - num) > 0.000001)
    approx = (approx + (num/approx))/2;
```

If a value is supplied for the variable `num` and the code executed, the value of the variable `approx` will become an approximation to the square root of `num`.

Applying this, we can construct a class `Sum1` to solve our problem (in the code for this class particular numbers have been assigned to a, b and c; any numbers could have been assigned):

```
public class Sum1 {

    /* The sum of the square root of three numbers. */

    public static void main (String [ ] args) {
        double a = 36.3;
        double b = 11.0;
        double c - 18.42;
        double sum = 0.0;
        double approx;

        //evaluate the square root of a and add it to sum
        approx = a/2;
        while (Math.abs(approx*approx - a) > 0.000001)
            approx = (approx + (a/approx))/2;
        sum = sum + approx;

        //evaluate the square root of b and add it to sum
        approx = b/2;
        while (Math.abs(approx*approx - b) > 0.000001)
            approx = (approx + (b/approx))/2;
        sum = sum + approx;
```

```
        //evaluate the square root of c and add it to sum
        approx = c/2;
        while (Math.abs(approx*approx - c) > 0.000001)
            approx = (approx + (c/approx))/2;
        sum = sum + approx;

        System.out.println(sum);
    }
}
```

The class Sum1 is in the folder *Sum Roots*. If you open this folder and run the class, 13.63342567411308 will be displayed in the Output window.

Using a method

The trouble here is that we had to repeat the code for calculating a square root. Copying is poor style, it is error prone, and even for moderately complex situations the programs we write would be long and repetitive.

It was precisely to tackle such situations that methods were originally created . A method is like a specialist in that it is able to accurately perform a particular task as often as required. Here is the code for a class Sum2 that makes use of a method `root` for calculating square roots.

```
public class Sum2 {

    public static void main (String [ ] args) {
        double a = 36.3;
        double b = 11.0;
        double c = 18.42;
        double sum;
        sum = Sum2.root(a) + Sum2.root(b) + Sum2.root(c);
        System.out.println(sum);
    }

    public static double root (double num) {
        double approx = num/2;
        while (Math.abs(approx*approx - num) > 0.000001)
            approx = (approx + (num/approx))/2;
        return approx;
    }
}
```

The class Sum2 is also in the folder *Sum Roots.* Run the class to confirm that we get the same output as before.

Notice that the class Sum2 has two methods, a main method and a root method.

Constructing methods

Consider in detail the structure of the root method:

```
public static double root (double num) {
    double approx = num/2;
    while (Math.abs(approx*approx - num) > 0.000001)
        approx = (approx + (num/approx))/2;
    return approx;
}
```

When constructing a method such as root there are several issues to resolve.

Availability

First, we have to decide on the public availability of the method. In the case of root, we want to be able to invoke the method by sending a message to the class that contains it. To achieve this we start the declaration of the method with the key-word public:

```
public static double root (double num) {
```

Almost all methods we shall construct will be public in this way. If we replace the key-word public by the key-word private then the method can be invoked only from other code inside the method's own class.

Class or instance

Next, we have to decide if a method is a class or instance method. A class method is invoked by sending a message to the method's class; an instance method is invoked by sending a message to an object of the method's class. The method root is a class method, and this is indicated by the inclusion of the key-word static as part of the declaration of the method:

```
public static double root (double num) {
```

Because of the use of the word static in this way, class methods in Java are known as *static* methods. If the method was an instance method then the key-word static would be omitted from the method's declaration. Instance methods will be discussed in more detail in Chapter 7.

Return type

Next, we must decide the type of result, if any, that is to be returned by the method. The `root` method returns a value of type `double`, namely, the square root of whatever number is supplied to the method when it is invoked. This return type is placed next in the method's declaration:

```
public static double root (double num) {
```

If no result is returned by a method, the key-word `void` is used in the method's declaration in place of the return type. Such methods are known as *void* methods. The `main` method, for example, is a void method.

Name

Next we must decide on a name for the method. In our case we have chosen to call the method `root`:

```
public static double root (double num) {
```

Any identifier that is not a Java reserved word can be chosen as the name for a method. It is convention that, as for variable names, the name of a method starts with a lower-case letter and the first letter of any subsequent sub-word is capitalised.

Parameters

Next, we must decide what, if any, information needs to be passed as input to the method when it is invoked. For the `root` method, the actual floating point number whose square root we wish to calculate needs to be supplied. This is indicated by the *parameter list* of the method:

```
public static double root (double num) {
```

In general, a method's parameter list (often called the *formal* parameter list) is a comma-separated list of parameters, where a parameter is a typed identifier of the form

type identifier

enclosed in brackets. In our case this list consists of just one parameter where *type* is `double` and *identifier* is `num`. The identifier `num` is effectively a variable of type `double` known locally within the code of the method. That is, the scope of `num` (that part of the program throughout which this identifier has its declared meaning and is recognised) is the method's code block. As we shall see, the value of `num` is initialised by the message that invokes the method.

If no information is to be passed as input to the method, the parameter list is empty. However, the brackets are still included as part of the declaration of the method even though they contain nothing between then but possibly white space. (We will meet examples of methods with no parameters and methods with more than one parameter later in this chapter.)

Code block

Finally, we have to construct the block of code that performs the method's specified task. In the case of `root`, we need code that takes the input number, computes the value of its square root, and returns this value. The block of code is placed within curly braces:

```
                              {
        double approx = num/2;
        while (Math.abs(approx*approx - num) > 0.000001)
            approx = (approx + (num/approx))/2;
        return approx;
    }
```

The code for the `root` method enables us to compute the square root of any number value of `num`. (Well, almost any value. We cannot use the `root` method to compute the (imaginary) square root of a negative number. We'll have a bit more to say about this issue later.)

Return statement

There is one new statement type in the code for the `root` method; to return the calculated square root we code

```
return approx;
```

The general syntax for a return-statement is

`return` *expression* ;

The type of *expression* must be the same as the return type of the method as given in the method's declaration (e.g. `double` in the case of the method `root`). The value of *expression* is computed and, as we shall see, sent back to the sender of the message which can now resume its own execution. The method itself terminates.

In general we may have several return-statements in the same method. For example, we may have code something like this:

`if (`*condition*`) return` *expression*$_1$
`else return` *expression*$_2$

The rule is that as soon as any return-statement is executed, the value of the appropriate expression is returned and the method itself stops execution.

A void method (i.e. one with the key-word `void` in place of a return type in its declaration) does not return a result and hence does not need to have a return-statement.

When the execution of a method ceases, either because a return-statement is executed or because there are no more statements in the method to be executed, the program resumes execution at the point immediately after the message whose sending originally invoked the method.

Invoking methods

To invoke a class method such as `root` we need to know

- the name of the class that contains the method;
- the name of the method;
- the method's result type;
- the number, types and order of the method's parameters.

The method `root` is invoked three times in the statement

```
sum = Sum2.root(a) + Sum2.root(b) + Sum2.root(c);
```

in the `main` method of the class Sum2. Let us look in detail at the first message, `Sum2.root(a)`. This message is of the form

$identifier_1.identifier_2$ (*expression*)

where

- $identifier_1$ is the receiver of the message; in this case, as `root` is a class method, the receiver is the class containing the code for the method, i.e. the class Sum2 itself;
- $identifier_2$ is the name of the method to be invoked; in this case `root`;
- *expression* is known as the *argument* of the message and its type is the same as the type of the parameter of the method; in this case `a` is of type `double` and that is the same as the type of the parameter `num` of the `root` method.

When the method `root` is invoked the value of the parameter becomes the value of *expression* and the code for the method is then executed; in this case `root` is executed with `num` set to the value of `a`, i.e. 36.3. The entire expression `Sum2.root(a)` then takes the value returned by the `root` method, i.e. the square root of 36.3.

Methods with 2 or more parameters

If the method has two parameters, say, then the message to invoke it has two arguments and is of the form

$$\mathit{identifier}_1.\mathit{identifier}_2\ (\ \mathit{expression}_1, \mathit{expression}_2\ )$$

where the type of $\mathit{expression}_1$ is the same as the type of the method's first parameter, and the type of $\mathit{expression}_2$ is the same as the type of the method's second parameter. This is generalised in the obvious way for methods with 3 or more parameters.

Methods with no parameters

If the method has no parameters, the message to invoke it has no arguments and is of the form:

$$\mathit{identifier}_1.\mathit{identifier}_2\ (\ )$$

Consider now the entire statement

```
sum = Sum2.root(a) + Sum2.root(b) + Sum2.root(c);
```

This sends to the class `Sum2` a message to invoke the `root` method three times, each time getting a value returned that is the square root we seek. The first message causes the value of the argument `a` to be assigned to `num` and `root` is then executed. When `root` finishes executing and returns the result (i.e. the square root of `a`), root is then executed with the value of the argument `b` assigned to `num` and then with the value of the argument `c` assigned to `num`.

[*An aside*: Method execution is a little more complex than we've indicated here. The values of the arguments are deposited in some known locations in the computer's memory. Execution control is then transferred to the method which allocates space for its parameters and local variables, initialises the parameter variables from the values of the arguments stored in the known locations, and executes its code. When it finishes, it puts the result in another specific known location and returns, effectively freeing the computer memory space it used for its own local variables including the parameters. The calling program collects the returned value from the known location and proceeds. *End aside*]

The total amount of code written can be significantly smaller when we make use of methods as we reduce the need to repeat code. Furthermore, methods enhance the generality of the code as parameters provide us with the ability to write methods that work regardless of the value of the argument passed.

Catching exceptions

On this issue of methods working regardless of the value passed as argument, if we pass a negative value to the method `root`, the while-loop will not terminate and consequently the method will go into an infinite loop and never return a value (try it and see). Of course, we created the method to be used only for finding the square root of non-negative numbers. But it is bad programming practice not to enforce this restriction as part of the code; once a method is created we have no control over where or when it may be invoked.

What we could do in this case is include the following line right at the beginning of the code in the `root` method:

```
if (num < 0) return -1.0;
```

If `num` is negative the method immediately returns the value -1.0 and terminates execution. This ensures that the while-loop will not be entered in the case when a negative number is supplied. Furthermore, whenever we invoke the `root` method we can test to see if the value returned is -1.0. If it is we know that a negative number was passed to the method and we can take appropriate steps to handle this exceptional case.

Eliding the receiver

One further point about this example is worth mentioning. In the statement

```
sum = Sum2.root(a) + Sum2.root(b) + Sum2.root(c);
```

the expression `Sum2.root(a)`, for example, is a message that is sent to the class `Sum2` and hence invokes the `root` method of that class. But the message `Sum2.root(a)` is itself within the class `Sum2` (within its `main` method to be precise). Because of this we could have alternatively coded:

```
sum = root(a) + root(b) + root(c);
```

That is, we are permitted in this case to omit the name of the receiver of the message. The understanding is that if the receiver of a message is missing, the method to be invoked is within the same class. Hence in our case, the compiler will automatically look within the class `Sum2` to find the method `root` to invoke. From now on we shall almost always make use of this abbreviation. If the method to be invoked by a message is in the same class as the message itself the receiver object will be omitted.

The following three problems explore and extend ideas to do with the construction and invocation of methods.

PROBLEM 1: converting Centigrade to Fahrenheit

A temperature measured in degrees Centigrade can be converted to degrees Fahrenheit by the formula $f = \frac{9}{5}c + 32$ where f denotes Fahrenheit and c Centigrade. Construct a method `cent2fah` which takes a floating point number representing a temperature in degrees Centigrade and returns the Fahrenheit equivalent.

Construct a class `Fever` which contains the method `cent2fah` together with a `main` method that makes appropriate use of the method `cent2fah` so that when the class is compiled and run the following table is displayed in the Transcript window:

```
Centigrade   Fahrenheit
    37.0        98.6
    37.2        99.0
    37.4        99.3
    37.6        99.7
    37.8        100.0
    38.0        100.4
```

In this table the Fahrenheit temperatures have been rounded correct to 1 decimal place.

For help with this problem see Hints.

□

In Section 4.3 we developed the following code to compute the greatest common divisor (gcd) of two positive integers `num1` and `num2`:

```
int num1 = ..;
int num2 = ..;
int temp;
if (num1 < num2) {
    temp = num1;
    num1 = num2;
    num2 = temp;
}
while (num2 != 0) {
    temp = num2;
    num2 = num1 % num2;
    num1 = temp;
}
```

After executing this code the gcd is the value of `num1`.

PROBLEM 2: gcd revisited

This problem involves constructing a method that has two parameters.

Make appropriate use of the code above to construct a method gcd which takes two integers and if both are greater than 0 returns their gcd, else returns 0.

In the folder *Testing Gcd* you will find a class TestingGcd with the following code:

```
import genesis.*;

public class TestingGcd {

    public static void main (String [] args) {
        int x = DialogBox.requestInt("First integer:");
        int y = DialogBox.requestInt("Second integer:");
        int result = gcd(x, y);
        if (result == 0)
            Transcript.println("Numbers not both positive.");
        else Transcript.println(result);
    }
}
```

Add your gcd method to this class and run it to test your method.

For help with this problem see Hints.

□

The next problem involves constructing a method that has no parameters.

PROBLEM 3: a method to toss a die

Construct a method tossDie which when invoked returns an integer randomly selected in the range 1 to 6.

Construct a class TestingTheToss which contains the method tossDie and a main method that makes appropriate use of the method tossDie so that when the class is compiled and run, 20 random integers in the range 1 to 6 are displayed in the Transcript window.

For help with this problem see Hints.

□

6.2 Methods and arrays

Methods are often useful when processing arrays. For example, consider the problem of displaying the elements of an array of numbers. As this is something we frequently want to do, why not create a method to do it? Here is the code for a class `ArrayMethods` that contains a method `displayIntArray`:

```
import genesis.*;

public class ArrayMethods {

    public static void main (String [] args) {
        int [] myArray = {36, 21, 15, 12, 57};
        displayIntArray(myArray);
    }

    public static void displayIntArray (int [] intArray) {
        for (int i=0; i<intArray.length; i++)
            Transcript.print(intArray[i]+" ");
        Transcript.println();
    }
}
```

When invoked, the method `displayIntArray` displays in the Transcript window the integers in the array `intArray`. The value of this array is passed as an argument to the method. Confirm this for yourself by running the class `ArrayMethods`; you will find this class in the folder *Array Methods.*

There are a few interesting issues raised by the method `displayIntArray`.

First, it is a void method, i.e. it does not return a value. You will notice that the method has no return-statement. This method is invoked to produce output, not to compute some value required by the message sender. Consequently, the invoking message, `displayIntArray(myArray)`, is a statement, not an expression. That is, it does not take a value.

Compare this with a message that invokes a non-void method. In such cases the message is part of some expression that takes some value as a consequence of the method's invocation.

Second, notice how the value `intArray.length` is used in the for-loop to determine the length of the array `intArray`. This demonstrates the power of using such an expression: the length of `intArray` will be the length of whatever array is passed as argument to the method. This length may well be different for each invocation of the method. Hence our method will work regardless of the actual length of the array whose elements we want to display.

Finally, notice that the elements of the array `intArray` are displayed spaced out on a line of the Transcript window, but then a new line is started (by the statement `Transcript.println()`) although nothing is yet displayed on this line. Why have we done this? If we didn't, then any subsequent output to the Transcript window would continue on the same line used to display the array elements, and usually this is not what we would want. There is a subtle programming rule here: make sure that when a method completes its execution, the environment is ready to continue with whatever task may follow.

PROBLEM 4: summing an array

Construct a method `sumIntArray` which when passed an array of integers returns the sum of the elements in that array.

To test your `sumIntArray` method, modify the class `ArrayMethods` by adding your method and then modifying the `main` method to invoke `sumIntArray` as appropriate so that when the class is compiled and run, the elements of the array `myArray` are displayed in the Transcript window, followed on a new line by the sum of these elements. (The class `ArrayMethods` is in the folder *Array Methods.*)

For help with this problem see Hints.

□

PROBLEM 5: chasing the tail

Given a non-empty array (i.e. one with length greater than 0), its *tail* is an array of length one smaller formed from the elements of the given array but with the first element discarded. For example, the tail of the array $\{36, 21, 15, 12, 57\}$ is $\{21, 15, 12, 57\}$, while the tail of $\{57\}$ is $\{\}$, the empty sequence.

Construct a method `tail` which when passed an array of integers returns the tail of that array.

To test your `tail` method, modify the class `ArrayMethods` by adding your method and then modifying the `main` method to invoke `tail` as appropriate so that when the class is compiled and run, the elements of the array `myArray` are displayed in the Transcript window, followed on a new line by the elements of the tail of this array. (The class `ArrayMethods` is in the folder *Array Methods.*)

For help with this problem see Hints.

□

PROBLEM 6: extracting data

Construct a method `getEven` which when passed an array of integers returns an array whose elements are all the even integers in the given array in the order in which they appear in that array. For example, if the array {36, 21, 15, 12, 57} is passed to the method, the array {36, 12} will be returned.

To test your `getEven` method, modify the class `ArrayMethods` by adding your method and then modifying the `main` method to invoke `getEven` as appropriate so that when the class is compiled and run, the elements of the array `myArray` are displayed in the Transcript window, followed on a new line by the elements of the array containing just the even integers in `myArray`. (The class `ArrayMethods` is in the folder *Array Methods*.)

For help with this problem see Hints.

□

PROBLEM 7: gcd of an array of integers

Suppose we want to find the gcd of a collection of positive integers, i.e. we want the largest integer which is a factor of each integer in the collection.

Suppose the numbers are all positive integers and are stored in an array. Consider the following strategy:

- start by taking the first integer in the array as the gcd so far;
- then step through the array and at each step if g, say, is the gcd of the integers looked at so far in the array, find the gcd of g and the next integer in the array.

Use this strategy to construct a method `gcdArray` which when passed an array of integers

- returns the gcd of these integers if all the integers are positive;
- returns 0 if the array is empty or if any integer is not positive.

When creating this method assume you already have available a method `gcd` which takes two integers and if both are greater than 0 returns their gcd, else returns 0 (see Problem 2 for such a `gcd` method).

To test your `gcdArray` method, modify the class `ArrayMethods` by adding both the method `gcdArray` and the method `gcd` (from Problem 2) and then modifying the `main` method to invoke `gcdArray` as appropriate so that when the class is compiled and run, the gcd of the integers in the array `myArray` is displayed in the Output window. (The class `ArrayMethods` is in the folder *Array Methods.*)

For help with this problem see Hints.

□

PROBLEM 8: arrays without duplications

Construct a method `hasNoDuplications` which when passed an array of integers returns the Boolean *true* if and only if the array of integers supplied has no duplicated elements, i.e. the integers in the array are all distinct .

When you have completed coding the method, test it by creating a class that contains this method together with a short `main` method.

For help with this problem see Hints.

□

PROBLEM 9: tossing four dice

Suppose we have 4 dice. On average, how many times do we need to simultaneously toss the 4 dice until the 4 numbers shown on the dice are all different? The aim of this problem is to use the computer to get a numeric estimate of this average.

Construct a class `FourDice` which simulates the simultaneous tossing of the 4 dice and counts the number of tosses required until the 4 numbers shown on the dice are all different. Repeat this 1,000 times and print out the average number of tosses required. In your code place the 4 tosses from each trial in an array of length 4 and make use of the method `hasNoDuplications` constructed in Problem 8 to test if the 4 tosses are distinct.

(Using elementary probability theory, its not too hard to calculate mathematically that the average number of tosses required is 3.6. If you fancy your mathematical skills you might like to try the calculation for yourself. How does the numeric estimate produced by the computer compare?)

For help with this problem see Hints.

□

6.3 Recursion

Problem 5 in the last section suggests an alternative way of summing a sequence of numbers based on the following simple observation. If *a* is a sequence of numbers, then to sum the elements in *a* all we need do is add the first element of *a* to the sum of all the other elements in *a*. That is,

$$sum(a) = a_1 + sum(tail(a))$$

where *tail*(*a*) is the sequence of integers formed from the elements of *a* but with the first element discarded. Of course, this only works if *a* is a non-empty sequence, i.e. it has length at least 1. If *a* is an empty sequence then its sum will be 0.

Let's now translate this idea into a method for summing an array of integers. Here is code for a method `sum` (it assumes there is already in the same class as `sum` a method `tail` that takes an array of integers and returns the tail of that array):

```
public static int sum (int [] intArray) {
    if (intArray.length == 0) return 0;
    else return intArray[0] + sum(tail(intArray));
}
```

The significant aspect of this code is the expression `sum(tail(intArray))`. When evaluated, this expression will invoke the method `sum` itself! That is, the method `sum` is *recursive*!

Can such code work? If a method invokes itself won't we just get into an endless loop? And anyhow, what does it mean? Here is the code for a class `SumByRecursion` that invokes the sum method:

```
public class SumByRecursion {

    public static void main (String [] args) {
        int [] myArray = {34, 21, 17, 55, 11};
        System.out.println(sum(myArray));
    }

    public static int sum (int [] intArray) {
        if (intArray.length == 0) return 0;
        else return intArray[0] + sum(tail(intArray));
    }
```

```
        public static int [] tail (int [] intArray) {
            if (intArray.length == 0) return intArray;
            int [] theTail = new int [intArray.length - 1];
            for (int i=0; i<theTail.length; i++)
                theTail[i] = intArray[i+1];
            return theTail;
        }
    }
```

This class is in the folder *Sum By Recursion*; open this folder and run the class. Experiment with modifying the array `myArray` to confirm to your satisfaction that the code works.

Executing recursive code

Consider the recursive method `sum`. If the array passed to the method `sum` has length 0, the method returns 0 without involving any recursion. This seemingly simple observation is crucial as it means that the method does not always invoke itself. This, as we shall see, gives us a way out of the recursion.

Next, suppose the array passed to the method `sum` has length greater than 0 (call this $invocation_1$ of the method). The first integer in the array is extracted and then the execution of $invocation_1$ pauses and the method is invoked once again (call this $invocation_2$). Notice, however, that the array passed to $invocation_2$ has a strictly smaller length. Once again the first integer is extracted and the execution of $invocation_2$ pauses. The element extracted at this stage is in fact the second integer of the original array.

This process continues until eventually the method `sum` is invoked (call this $invocation_k$) and the array passed to this invocation has length 0. In this case at last a value (namely, 0) is returned without any new invocation of the method. This result (0) is returned to $invocation_{k-1}$ and this invocation can resume execution. The result from this invocation (namely, the value of the last integer (added to 0) in the original array) will now be returned to $invocation_{k-2}$ and this invocation can resume execution. The result from this invocation (namely, the sum of the last two integers in the original array) will now be returned to $invocation_{k-3}$ and this invocation can resume execution.

This continues until eventually a result is returned to $invocation_1$ and this invocation resumes execution. This original invocation will in its turn return its result (namely, the sum of all the integers in the original array) and the computation is completed.

Note: although the code for a recursive method such as `sum` is very neat and concise, the nested invocation involved in executing the code can sometimes lead to inefficiencies. When creating a recursive method you need to keep in mind this trade-off between succinct code and implementation efficiency.

PROBLEM 10: computing factorials recursively

In Problem 17 of Chapter 3 we constructed a class `Factorial` to calculate the factorial of a given positive integer. Here we revisit the problem but use recursion to do the same calculation.

The factorial of a positive integer n can be defined recursively as follows:

$$factorial(n) = 1 \quad \text{if } n = 0$$
$$factorial(n) = n * factorial(n-1) \quad \text{if } n \geqslant 1$$

Use this definition to construct a recursive method `factorial` which when passed an integer returns 0 if the integer is negative, but otherwise returns the factorial of the integer.

Test this method by constructing a class `RecursiveFactorial` containing this method and a short `main` method which when compiled and run opens a dialog box requesting the user supply a positive integer, and when this integer is supplied displays its factorial in the Transcript window.

As the factorial of a number can be very large, do the calculations using floating point arithmetic.

For help with this problem see Hints.

□

6.4 Passing arguments to parameters

Variables and parameters declared within a method have what is known as *local scope.* They are created each time the method is invoked and have meaning only within the code of the method. They cease to exist when the method finishes its task, i.e. completes execution. The parameter variables are initialised with the argument values passed by the message that invokes the method.

The important issue of what happens when we use an argument of a message to pass a value to a parameter of a method is not as straightforward as may at first appear. Recall that when discussing the assignment operator in Section 5.1 we distinguished assignment of primitive types and assignment of objects. Again, when passing argument values to parameters we distinguish these two categories, primitive types and objects.

Passing a primitive type

When the formal parameter is a primitive type, the argument passed is a value of that type. When the method starts to execute, it assigns this value to the corresponding parameter which is effectively a local variable existing for the duration of the method's execution. We can use the variable like any other, e.g. we can assign to it. But these effects are isolated from the sender of the message which invoked the method. This is akin to assigning the value of the argument to the formal parameter. It obeys the rules for primitive value assignment discussed earlier.

Example: what is output by:

```
        int j = 7;
        System.out.println(add2(j) + " and " + j);
        ...

    public static int add2 (int i) {
        return i + 2;
    }
```

Answer:

9 and 7

Explanation: the value 7 is sent to the method which copies the value into the local `int` variable `i` (recall parameters are effectively local variables). Two is added to the value of `i` and the result returned, but the value of `j` does not change. In this case, 9 is returned. Note `i` and `j` are two distinct variables; `i` exists only for the duration of the method call. Note also that what happens is independent of the name of the parameter. If we replace `i` by `j` in the method `add2` the effect would be exactly the same.

Passing an object type

If the argument of a message is an object (e.g. an array), the object reference is passed to the method. This reference is assigned to the corresponding formal parameter. Again, the parameter is identical to a local variable whose value is initialised to the value passed to the method (in this case an object reference). Again, just as for object assignment, this parameter identifier is an alias to the underlying object. The object itself is not cloned (a duplicated copy is not created) and passed.

Consequently, if a message argument is of object type the corresponding parameter in the method becomes an alias for that object and any changes to the object within the method will be reflected as changes to the original argument.

Example: what is output by:

```
        int [] myArray = {0, 1, 2, 3};
        add2(myArray);
        for (int i =0; i < myArray.length; i++) {
            System.out.println(myArray[i]);
        }

        ...

    public static void add2 (int [] intStuff) {
        for (int i=0; i < intStuff.length; i++)
            intStuff[i] = intStuff[i] + 2;
    }
```

Answer:

2
3
4
5

Explanation: When the message add2(myArray) is sent, a reference to the array myArray is sent to the method. While the method is active, both the variables myArray and intStuff reference the same underlying array of values. The method adds 2 to each element in this array.

PROBLEM 11: rounding off

Construct a method roundToOne which when passed an array of floating point numbers of type double rounds each number in the array correct to 1 significant digit. For example, if the array

{37.2, 2.0, 0.017, 405.6}

is passed to the method, it becomes the array

{40.0, 2.0, 0.02, 400.0}.

For help with this problem see Hints.

□

Discussion

Problem 11 illustrates an important side-effect of passing an array to a method. If the role of the method is to alter the values of the elements of the array, the method does not need to return the changed array. Changes to the array in the method will automatically be changes to the original array.

Chapter 6 self-check

Can you describe

- the overall structure of a method?
- how arguments of primitive type are passed to a method?
- how array arguments are passed to a method?
- the role played by the parameters of a method?
- how a return type for a method is declared?
- how a value is returned by a method?
- the distinction between method arguments and message parameters?
- the scope of a local variable declared in a method?

Objects and classes 7

Prerequisites

Before commencing Chapter 7, you will need to be familiar with:

- control constructs, as covered in Chapter 4;
- methods, as covered in Chapter 6.

In particular, you will need to be familiar with how arguments are passed to parameters when sending a message to invoke a method, and how a value can be returned by a method. Arrays (Chapter 5) will also be used occasionally.

Overview

So far in *Java Genesis* we have concentrated on the role of a class as a repository for code that is invoked directly by an application. For example, the `main` method of a class is invoked when that class is run. In Chapter 6 we saw how other methods can be added to this class and invoked from the `main` method. These methods all contain the key word `static` indicating that they are *class* methods, i.e. methods that are invoked either from some other method in the class, or by sending a message directly to the class. All the methods in the classes we have coded so far have been static methods.

In this Chapter we begin to look at the other fundamental role of a class: as a 'factory' for defining, building and managing its own objects. Not all classes undertake this role: the classes we have coded so far to contain the `main` method do not. But these are the exception. When constructing applications, a central task will be to code classes that, among other things, define, build and manage their own objects. Indeed the key to object-oriented software development is to create classes whose objects cooperate to perform the desired application. The code within a class that is directly responsible for its objects is distinguished by *not* having the key word `static`.

The approach adopted in this unit is to illustrate the general role played by objects and classes by looking at some particular applications. We begin by developing a class whose objects model points in a plane. These objects are then applied in two case studies involving the animation of simple graphics. We then develop a case study based on a credit-card banking system. The chapter ends with some best-practice guidelines to be followed when coding classes.

7.1 Objects and classes

The role played by objects and the classes that define, build and manage them is illustrated by looking at a specific example: a class whose objects model points in a plane. This example illustrates various concepts, including instance variables, constructor methods, setter and getter methods, and the distinction between methods that modify the receiver object and those that return a value to the sender object.

Problems:

1 declaring planar points

2 exploring object equality

3 modify receiver vs return a value

7.2 Case study: drawing polygons

We use the ideas about objects and classes introduced in the previous section to construct a simple animation application.

Problems:

4 drawing a triangle

5 drawing regular polygons

6 rotating a regular polygon

7 rotating a star

7.3 Case study: bouncing a ball

We consider another animation problem, and in the process discuss a systematic approach to the coding of applications in general.

Problem:

8 bouncing the ball

7.4 Case study: credit-card accounts

In this section we investigate further the coding of classes whose core role is to define, build and manage its objects. Through the construction of a class whose objects model credit-card bank accounts we get to examine carefully the processes involved in constructing classes.

Problem:

9 testing the `CreditCard` class

7.5 Some best-practice patterns

This short finale brings together many of the ideas about classes and objects met in the earlier sections, and presents them in the form of a guide to best practice when constructing classes.

Problem:

10 savings accounts

Learning outcomes

At the conclusion of Chapter 7 you will understand:

- how to declare a variable whose type is a given class;
- how to use the key word `new` to construct a new object of a given class;
- the role of a constructor method in defining a new object;
- how to code a class so that objects of that class can be defined, built and managed;
- how to declare instance and class variables;
- how to get the current values of an object's variables by invoking a *getter* method;
- how to set the values of an existing object's variables by invoking a *setter* method;
- the distinction between methods that modify the state of an object, and those that extract and return information about the state of an object;
- how to output information about an object;
- how to restrict access to variables;
- the distinction between *class* (static) variables and methods, and *instance* (non-static) variables and methods, and the circumstances under which each is used;
- how to approach the construction of a class in a systematic way.

7.1 Objects and classes

In this section we begin a detailed examination of the role objects play in applications. Each object in Java is associated with a class that determines the type of the object, and this class takes responsibility for defining, building and managing its objects.

The role of objects and classes is motivated and illustrated in this section through a specific example: a class that models points in a plane.

Modelling planar points

When building graphical images or doing computer animation, it is often necessary to refer to specific positions within a window. As explained in Section 2.1, a position in a window is identified by a so-called *grid* position, i.e. a pair (x, y) of integers, where x denotes the horizontal and y the vertical distance (in pixels) from the upper-left corner of the window. Clearly therefore, when building complex images and in particular when animating those images, it will be necessary to work with such pairs of integers.

However, many of the graphical operations we may want to perform (e.g. moving a figure an arbitrary distance in an arbitrary direction) cannot be easily captured by integer arithmetic. It is more convenient to work with floating point number pairs and only round these number pairs to the nearest grid positions when we want to draw images on the screen.

To facilitate working with floating point number pairs we have coded a class `PlanarPoint` whose objects represent points in the plane. Such points are number pairs (x, y) where x and y are floating point numbers of type `double`. This class has been placed in the *genesis* package so that our applications can readily make use of it.

We will shortly examine in detail the code for the class `PlanarPoint` but for now let's experiment with declaring and using objects of this class.

PROBLEM 1: declaring planar points

The class `DeclaringPlanarPoints` whose code is given at the top of the next page declares two objects of the class `PlanarPoint` and displays details of these objects in the Transcript window.

This class is in the folder *Declaring Planar Points.* Open the folder and run the class.

Experiment with modifying the code for this class so as to declare points `p1` and `p2` with different coordinates.

```
import genesis.*;

public class DeclaringPlanarPoints {

    /*
    Declaring a couple of planar points.
    */

    public static void main (String [] args) {
        PlanarPoint p1;
        p1 = new PlanarPoint(12, -3.4);
        Transcript.println("p1 is the point "+p1);
        PlanarPoint p2 = new PlanarPoint();
        Transcript.println("p2 is the point "+p2);
    }
}
```

□

Discussion

In the class `DeclaringPlanarPoints`, two local variables `p1` and `p2` of class type `PlanarPoint` are declared and assigned values. Colloquially, we say that `p1` and `p2` are *objects* of the class `PlanarPoint`. Notice that the statement

```
PlanarPoint p1;
```

declaring the variable `p1` to be of type `PlanarPoint` has the same syntax as statements we saw in Chapter 3 declaring variables of type `int`, `double`, `char` or `String`, namely:

type identifier ;

The difference comes, however, when we assign initial values to the declared variables. In the case of the variable `p1`, this is the statement

```
p1 = new PlanarPoint(12, -3.4);
```

The key word `new` is used to indicate that we are creating a completely new object of the class `PlanarPoint`. This key word is followed by the message `PlanarPoint(12, -3.4)` which invokes the corresponding method, known as a *constructor* method, in the class `PlanarPoint`. As we shall confirm when we look in detail at the code for the class `PlanarPoint`, this constructor method builds a number pair whose x- and y-coordinates are respectively the numbers

12.0 and -3.4 of type `double`. The name of a constructor method is always the same as the name of its class (`PlanarPoint` in this case).

As with other types, the declaration of an object variable and the assignment of initial values to the variable can be done in the one statement, as is illustrated by the declaration of the object p2:

```
PlanarPoint p2 = new PlanarPoint();
```

In this case the constructor method builds a number pair whose x- and y-coordinates are both 0. We will have quite a lot more to say about constructor methods both later in this chapter and in Chapter 8.

Consider now the complete code for the class `PlanarPoint`. Various aspects of this code will be explored in the discussion that follow.

```
package genesis;

public class PlanarPoint {

    /*
    Objects of this class denote points in the plane.
    */

    // instance variables

    private double x;  // x-coordinate of the point
    private double y;  // y-coordinate of the point

    // -------------------------------------------

    // constructors: the following two methods set the
    // values of the instance variables for a new object

    public PlanarPoint (double a, double b) {
        x = a;
        y = b;
    }

    public PlanarPoint ( ) {
        x = 0;
        y = 0;
    }

    // -------------------------------------------
```

```
// setters: the following two methods set the values
// of the instance variables of the receiver

public void setX (double a) {
    x = a;
}
public void setY (double b) {
    y = b;
}

// ---------------------------------------------

// getters: the following two methods return current
// values of the instance variables of the receiver

public double getX ( ) {
    return x;
}

public double getY ( ) {
    return y;
}

// ---------------------------------------------

public void translate (PlanarPoint p) {
    // modifies the receiver by adding to it point p
    setX(x + p.x);
    setY(y + p.y);
}

public PlanarPoint add (PlanarPoint p) {
    // returns the result of adding the receiver to the
    // point p; the receiver itself is not modified
    PlanarPoint result =
        new PlanarPoint(x + p.x, y + p.y);
    return result;
}

public PlanarPoint rounded ( ) {
    // returns the nearest grid point to the receiver;
    // the receiver itself is not modified
    PlanarPoint result =
        new PlanarPoint(Math.round(x), Math.round(y));
    return result;
}
```

```
        public String toString ( ) {
            // returns a string representation of the receiver
            return "("+x+", "+y+")";
        }
    }
```

Let us look at some aspects of the code for this class before we apply it in applications involving planar points.

To begin, notice that the key word `static` does not appear anywhere within the code. In particular, there is no `main` method. Hence the class `PlanarPoint` is exclusively concerned with defining, building and managing its objects. Code within the class can be invoked only when a new object of the class is created (as was done in the `main` method of the `DeclaringPlanarPoints` class) or when an existing object of the class is sent a message.

Instance methods

Methods that do not contain the `static` key word are known as *instance* methods. These methods can only be invoked by sending an object of the class an appropriate message. Each method in the class `PlanarPoint`, for example, is an instance method. The name 'instance' is used because an object of a class is often referred to as an *instance* of the class.

On the other hand, messages that do contain the key word `static` are known as *class* (or *static*) methods. It is with class methods that we have been mostly concerned in earlier chapters; e.g. `main` is a class method. When the class itself (as distinct from an object of the class) is sent a message, it is a class method that is invoked.

At this point it is worth digressing slightly to discuss the way instance methods are associated with objects. When an object is created it is assigned space in memory where values of variables unique to that object can be stored. (These are the object's instance variables; we discuss them in detail below.) But the code of the methods invoked when the object receives a message (i.e. the object's instance methods) are not stored with the object. Instead these instance methods are stored with the class where, as we remarked above, they are distinguished by not having the key work `static`.

The great advantage of this is that although within a software system there may exist many objects of a given class, we need store the code for the instance methods of these objects once only. Of course, nothing comes for free; for this to work the instance methods must be coded in such a way that they can be applied to any object of the class regardless of the values of the object's unique instance variables.

When an object receives a message the appropriate instance method is invoked and the code for that method is interpreted uniquely for that particular object. For example, if we send a planar point object *p*, say, the message `getX()`, the method `getX` in the class `PlanarPoint` is invoked. The only line of code in this method is

```
return x;
```

When this code is executed, the `x` is interpreted as referring to the unique instance variable of that name associated with the object *p* that received the message. In this context *p* is called the *receiver* object. That is, when an instance method is invoked it is interpreted with respect to the receiver object. Perhaps as a consequence the values of the receiver object's instance variables are changed, perhaps information about the receiver object is extracted. It will all depend upon the role of the invoked instance method.

We will revisit and elaborate upon these issues several times in the discussion below.

Instance variables

The statements

```
private double x;  // x-coordinate of the point
private double y;  // y-coordinate of the point
```

in the class `PlanarPoint` declare *instance* variables `x` and `y` of type `double`. Instance variables are much like local variables but differ in three important respects.

Values exclusive to an object

Firstly, each object of the class `PlanarPoint` has its own exclusive set of these instance variables. Hence, if `p` is an object of the class `PlanarPoint`, `p` will have a pair `x` and `y` of instance variables of type `double` associated with it, and these variables will be distinct from the instance variables associated with any other planar point. (Although the instance variables associated with distinct objects are distinct, the values taken by these variables need not be. We discuss this issue in more detail below.) Within the class `PlanarPoint`, the actual floating point number values of the variables `x` and `y` for an object `p`, say, of the class `PlanarPoint` can be referred to by the expressions `p.x` and `p.y` respectively (e.g. see the method `add` where `p` is the parameter).

As we shall see, some of the messages that can be sent to an object p of the class PlanarPoint have the effect of changing the values of p's x and y variables. Nevertheless, p remains the same object — only the values of its instance variables have changed. The values of the variables x and y for any other planar point would be unaffected.

To give an analogous example, each person object has an associated instance variable address denoting where they live. A person may change his or her address, but remains the same person, and the addresses of all other people are unaffected. Even if two distinct people have the same address (which often happens!), they remain distinct objects. That is, each person object has its own version of the instance variable address, and even if two people have the same value for this variable they remain quite distinct people.

Scope

Secondly, unlike local variables that are declared within some block within some method and have that block as their scope, instance variables are declared outside any method and include every instance method in the class in their scope. That is, instance variables can be accessed and modified by any instance method in the class. In the case of the class PlanarPoint, as all the methods are instance methods, each can access and even modify directly the instance variables x and y, as can be readily confirmed by looking at the code for these methods.

Accessibility

Thirdly, the declaration of an instance variable starts with a key word to indicate its accessibility. In the case of the instance variables for the class PlanarPoint, the key word is private. This indicates that the values of these instance variables are private to the class PlanarPoint and cannot be accessed directly except within the class PlanarPoint itself. Hence for an object p of type PlanarPoint declared within the class PlanarPoint itself, the values of x and y are given by the expressions p.x and p.y respectively (as, for example, in the add method). But for an object p of type PlanarPoint declared within the code of any class other than PlanarPoint, the expressions p.x and p.y are not permitted and the Java compiler would reject them.

Why do we do this? The reason is *encapsulation*. The idea is that the values of an object's instance variables can be considered to be a private matter for the object. That is, an object may encapsulate (hide) these values and access to them should be restricted. In fact, as we shall see, if there exists an appropriate 'getter' method we can still get access to the values of an object's private instance variables. Access is obtained by sending an appropriate message to the object. (Getter methods are discussed further below.)

This restriction can be overcome in Java by declaring an instance variable to be `public`. If this is done, expressions such as `p.x` would then be valid in any class. However, making instance variables public in this way is generally considered bad programming practice as it violates the principle of encapsulation.

Constructor methods

The class `PlanarPoint` contains two constructor methods. The role of a constructor method is to set the initial values of the instance variables when a new object of the class is created. As mentioned before, the name of a constructor method must be the same as the name of its class (`PlanarPoint` in this case). So we have the situation where both constructor methods have the same name!

Overloading the method name

The situation whereby more than one constructor method has the same name is known as method *overloading*. In such a situation, how can the compiler tell which constructor method to invoke in response to receiving a message? The answer lies in the types of the arguments the message contains. Just so long as the argument types uniquely correspond to the parameter types for some version of the associated constructor method, the compiler will give us no hassle. It will correctly deduce which constructor method to invoke.

In the case of the constructor methods for planar points, if the message contains two arguments of type `double`, the first constructor method is invoked, but if the message contains no arguments the second constructor method is invoked. (If the constructor message argument is neither of these two cases, the compiler will signal an error.)

[*An aside*: Any method, not just constructor methods, can be overloaded in this way. It is permissible to have several methods with the same name within the one class provided these same-named methods can be uniquely differentiated by their parameter lists. That is, the parameter lists of any two methods with the same name must either have a different number of parameters, or the sequence of parameter types (taking order into account) must be different. *End aside*]

Default constructor

A constructor with no parameters, such as the second constructor in the class `PlanarPoint`, is called a *default* constructor. If no constructors are explicitly coded, Java provides a default constructor that assigns default values to the instance variables. However, you are strongly advised not to rely on this feature of Java, but always code explicit constructors and, in particular, always code an explicit default constructor.

Notice that the constructor methods do not reference any return type. Essentially they return the constructed object, but as this type is obvious from the constructor's name, the return type is *not* included as part of a constructor method's declaration.

Object equality

Consider the class ExploringObjectEquality:

```
import genesis.*;

public class ExploringObjectEquality {

    /*
    Exploring the equality of planar point objects.
    */

    public static void main (String [] args) {
        PlanarPoint p1 = new PlanarPoint(3, -4);
        PlanarPoint p2 = new PlanarPoint(3, -4);
        Transcript.println("p1 equals p2? "+(p1 == p2));

        p1.setX(9);
        Transcript.println("p1 is now the point "+p1);
        Transcript.println("p2 is now the point "+p2);
        Transcript.println("The x-coord of p2 is "+p2.getX());

        p1 = p2;
        PlanarPoint p3 = new PlanarPoint(1, 1);
        p1.translate(p3);
        Transcript.println("p1 is now the point "+p1);
        Transcript.println("p2 is now the point "+p2);
        Transcript.println("p1 equals p2? "+(p1 == p2));
    }
}
```

PROBLEM 2: exploring object equality

Without actually running the class ExploringObjectEquality, try to deduce what would be displayed in the Transcript window if the class was run.

The class ExploringObjectEquality is in the folder *Exploring Object Equality*. Now run this class to test your deductions.

□

Discussion

The code of the `ExploringObjectEquality` class begins by creating two new planar point objects `p1` and `p2` whose `x` and `y` variables take the same values. Hence `p1` and `p2` are such that `p1.x` equals `p2.x` and `p1.y` equals `p2.y`, i.e. both `p1` and `p2` denote the same planar point because their x- and y-coordinates agree.

Nevertheless, `p1` and `p2` are distinct objects of the class `PlanarPoint`. Hence the expression `p1 == p2` evaluates to *false* as the '==' operator tests for object equality, i.e. the expression evaluates to *true* if and only if `p1` and `p2` are the same object. That `p1` and `p2` are not the same object is further confirmed by executing the expression

```
p1.setX(9);
```

which sets the x-coordinate of `p1` to be 9 but leaves the coordinates of `p2` unchanged.

Object aliasing

If we want `p1` and `p2` to be the same object we simply need to execute the assignment

```
p1 = p2;
```

which has the effect that the object identified by `p1` becomes the same object already identified by `p2`, i.e. `p1` and `p2` now become alternative names (aliases) for the same object. (As an analogy, it is as if a person is given two names and either can be used to refer to the person.)

If we now increase both the x- and y-coordinates of `p1` by 1 by executing the statement

```
p1.translate(p3);
```

the coordinates of `p2` change in exactly the same way because `p2` is just another name for the same object. **Be warned!!** As we saw with arrays in Section 5.1, if `ob1` and `ob2` are objects (i.e. variables whose values are objects of a given class), the assignment statement

```
ob1 = ob2
```

effectively says that `ob1` is now just another name for the object already named by `ob2`.

Having distinct variables refer to the same object in this way is known as *aliasing*. It can pose serious risks when programming because if we are unaware that `ob1` and `ob2`, say, are aliases for the same object, we may not realise that sending a message to change the state of `ob1` will change the state of `ob2` in the same way.

Setter methods

The instance method `setX`, as invoked by the expression `p1.setX(9)`, is known as a *setter* (or *mutator*) method because it sets the value of the instance variable `x` in the receiver object (`p1` in this case). A setter method is needed to set the value of the instance variable `x` of `p1` as `x` is declared `private` in the class `PlanarPoint` and so cannot be modified directly by code in any other class and, in particular, not in the class `ExploringObjectEquality`.

Setter methods are void as they do not return a value. Rather they change the state of an object.

Getter methods

The instance method `getX`, as invoked by the expression `p2.getX()` in the `ExploringObjectEquality` class, is known as a *getter* (or *accessor*) method because it returns (i.e. gets) the current value of the instance variable `x` of the receiver object (`p2` in this case). A getter method is needed to get the value of the instance variable `x` of `p2` as `x` is declared `private` in the class `PlanarPoint` and so cannot be accessed directly by code in the class `ExploringObjectEquality`. As getter methods return a value, they are not void, but instead have as return type the type of the instance variable whose value they are getting.

[*An aside*: If instance variables are declared `public` rather than `private`, then they can be accessed from any class and hence there is no need to define setter and getter methods. However, as we remarked before, declaring such variables `public` is considered to be very poor programming practice. *End aside*]

Invoking instance methods

Let us return and look in detail at what happens when we execute the statement

```
p1.translate(p3);
```

in the code for the class `ExploringObjectEquality`. The object `p1` of type `PlanarPoint` receives the message `translate(p3)`, and so the code for the instance method `translate` in the class `PlanarPoint` is invoked with the object `p3` of type `PlanarPoint` passed as argument. The code for the method `translate` is:

```
public void translate (PlanarPoint p) {
    // modifies the receiver by adding to it point p
    setX(x + p.x);
    setY(y + p.y);
}
```

Hence, as we discussed in Section 6.4, when this code is invoked by the message `translate(p3)`, the parameter `p` in the method will refer to (i.e. be an alias for) the object identified by `p3`. Furthermore, the unreferenced variables `x` and `y` (i.e. those without the '`p.`' in front) in the method's code represent the instance variables of the receiver object `p1`. Consequently, when evaluating the statement

```
p1.translate(p3);
```

what is in fact evaluated are the statements

```
setX(p1.x + p3.x);
setY(p1.y + p3.y);
```

i.e. the `x` value of `p1` is increased by the `x` value of `p3` and the `y` value of `p1` is increased by the `y` value of `p3`.

The general rule is this:

when invoking an instance method, any unreferenced instance variable in that method takes the value of that variable in the receiver object.

In Java it is possible to emphasise this rule by using the key word `this`. Within a method, `this` refers to the receiver object. Hence the code for the `translate` method could have been written as

```
public void translate (PlanarPoint p) {
    // modifies the receiver by adding to it point p
    setX(this.x + p.x);
    setY(this.y + p.y);
}
```

and the meaning would have been identical. When we execute the code, `this` is replaced by the receiver object. As the key word `this` can be inferred by the compiler in this case, it is common programming practice to omit it in such circumstances.

Comparing void with non-void methods

Consider the class `ModifyOrReturn` whose code is given at the top of the next page.

PROBLEM 3: modify receiver vs return a value

Without actually running the class `ModifyOrReturn`, try to deduce what would be displayed in the Transcript window if the class was run.

```
import genesis.*;

public class ModifyOrReturn {

    /*
    Exploring method side effects.
    */

    public static void main (String [] args) {
        PlanarPoint p1 = new PlanarPoint(1, 7);
        PlanarPoint p2 = new PlanarPoint(-1, 2);
        PlanarPoint p3;
        p3 = p1.add(p2);
        p1.translate(p2);
        Transcript.println("p1 is the point "+p1);
        Transcript.println("p2 is the point "+p2);
        Transcript.println("p3 is the point "+p3);
    }
}
```

The class ModifyOrReturn is in the folder *Modify Or Return.* Now run this class to test your deductions.

□

Discussion

The class ModifyOrReturn illustrates the distinction between instance methods that return a value and do not modify the receiver object (such as the method add of the class PlanarPoint), and those that do not return a value but instead modify the receiver object (such as the method translate of the class PlanarPoint). For example, the expression

```
p1.add(p2)
```

does not modify p1 or p2 but returns a new object of the class PlanarPoint. In the class ModifyOrReturn this returned value is assigned to p3 via the assignment

```
p3 = p1.add(p2);
```

On the other hand, the statement

```
p1.translate(p2);
```

modifies `p1` and does not return any value. Notice that in the `ModifyOrReturn` class this phrase stands in its own right and does not need to be associated with some expression, indicating it is a statement.

It is important when writing or using code to be clear about the role of a method, i.e. whether it returns a value or modifies the receiver object. In fact, in Java it is quite possible to code a method that both modifies the receiver object and also returns a value. However, this is considered bad programming practice; as a rule methods should do one or the other, but not both.

[*An aside*: More generally, the notion of 'separation of concerns' suggests that we should separate distinct tasks into distinct methods. Good programming practice suggest that a method should be designed to do essential just one thing. If we want to do more than one thing, create more than one method. *End aside*]

In the case of the class `PlanarPoint`, why bother to have both of the methods `add` and `translate`? After all, they both simulate the same thing: the vector addition of planar points. We use `add` when we want to output a new planar point based on the vector addition of existing points and when we do not want to change the existing points. For example, perhaps we want to extend a geometric figure by starting with some existing points and then computing extra points to be added to the figure.

On the other hand, we use `translate` if we want to change the point denoted by the receiver object. For example, perhaps we want to translate (i.e. move rigidly in some direction) a given geometric figure, in which case each of the existing points in the figure needs to be modified to reflect the translation.

This example illustrates the importance of making a clear distinction between methods that return a value and those that modify the receiver object.

Printing a string representation of an object

Consider the statement

```
Transcript.println("p1 is the point "+p1);
```

which appears in the class `DeclaringPlanarPoints`. When evaluating the string `"p1 is the point "+p1`, Java appends a string representation of the object `p1` to the string `"p1 is the point "`. To get a string representation of the object `p1`, the expression `p1.toString()` is automatically evaluated by the underlying Java system, i.e. the `toString` method is invoked with `p1` as the receiver object. This method returns a string, and it is this string which is appended. For the class `PlanarPoint`, the `toString` method is:

```
public String toString ( ) {
    // returns a string representation of the receiver
    return "("+x+", "+y+")";
}
```

That is, the string returned by the method `toString`, is the string (a, b) where a and b are respectively the values of the object's x and y instance variables.

In general, we can code the `toString` method to return any appropriate string representation of our objects — it all depends which features of the object we want to display in string form in the window. There is a default `toString` method defined by the system which will be invoked if we do not define our own `toString` method in the object's class, but this default is often not useful.

As a general rule, it is good programming practice to always code a specific `toString` method when constructing a class so that information about any particular object can be readily output.

We finish this section by giving a brief and informal specification of each of the instance methods in the class `PlanarPoint`. In the next two sections we shall make use of objects of this class to develop a couple of case studies involving the animation of simple graphics.

Specification of methods in the class `PlanarPoint`

constructor methods

```
public PlanarPoint (double a, double b)
```

sets the x and y variables of a new object to be a and b respectively

```
public PlanarPoint ( )
```

sets both the x and y variables of the new object to be 0

setter methods

```
public void setX (double a)
```

sets the x variable of the receiver object to be a

```
public void setY (double b)
```

sets the y variable of the receiver object to be b

getter methods

`public double getX ( )`

returns the value of the `x` variable of the receiver object

`public double getY ( )`

returns the value of the `y` variable of the receiver object

other methods

`public void translate (PlanarPoint p)`

modifies the receiver object by adding to it the object `p` using vector addition; if the receiver denotes the point (a, b) and `p` denotes the point (c, d), then the variables of the receiver are changed to denote the point $(a + c, b + d)$

`public PlanarPoint add (PlanarPoint p)`

returns a new object denoting the point obtained by adding the receiver object to the object `p` using vector addition; the receiver is unchanged

`public PlanarPoint rounded ( )`

returns a new object denoting the point obtained by rounding the point denoted by the receiver object to the nearest grid point, e.g. if the receiver object denotes the point $(3.45, 7.6)$, then the object returned denotes the point $(3.0, 8.0)$; the receiver is unchanged

`public String toString ( )`

returns a string representation of the receiver object, e.g. if the receiver denotes the point $(3.45, 7.6)$, the string "(3.45, 7.6)" is returned

7.2 Case study: drawing polygons

The aim of this case study is to further explore the way objects can be used in Java to build applications, and in the process examine some issues to do with simple animation.

The *genesis* package contains the class `PolyFigure` which can be used to display a polygon in a window. There are three messages that can be sent to this class:

- `create()` takes no arguments; it needs to be sent to the class `PolyFigure` before any other message as it creates and opens the window in which the polygon will be drawn.
- `draw(..)` takes as argument an array of planar points (i.e. an array of objects of the class `PlanarPoint`). When this message is sent to the class `PolyFigure`, anything previously drawn in the window is erased and a hollow red polygon whose vertices are at the positions given by the planar points in the array supplied as the argument is drawn.
- `fill(..)` is similar to `draw` above except that the red polygon is drawn solid rather than hollow.

PROBLEM 4: drawing a triangle

The class `Triangle` displays a solid red triangle in a window:

```
import genesis.*;

public class Triangle {

    /*
    Draw a solid red triangle.
    */

    public static void main (String [] args) {
        PolyFigure.create();
        PlanarPoint [] vertices = new PlanarPoint[3];
        vertices[0] = new PlanarPoint(200, 80);
        vertices[1] = new PlanarPoint(250, 180);
        vertices[2] = new PlanarPoint(150, 180);
        PolyFigure.fill(vertices);
    }
}
```

Open the folder *Triangle* and run the class `Triangle`.

Modify the code so that a different triangle is drawn. In particular, experiment with the message `draw` as well as `fill`.

Now modify the code so that a polygon other than a triangle is drawn. In particular, try drawing a regular polygon (such as a square or a regular pentagon).

□

Drawing regular polygons

Let us consider in some detail the problem of drawing a regular polygon (i.e. a polygon with a common length for each edge and a common angle between any two adjacent edges). One approach is to start with the coordinates for the centre of the polygon, together with the radius of the polygon (i.e. the common distance from this centre to any vertex), and from this construct coordinates for the vertices. To do this we need to apply some elementary trigonometry and vector arithmetic. We'll take this gently so that if you can recall your school trigonometry you will be able to check the details for yourself; otherwise, just take the expressions that follow on trust. All we need in the end is the Java method `getVertex` whose code is given below.

The diagram below indicates how the coordinates of a vertex can be calculated. For example, suppose the centre of the polygon is the planar point (a, b) and its radius is the distance r. Suppose also that a vertex of the polygon is such that the line from the polygon's centre to that vertex makes an angle α with the direction of the x-axis. Then the vertex is the planar point

$$(a + r\cos\alpha, b + r\sin\alpha).$$

That is, the x-coordinate of the vertex is $a + r\cos\alpha$ and the y-coordinate is $b + r\sin\alpha$. (The direction of the x- and y-axes as given in the following diagram corresponds to the way the axes are aligned in a window, i.e. with the origin at the upper-left corner and with x denoting horizontal distance and y vertical distance.)

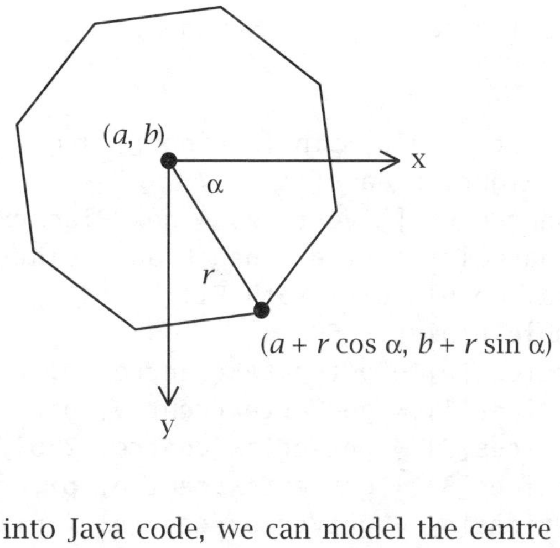

To translate this into Java code, we can model the centre (a, b) as a planar point object `c` of the class `PlanarPoint`, and using the methods defined in this class, the vertex becomes the point

```
(c.getX()+r*Math.cos(alpha), c.getY()+r*Math.sin(alpha))
```

where alpha denotes an angle measured in radians.

We can summarise all this by coding a method getVertex to perform this computation:

```
public static PlanarPoint getVertex
                (PlanarPoint c, double alpha, double r) {
    double x = c.getX()+r*Math.cos(alpha);
    double y = c.getY()+r*Math.sin(alpha);
    PlanarPoint v = new PlanarPoint(x, y);
    return v;
}
```

This method takes an object c of type PlanarPoint (denoting the centre of the polygon), a floating point number alpha (denoting the angle in radians) and another floating point number r (denoting the radius), and returns an object of type PlanarPoint (denoting the vertex of the polygon).

Let us now apply this. Here is the code of the class Hexagon which when run draws a regular hexagon:

```
import genesis.*;

public class Hexagon {

    /*
    Draw a solid red regular hexagon.
    */

    public static void main (String [] args) {
        PolyFigure.create();
        PlanarPoint [] vertices = new PlanarPoint[6];
        PlanarPoint centre = new PlanarPoint(195, 135);
        final double pi = Math.PI;
        double radius = 50;
        vertices[0] = getVertex(centre, 0, radius);
        vertices[1] = getVertex(centre, pi/3, radius);
        vertices[2] = getVertex(centre, 2*pi/3, radius);
        vertices[3] = getVertex(centre, pi, radius);
        vertices[4] = getVertex(centre, 4*pi/3, radius);
        vertices[5] = getVertex(centre, 5*pi/3, radius);
        PolyFigure.fill(vertices);
    }
```

```
        public static PlanarPoint getVertex
                (PlanarPoint c, double alpha, double r) {
            double x = c.getX()+r*Math.cos(alpha);
            double y = c.getY()+r*Math.sin(alpha);
            PlanarPoint v = new PlanarPoint(x, y);
            return v;
        }
    }
```

In this code we declare `vertices` to be an array of planar points (i.e. an array of objects of the class `PlanarPoint`) and set the length of the array to be 6. This array will store the vertices of the hexagon. The centre of the hexagon is declared to be the point $(195, 135)$ (which is approximately the centre of the window) and the radius of the hexagon is declared to be 50.

Declaring a constant

In the declaration

```
    final double pi = Math.PI;
```

the expression `Math.PI` gives a value for π and is denoted in this class by the identifier `pi`. The key word `final` at the beginning of the declaration indicates that `pi` denotes a constant; Java will not permit its value to be changed.

The vertices are computed by making 6 invocations of the method `getVertex`, with the angles from the centre taken to be

$$0, \pi/3, 2\pi/3, \pi, 4\pi/3, 5\pi/3$$

respectively, i.e. the angle from the centre between successive vertices is $\pi/3$ radians (or 60 degrees; recall there are 2π radians in 360 degrees).

PROBLEM 5: drawing regular polygons

Open the folder *Hexagon* and run the class `Hexagon`. Modify this code to construct a class `Pentagon` that when compiled and run draws a regular pentagon (i.e. a regular 5-sided polygon).

Further modify the code to construct a class `RegularPolygon` that when compiled and run opens a dialog box requesting the number of edges. When this number has been supplied by the user, a regular polygon with the given number of edges is drawn. For help with this problem see Hints.

□

Now that we can readily draw polygons, it's time to try a bit of animation. To begin, consider the problem of rotating a square about its centre. We know how to construct a square with one of its vertices on a horizontal line with the centre (so that the square when drawn looks like a diamond). Here is the `main` method that does it (the method `getVertex` is as before):

```
PolyFigure.create();
PlanarPoint [] vertices = new PlanarPoint[4];
PlanarPoint centre = new PlanarPoint(195, 135);
final double pi = Math.PI;
double radius = 100;
for (int i=0; i<4; i++)
    vertices[i] = getVertex(centre, i*pi/2, radius);
Polyfigure.fill(vertices);
```

To get a square drawn at a different orientation, all we need to do is add an angle:

```
PolyFigure.create();
PlanarPoint [] vertices = new PlanarPoint[4];
PlanarPoint centre = new PlanarPoint(195, 135);
final double pi = Math.PI;
double radius = 100;

double angle = 1;    // this line is new

for (int i=0; i<4; i++)
    vertices[i] = getVertex(centre, i*pi/2 + angle, radius);

PolyFigure.fill(vertices);
```

The effect is that this draws a square that has been rotated clockwise by an angle of 1 radian (about 57 degrees) compared with the previous square.

To animate the rotating square, all we need to do is perform this rotation a bit at a time, pausing briefly to redraw the square at each stage.

PROBLEM 6: rotating a regular polygon

The code to animate the rotating square is at the top of the next page. Notice that because of the `while (true)` statement, the square will continue to rotate until the program is terminated.

This code can be found in the class `RotatingSquare` in the folder *Rotating Square*. Run this class and notice the effect.

```
PolyFigure.create();
PlanarPoint [] vertices = new PlanarPoint[4];
PlanarPoint centre = new PlanarPoint(195, 135);
final double pi = Math.PI;
double radius = 100;
double angle = 0;
while (true) {
    for (int i=0; i<4; i++)
        vertices[i] =
                getVertex(centre, i*pi/2 + angle, radius);
    PolyFigure.fill(vertices);
    angle = angle + 0.01;
    Delay.milliseconds(5);
}
```

By adjusting the delay or the change in angle, modify the code so that the square rotates faster/slower.

Modify the code to construct a class `RotatingPolygon` that when compiled and run opens a dialog box requesting the number of edges. A regular polygon with the given number of edges is then drawn and rotates about its centre.

For help with this problem see Hints.

□

To finish this section, here is a problem that is a little more challenging.

PROBLEM 7: rotating a star

Construct a class `RotatingStar` which when compiled and run opens a window displaying a rotating 6-pointed star.

To give you an idea of what is expected, open the folder *Rotating Star Demo* and run the class `RotatingStarDemo`. This class was compiled and then its code deleted but the compiled code was left in the *.class* file in the folder. Your task is to construct the class `RotatingStar` so that when executed it has the same effect.

For help with this problem see Hints.

□

7.3 Case study: bouncing a ball

In Section 2.4 we introduced the class `CircleFigure` that enables us to draw a circle in a window. From time to time since then we have returned to this example to illustrate various aspects of Java coding. Now that we have at our disposal the class `PlanarPoint` whose objects enable us to work with points in the plane, we can return to the `CircleFigure` class and consider the animation problem of moving the circle in any direction and bouncing it off the edges of the window like a billiard ball bounces off the edges of the billiard table.

Like the previous case study in Section 7.2, this case study requires a small bit of trigonometry and vector arithmetic. If you are not familiar with these topics, take the technical detail on trust and concentrate instead on the way the code is structured.

Towards a software development strategy

The case study in this section also gives us an opportunity to illustrate various aspects of how to systematically approach the coding of an application. The procedure involves starting with an informal high-level description of the problem we want to solve. This description is then refined into a more detailed yet informal scenario that summarises in outline form the steps (algorithm) that will be coded in order to solve the problem. Finally, this scenario is refined to code that can be tested and modified as required to give the completed program.

In practice, when coding a real-world problem the steps involved would be more complex and detailed, and would involve many iterations as the software evolves. The approach described here, however, works well for our small case study and suggests a more general procedure that could be expanded to apply to larger software engineering projects.

Before beginning this case study, we suggest you turn back to Section 2.4 and remind yourself of the messages that can be sent to the class `CircleFigure`.

High-level description of the problem

We want to construct code to animate the circle so that it can start moving in any direction and when it reaches an edge of the window, bounce off that edge just as a billiard ball bounces off the edge of the table. In fact, our bouncing circle will be unlike the billiard ball in so far as the circle's speed will remain constant. It does not slow down and eventually stop because of friction as would a billiard ball.

Informal scenario

1. Determine the dimensions of the window's display area and decide the radius and starting position of the circle.
2. Decide the direction in which the circle will initially move.
3. Decide the distance which the circle will move at each step in the given direction. If this step distance is small the motion will be slow but smooth; if large the motion will be quicker but possibly less smooth.
4. Decide how long to delay between circle moves. If the delay is small the motion will be fast; if large the motion will be slow but possibly less smooth.
5. If the circle were to move by the given step distance in the given direction, compute what its next position would be.
6. Check to see if the circle's proposed next position is within the display area of the window. If not (i.e. if the proposed move would take the circle to an edge of the window), detect which edge (or edges) of the window would be crossed and as a consequence modify the Circle's direction of motion to simulate the way a billiard ball bounces off the edge of the table. In this case recompute the next position of the window using this new direction.
7. Move the circle to the next position.
8. Repeat the process from step 5.

Refining the scenario to code

The scenario above gives some idea of the steps required to write the code but clearly quite a lot of detail needs to be included. We will follow the steps outlined in the scenario and expand them as necessary.

1. We need to determine the dimensions of the window's display area. The window as a whole is 400 pixels wide and 300 pixels high, but allowing for the window's border we get a display area approximately 392 pixels wide and 268 pixels high. We declare local variables of type `int` to record these dimensions:

   ```
   int winWidth = 392;
   int winHeight = 268;
   ```

   [*An aside*: The actual dimensions of the display area will depend on the size of the window's borders, and these are slightly different for each underlying operating system. We will see in Chapter 9 how these dimensions can be exactly determined. In any case, the dimensions given above will be sufficiently accurate for this case study. *End aside*]

We also need to create the window and decide on the radius and initial starting position for the circle. Any reasonable radius for the circle will do, so take it to be 25 pixels. Similarly, any reasonable starting position for the window's centre will do, so why not take it to be (195, 135) as that is near the centre of the window. Anyhow, it will do for testing the code and we can change it later after the code is working properly. Again, we need local variables to record this information:

```
int radius = 25;
int startX = 195;
int startY = 135;
```

We now create the window and place a circle with the given radius at the given starting position:

```
CircleFigure.create();
CircleFigure.moveTo(startX, startY);
CircleFigure.setRadius(radius);
```

2. The initial direction in which to move can be determined by selecting an angle. Any angle will do, so why not take $\pi/6$ (measured from the x-axis — see the figure below) just to test out the code. A local variable of type `double` is needed to record this angle. The value of π needs to be declared as a constant:

```
final double pi = Math.PI;
double alpha = pi/6;
```

3. The step distance can be any value, so why not take it to be 2 pixels and see what happens; we can experiment with different values to see the effect once the code is working. A local variable of type `int` is needed to record this distance:

```
int stepDistance = 2;
```

Now that we have the angle and the step distance, we can create a vector (i.e. a planar point object of the class `PlanarPoint`) to represent the direction and distance moved at each step. We can use the trigonometric ideas we met in Section 7.2:

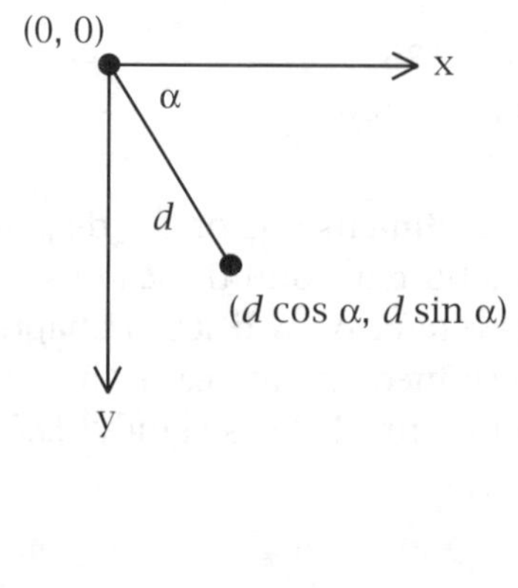

In this diagram d denotes the step distance and the angle α denotes the direction in which the circle is moving. Hence the point $(d \cos \alpha, d \sin \alpha)$ is a vector representing both the distance and the direction in which we want the circle to move. Converting this to code gives:

```
double stepX = stepDistance*Math.cos(alpha);
double stepY = stepDistance*Math.sin(alpha);
PlanarPoint step = new PlanarPoint(stepX, stepY);
```

4. Now we can consider the iterative part of the program. First, decide how long we need to delay between circle moves. Any time delay will do, so why not take 5 milliseconds and just observe the effect. We can experiment with this value later once the code is working:

```
Delay.milliseconds(5);
```

5. Now calculate the next position of the circle if it were to move the given distance in the current direction. To do this calculation we make use of the method `add` of the class `PlanarPoint`:

```
PlanarPoint nextPosn = currentPosn.add(step);
```

6. We now test to see if the proposed next position of the circle is within the window.

   If the next position would move the circle to the left or right edge of the window, reverse the x-component of the motion (i.e. 'bounce' off the appropriate vertical edge of the window):

```
boolean atEdge = false;
if (nextPosn.getX() <= radius
            || nextPosn.getX() >= winWidth-radius) {
    atEdge = true;
    step.setX(-step.getX());
}
```

   In this code the Boolean `atEdge` is set to *true* if and only if the circle is at the window's edge.

   If the next position would move the circle to the top or bottom edge of the window, reverse the y-component of the motion (i.e. 'bounce' off the appropriate horizontal edge of the window):

```
if (nextPosn.getY() <= radius
            || nextPosn.getY() >= winHeight-radius) {
    atEdge = true;
    step.setY(-step.getY());
}
```

If the circle is in fact at the window's edge (i.e. if atEdge is *true*), recompute the proposed next position of the circle:

```
if (atEdge) nextPosn = currentPosn.add(step);
```

7. Move the circle to the next position. In fact, as we can only move to grid positions, we need to first find the grid position nearest to the next position and move there:

```
PlanarPoint roundedPosn = nextPosn.rounded();
int gridXPosn = (int)roundedPosn.getX();
int gridYPosn = (int)roundedPosn.getY();
CircleFigure.moveTo(gridXPosn, gridYPosn);
```

8. We need to set currentposn to be the circle's new position

```
currentPosn = nextPosn;
```

and find the new next position that results as a consequence

```
nextPosn = currentPosn.add(step);
```

before repeating the whole move procedure.

The complete code is in the class BouncingBall:

```
import genesis.*;

public class BouncingBall {

    /* Bounce the circle in its window like a ball. */

    public static void main (String [ ] args) {

        // determine the dimensions of the window's
        // display area, the circle's radius,
        // and the circle's starting position
        int winWidth = 392;
        int winHeight = 268;
        int radius = 25;
        int startX = 196;
        int startY = 134;

        // create the window and display the
        // circle in its starting position
        CircleFigure.create();
        CircleFigure.moveTo(startX, startY);
        CircleFigure.setRadius(radius);
```

```
// set current position to this starting position
PlanarPoint currentPosn =
            new PlanarPoint(startX, startY);

// decide on a direction in which to move
final double pi = Math.PI;
double alpha = pi/6;

// decide on a step distance
int stepDistance = 2;

// compute the step vector moved by the circle
double stepX = stepDistance*Math.cos(alpha);
double stepY = stepDistance*Math.sin(alpha);
PlanarPoint step = new PlanarPoint(stepX, stepY);

// constantly move the circle
while (true) {

    // delay for a while
    Delay.milliseconds(5);

    // compute the window's next position
    PlanarPoint nextPosn = currentPosn.add(step);

    // check if moving to the next position would
    // bring the circle to the window's edge; if so
    // change the step direction:

    // if next position is at the left or
    // right window edge, reverse x direction
    boolean atEdge = false;
    if (nextPosn.getX() <= radius
          || nextPosn.getX() >= winWidth-radius) {
        atEdge = true;
        step.setX(-step.getX());
    }

    // if next position is at the top or
    // bottom window edge, reverse y direction
    if (nextPosn.getY() <= radius
          || nextPosn.getY() >= winHeight-radius) {
        atEdge = true;
        step.setY(-step.getY());
    }
```

```
                // if at window's edge recompute next position
                if (atEdge) nextPosn = currentPosn.add(step);

                // move circle to the grid position
                // nearest to the next position
                PlanarPoint roundedPosn = nextPosn.rounded();
                int gridXPosn = (int)roundedPosn.getX();
                int gridYPosn = (int)roundedPosn.getY();
                CircleFigure.moveTo(gridXPosn, gridYPosn);

                // set current position to circle's new position
                currentPosn = nextPosn;

                // compute the new next position and loop again
                nextPosn = currentPosn.add(step);
            }
        }
    }
```

Notice how detailed comments have been placed in this code to help the reader. In fact, there are almost as many lines of comment as lines of code!

PROBLEM 8: bouncing the ball

Open the folder *Bouncing Ball* and run the class `BouncingBall`.

Modify the code so as to create a class `RandomBouncingBall` so that when it is compiled and run:

- the angle determining the initial direction in which to move is randomly selected between 0 and 2π (i.e. between 0 and 360 degrees);
- the initial position (x, y) of the centre of the circle is randomly selected so that x lies between 100 and 300 and y lies between 100 and 200;
- whenever the circle bounces off the top or bottom edges of the window it turns blue, but reverts to red whenever it bounces off the right or left edges.

Experiment with making the ball move faster/slower.

For help with this problem see Hints.

□

7.4 Case study: credit-card accounts

The main aim of this section is to further investigate the coding of a class and the subsequent use of objects of that class in building applications. We have already seen this with the class `PlanarPoint` introduced in Section 7.1. The earlier case studies in Sections 7.2 and 7.3 use objects of this class to build graphical applications. In this section, however, we want to look more carefully at the process we undergo when constructing classes. The ideas will be illustrated by constructing a class `CreditCard` whose objects model the credit-card accounts that may be found within an actual banking system. In reality, credit-card accounts come in many variations and have sophisticated rules and regulations. So that we do not get bogged down in detail, we consider here only a very simplified type of credit-card account.

The class `CreditCard`, like the class `PlanarPoint` before, is exclusively concerned with defining, building and managing objects. However, unlike the class `PlanarPoint`, it has both instance and class variables and methods. In this section we will compare the role played by these features and gain some understanding about the appropriate circumstances under which to use class variables and methods as distinct from instance variables and methods.

A strategy for software development

The process undertaken to construct the class `CreditCard` begins with a general problem statement outlining in very broad terms the role of the class. This is then followed by an informal description (specification) of the properties and features required both of the class itself and of objects of the class. These required features are then refined and developed in such a way that they can be expressed using Java code fragments. For example, some fragments will capture the declaration of variables; others will be broader in scope capturing methods of the class or its instances. The code fragments are then pieced together to construct the class. Finally, the class is tested and, if necessary, modified.

The class `CreditCard` is sufficiently simple that we can code it successfully in the fashion just described. A larger real-world software engineering project may consist of many classes, possibly in total running to thousands of lines of code. In such cases, the process described here would need to be much more sophisticated, with testing and modification of code occurring at all stages of development.

General problem statement

Customers of a bank can be issued with credit cards and the bank needs software to manage these accounts. Our task is to construct a class `CreditCard` whose objects are credit-card accounts.

Informal requirements

State properties

We shall make the following assumptions about the state properties of the credit-card account system:

- each credit-card account object has an associated
  - name, denoting the name of the person who holds the account;
  - identification code, by which the account can be easily distinguished;
  - balance, denoting the (possibly negative) amount currently held in the account;
  - credit limit, denoting the maximum amount the account may be overdrawn;
- the credit limit must be one of the values $1,000, $2,000, $5,000 or $10,000;
- the rate of interest charged on overdrawn accounts is currently 12.75% and is common for all accounts.

Dynamic properties

We shall make the following assumptions about the operations that can be applied within the credit-card account system:

- new credit-card account objects can be created;
- the credit limit of a credit-card account can be changed but only to one of the allowable limits;
- account details can be output;
- money can be deposited into a credit-card account;
- money can be withdrawn from a credit-card account provided the balance does not fall below the credit limit;
- interest at the current rate can be charged on an overdrawn account;
- the common interest rate can be changed.

Developing the code: state properties

The state properties are captured either by instance or by class variables.

The name, identification code, balance and credit limit are associated with individual credit-card account objects and will in general be different for different accounts. Therefore, they need to be captured in the code by *instance* variables:

```
protected String name;
protected String ident;
protected int balance = 0;
protected int creditLimit;
```

The variables `name` and `ident` are declared to be of type `String`. In reality, the account identifier is often a number (e.g. the number embossed on the actual plastic credit card). However, we may well want to use characters other than digits, and anyhow, we do not want to do arithmetic with account identifiers (there would be no sense in adding account identifiers). For these reasons it is best to declare the identifier as type `String` rather than `int`.

The variable `balance` is declared to be of type `int` to simplify the code. We shall suppose all transactions are done in whole dollars (i.e. cents are discarded). The initial value of `balance` is set at 0 to model the idea that a new credit-card account starts with a zero balance when first created. The values of the other instance variables will be set by the constructor method when a new credit-card account object is created: they cannot be set in advance as it is not known what their values will be initially.

Protected

The modifier `protected` indicates that the variables are private to the class `CreditCard` and cannot be accessed directly by any other class, except for a subclass of `CreditCard` or for a class in the same package. We will have much more to say about subclasses when we study inheritance in Chapter 8. For now, just think of `protected` as being the same as `private` except in special circumstances which won't arise in this chapter.

Class variables

The interest rate, whose initial value is set as 12.75%, is something that is common to all credit-card account objects. As it is shared by all the objects it is best captured in the code by a *class* variable:

```
protected static double interestRate = 12.75;
```

Class variables are like instance variables in that they are declared outside any method, but differ from instance variables in two major ways. First, their declaration includes the key word `static`. Second, they include every class and instance method in their scope (recall that an instance variable includes only the instance methods in its scope). Hence a class variable can be accessed and modified by any method in the class. Consequently, a class variable is shared by each object of the class, unlike an instance variable which is unique to each object. Class variables are used to record values common to all the objects; the interest rate above is a good example of this.

A side effect of this is that if the value of a class variable changes, it changes for every object. **Be warned!!**

Capturing conditions on state properties

The various conditions associated with the state properties, e.g. that money cannot be withdrawn from an account if the balance will fall below the credit limit, or that the credit limit must be one of the allowable limits, will be captured within the code for the appropriate methods of the class.

Dynamic properties

Creating new credit-card account objects

A constructor method is needed so that the values of the instance variables can be set when a new credit-card object is created. There are various ways that this could be done and we give two possibilities here. The first constructor has parameters which enable the name, identifier and initial credit limit of a new account to be passed as arguments. The second constructor is the so-called default constructor as it has an empty parameter list. It uses dialog boxes to extract the required information from the user:

```
public CreditCard
        (String aName, String anIdent, int aLimit) {
    name = aName;
    ident = anIdent;
    setCreditLimit(aLimit);
}

public CreditCard ( ) {
    name = DialogBox.request("Name of account holder:");
    ident = DialogBox.request("Account Identification:");
    setCreditLimit(DialogBox.requestInt("Credit limit:"));
}
```

Notice that in order to set the credit limit of the new account object we invoke the method `setCreditLimit` defined below.

Setting the credit limit

A setter method is required to enable the value of the credit limit to be set. The method needs to ensure that the credit limit is set to one of the four allowable limits:

```
public void setCreditLimit (int limit) {
    if (limit == 1000 || limit == 2000 ||
        limit == 5000 || limit == 10000) creditLimit = limit;
    else setCreditLimit(DialogBox.requestInt
        ("Invalid credit limit. Try again"));
}
```

Notice that this method is recursive—it invokes itself! If the proposed credit limit is invalid, a request is made for a new proposed limit, and when this is supplied setCreditLimit is invoked again with the new value passed as argument. Only when a valid credit limit is supplied will the looping stop.

Getter methods

Although not specifically mentioned in the informal requirements, getter methods are needed so that the values of the instance variables of any credit-card account object can be extracted:

```
public String getName ( ) {
    return name;
}

public String getIdent ( ) {
    return ident;
}

public int getBalance ( ) {
    return balance;
}

public int getCreditLimit ( ) {
    return creditLimit;
}
```

Printing account details

In order to enable details of a credit-card object to be easily printed in either the Output or Transcript window, a toString method needs to be coded that returns a string containing the relevant information:

```
public String toString ( ) {
    return "credit card account details:\n"
        +"  name:  "+name+"\n"
        +"  identification:  "+ident+"\n"
        +"  balance:  "+balance+"\n"
        +"  credit limit:  "+creditLimit+"\n"
        +"  interest rate:  "+interestRate;
}
```

Notice that, for completeness, the current interest rate is included as relevant information about an object even though interestRate is a class variable, not an instance variable. That is, the interest rate is class information rather than instance information and hence its common value is shared by all the objects.

Depositing money

When money is deposited into an account, the balance is increased by that amount:

```
public void deposit (int amount) {
    if (amount > 0) balance = balance + amount;
    else DialogBox.warn("Must deposit a positive amount");
}
```

In our system, only positive integer amounts can be deposited.

Withdrawing money

When money is withdrawn from an account, the balance is reduced by that amount. However, if the balance would as a consequence fall below the account's credit limit, the withdrawal is rejected:

```
public void withdraw (int amount) {
    if (amount > 0) {
        int newBalance = balance - amount;
        if (newBalance + creditLimit >= 0)
            balance = newBalance;
        else DialogBox.warn
                ("Insufficient funds for the withdrawal.");
    }
    else DialogBox.warn("Must withdraw a positive amount.");
}
```

In our system, only positive integer amounts can be withdrawn.

Charging interest

Interest can be charged on an overdrawn account. The balance of the account is reduced by the amount of interest payable (even if the balance were as a consequence to fall below the account's credit limit):

```
public void chargeInterest ( ) {
    if (balance < 0)
      balance = balance + (int)(balance*(interestRate/100));
}
```

In practice, interest would be charged periodically but this aspect is ignored in our simple system. Notice that the code here casts to `int` in order to discard any fractional part of a dollar that may result from the calculation of the interest payable.

Setting the interest rate

The interest rate can be changed, with the consequence that as the rate is shared by all the objects, the new rate will apply to each object. As the variable `interestRate` is a class variable, we code a class method to set its value:

```
public static void setInterestRate (double newRate) {
    if (newRate >= 0) interestRate = newRate;
    else DialogBox.warn("Interest rate cannot be negative.");
}
```

To invoke this method we can send a message `setInterestRate(..)` directly to the class `CreditCard` rather than to an object of the class, i.e.

```
CreditCard.setInterestRate(...)
```

Getting the interest rate

Again it is not specifically mentioned in the informal requirements, but a getter method is needed if we want to extract the current value of the interest rate:

```
public static double getInterestRate ( ) {
    return interestRate;
}
```

Constructing the class

Now that we have the code fragments, it is not difficult to piece it all together to get the `CreditCard` class. We need to import the *genesis* package as it contains the `DialogBox` class. Here is the complete code:

```
import genesis.*;

public class CreditCard {

    /* Objects of this class are credit-card accounts */

    // instance variables
    protected String name;
    protected String ident;
    protected int balance = 0;
    protected int creditLimit;

    // class variable
    protected static double interestRate = 12.75;
```

```
// constructors

public CreditCard
        (String aName, String anIdent, int aLimit) {
    name = aName;
    ident = anIdent;
    setCreditLimit(aLimit);
}

public CreditCard ( ) {
   name = DialogBox.request("Name of account holder:");
   ident = DialogBox.request("Account Identification:");
   setCreditLimit(DialogBox.requestInt("Credit limit:"));
}

// instance methods

public void setCreditLimit (int limit) {
    // set credit limit
    if (limit == 1000 || limit == 2000 ||
                limit == 5000 || limit == 10000)
        creditLimit = limit;
    else setCreditLimit(DialogBox.requestInt
                ("Invalid credit limit. Try again"));
}

public String getName ( ) {
    // get name
    return name;
}

public String getIdent ( ) {
    // get ident
    return ident;
}

public int getBalance ( ) {
    // get balance
    return balance;
}

public int getCreditLimit ( ) {
    // get creditLimit
    return creditLimit;
}
```

```
public String toString ( ) {
    // credit card information
    return "credit card account details:\n"
        +"  name:  "+name+"\n"
        +"  identification:  "+ident+"\n"
        +"  balance:  "+balance+"\n"
        +"  credit limit:  "+creditLimit+"\n"
        +"  interest rate:  "+interestRate;
}

public void deposit (int amount) {
    // deposit amount
    if (amount > 0) balance = balance + amount;
    else DialogBox.warn
            ("Must deposit a positive amount.");
}

public void withdraw (int amount) {
    // withdraw amount if sufficient funds
    if (amount > 0) {
        int newBalance = balance - amount;
        if (newBalance + creditLimit >= 0)
            balance = newBalance;
        else DialogBox.warn
            ("Insufficient funds for the withdrawal.");
    }
    else DialogBox.warn
            ("Must withdraw a positive amount.");
}

public void chargeInterest ( ) {
    // interest is charged if account overdrawn
    if (balance < 0)
        balance =
            balance + (int)(balance*(interestRate/100));
}

// class methods

public static void setInterestRate (double newRate) {
    // set interest rate
    if (newRate >= 0) interestRate = newRate;
    else DialogBox.warn
            ("Interest rate cannot be negative.");
}
```

```
    public static double getInterestRate ( ) {
        // get interest rate
        return interestRate;
    }
}
```

Testing the class

To test the class CreditCard we construct a purpose-built class TestCreditCard with a main method that creates a couple of objects of the class CreditCard and then sends these objects various messages. By modifying the code for the class TestCreditCard we can test each of the features of the class CreditCard and its objects. Here is our code for a TestCreditCard class:

```
import genesis.*;

public class TestCreditCard {

    /*
    Test the CreditCard class.
    */

    public static void main (String [] args) {
        CreditCard cc1 = new CreditCard("Bill", "34", 1000);
        CreditCard cc2 = new CreditCard("Joan", "81", 6000);
        cc1.deposit(500);
        cc2.withdraw(750);
        Transcript.println(cc1);
        Transcript.println(cc2);
        cc1.chargeInterest();
        cc2.chargeInterest();
        Transcript.println(cc1);
        CreditCard.setInterestRate(10);
        Transcript.println(cc2);
    }
}
```

PROBLEM 9: testing the CreditCard class

Open the folder *Credit Card*. This folder contains the classes CreditCard and TestCreditCard. By modifying the class TestCreditCard as appropriate, test the various features of the class CreditCard. In particular,

- try to set the credit limit to a value other than \$1,000, \$2,000, \$5,000 or \$10,000 to confirm that it is not permitted;
- try to withdraw an amount from an account that would result in the balance of the account falling below the credit limit to confirm that the withdraw is rejected.

□

7.5 Some best-practice patterns

We finish this unit by collecting together, in note form, many of the observations we have made about objects and classes. Treat the list of suggestions given here as a best-practice guide to the construction of classes.

- Before beginning to code a class, analyse the overall role of the class and its objects. In particular, clearly distinguish between the following:
  - state properties of the class (to do with describing the state of the class and its objects);
  - dynamic properties of the class (to do with the way the state of a class and its objects can change).
- Name the class after the objects it produces.
- Create instance variables to capture the state properties associated with individual objects of the class, i.e. declare a variable as an instance variable if each object of the class takes its own value for the variable.
- Create class (static) variables to capture the state properties shared between all the objects of the class. That is, declare a variable as a state variable if its common value is shared by all the objects of the class.
- Class and instance variables should be declared `private` (or `protected` if we expect to later require access from a subclasses of this class — see Chapter 8).
- Name a variable after its role.
- Choose meaningful names (identifiers) for variables.
- A variable name should start with a lower-case letter but have the first letter of each subsequent sub-word capitalised.
- Initialise the values of the instance variables within the code of a constructor method. In particular, always supply a default constructor, i.e. a constructor whose parameter list is empty.
- Any method that accesses or modifies an instance variable will need to be an instance method.
- Any method that accesses or modifies only class variables should be a class (i.e. static) method.

- A method that returns a value should not also modify the receiver object.
- Add a getter method for each private or protected variable so that the value of the variable can be accessed from outside the class by sending the appropriate getter message. A method that returns the value of an instance variable will be an instance method. A method that returns the value of a class variable should be a class method.
- Add a setter method for each private or protected variable whose value you may want to change by sending the appropriate setter message from outside the class. A method that sets the value of an instance variable will be an instance method. A method that sets the value of a class variable will in general be a class method.
- Add a `toString` method to a class so that a string representation of objects of the class can be printed in an output window.
- Name a method so as to suggest the effect of performing it.
- Name a method parameter after the generic role it plays in the method.
- Create a method so as to perform just one task. Methods that perform more than one task should be decomposed into smaller methods.

PROBLEM 10: savings accounts

A bank allows customers to open and operate savings accounts and requires software to manage these accounts. Real savings accounts can be quite sophisticated. So that our programming task is not too complicated, we consider here a very simplified type of savings account.

Informal requirements

- each savings account has an associated
  - name;
  - identification code;
  - balance;
- any (positive) amount of money can be deposited into an account;
- if money is withdrawn from an account, a bank charge is levied; this charge is the same for all accounts, and is a fixed amount regardless of the amount withdrawn;
- money can be withdrawn from an account provided the sum withdrawn is at least $50 and the balance does not as a consequence fall below zero when the balance is adjusted for the amount withdrawn together with the bank charge;
- the bank charge for withdrawals is currently $2 but can be set to a new value if required.

Construct a class `SavingsAccount` whose objects are savings accounts as specified above.

Your code should give a warning if an attempt is made to deposit a negative amount or withdraw less than $50, or if the balance of the account would fall below zero.

Your class should have a method `toString` which returns a string version of a savings account object containing relevant information about the object.

Also construct a class `TestSavingsAccount` that has a `main` method that creates a couple of objects of the class `SavingsAccount` to test the features of this class and its objects.

For help with this problem see Hints.

□

Chapter 7 self-check

Can you

- declare a variable whose type is a given class?
- use the key word `new` together with a constructor to initialise a new object of a given class?
- explain the role of the `toString` method?

Do you understand the terms

- constructor method?
- default constructor?
- instance method?
- instance variable?
- class method?
- class variable?
- setter and getter methods?
- private variables?
- method overloading?

What is the distinction between

- instance and class variables?

- instance and class methods?
- setter and getter methods?
- public and private variables?
- methods that modify the receiver object, and those that return a value?

How do you

- construct a class so that objects of that class can be defined, built and managed?
- extract the value of a private variable from outside the class?
- set the value of a private variable from outside the class?
- display in the Output or Transcript window relevant information about objects of a class?

Inheritance 8

Prerequisites

Chapter 8 assumes an understanding of the basic Java language constructs. In particular, you will need to be familiar with:

- Java control constructs (Chapter 4);
- arrays(Chapter 5);
- the construction of classes (Chapter 7);
- how to define, build and manage objects (Chapter 7).

In addition, use will be made of the classes `PlanarPoint`, `CreditCard` and, to a lesser extent, `SavingsAccount` introduced in Chapter 7. If you are unsure of any of these topics, revise the appropriate sections of *Java Genesis* before beginning this chapter.

Overview

The technique of inheritance enables us to take an existing class, called the *superclass* (or *parent* class), and extend and/or redefine features of it to construct a new class, called the *subclass* (or *child* class). The new class will have

- all the instance and class variables of the original class;
- possibly extra variables not in the original class;
- all the instance and class methods of the original class, some of which may have been redefined to exhibit different behaviour;
- possibly extra methods not in the original class.

There are two main benefits of being able to do this. First, it enables us to create a new class (the subclass) that not only 'inherits' the features of an existing class (the superclass), but also extends and specialises these features in various ways. For example, objects of the subclass will be able to receive and understand

- any message that can be sent to objects of the superclass, although the response to these messages may be different;
- possibly new messages not understood by objects of the superclass.

Second, inheritance enables us to organise classes related by inheritance into hierarchies with the common features of objects of the different classes extracted into a superclass, simplifying somewhat the overall programming task. It also enables us to create a clean architectural structure when building software systems, a property that can greatly improve our ability to understand, maintain and reuse the software system.

Furthermore, by arranging our classes into suitable 'inheritance hierarchies', we can introduce a notion of 'subtype' enabling us to weaken slightly the strict typing system of Java and treat in a common way objects from any of the classes in the hierarchy. The idea behind subtyping is that even though the program code may declare a variable to be of a particular class type, when the program is run an object of a subclass can be assigned to that variable instead. This enables us to construct systems containing objects whose precise class need not be known when the code is compiled, making the code more generic and hence more widely applicable.

We can write code to send a message to an object whose type is declared to be of a particular class. When the code is run, however, an object of a subclass may be substituted and receive the message instead. Therefore the method to be invoked by the message cannot be determined when the code is compiled but can only be determined at run-time when the actual type of the receiver object is revealed. This is known as *dynamic binding.*

Each of these aspects of inheritance is considered in this chapter. Inheritance is a crucial concept at the very heart of object-oriented software development. Although it is a big topic, the main aspects of inheritance in Java are introduced here and most will be applied in later chapters of *Java Genesis.*

8.1 Inheritance as class extension

We begin by looking at how we can construct a class that inherits unaltered the features of an existing class, but has in addition extra features not in the original class.

Problems:

1. testing the class `RandomPlus`

2 detecting repetitions

3 extending `SquareFigure`

8.2 Inheritance as class specialisation

We look at how inheritance allows us to create a subclass that redefines some of the methods of the superclass.

Problems:

4 testing the class `SilverCreditCard`

5 redefining `SquareFigure`

8.3 Constructor methods and inheritance

Java follows a well defined, but not necessarily intuitive, procedure in order to construct a subclass object. For example, every constructor method of a subclass must invoke a constructor method in its superclass, either explicitly or implicitly. We consider the way Java interprets constructor methods in a subclass and look at the consequences.

Problem:

6 assessing property taxes

8.4 Subclasses of subclasses

There is no need to stop the process of inheritance once we have a subclass of a superclass. We can continue, constructing a subclass of a subclass, and so on.

Problem:

7 testing the class `GoldCreditCard`

8.5 Polymorphism, subtyping and casting

Because a subclass inherits all the class and instance variables of its superclass and either inherits or redefines all the methods of its superclass, any message that can be understood by an object of the superclass can also be understood by an object of the subclass. The method invoked by a message depends only on the class of the receiver object. This polymorphic idea leads naturally to the idea of subtyping: that an object of a subclass can be supplied where an object of a superclass is expected.

Problems:

8 testing the class `ComplexNumber`

9 spiraling away

10 type-casting demonstration

11 making use of casting

8.6 Inheritance hierarchies

We look at how classes can be organised into hierarchies based on inheritance. In the process we meet abstract classes whose role is to act as a repository for common code. As a consequence, abstract classes help determine the overall architectural structure of the inheritance hierarchy.

Problems:

12 `CreditCard` as a subclass of `BankAccount`

13 testing the bank-account hierarchy

14 working with abstract classes

Learning outcomes

At the conclusion of Chapter 8 you will understand:

- how to use inheritance to create a new class that extends and/or redefines features of an existing class;
- the relationship between a superclass and its subclasses;
- how to code a constructor method for a subclass;
- the role of the super-statement when coding a constructor method in a subclass;
- the role of the `super` pseudo-object when coding instance methods in a subclass that modify instance methods inherited from the superclass;
- how to create and use inheritance hierarchies;
- the idea of polymorphism whereby the same message can be sent to objects of different classes and result in different methods being invoked;
- the role of subtyping in weakening the type system of Java when working with objects of classes within an inheritance hierarchy;
- the way type casting can be used to re-establish the type of an object masquerading as an object of its superclass;
- the role of the key word `protected` in enabling instance and class variables of the superclass to be directly available to a subclass;

- how an inheritance hierarchy is searched to find the method to invoke when an object whose class is in the hierarchy receives a message;
- the role of abstract classes.

8.1 Inheritance as class extension

Example: generating a random integer

So far throughout *Java Genesis* we have often generated random integers in some given range. For example, to simulate the tossing of a die we generated random integers in the range 1 to 6. As this is a task undertaken frequently, why not write a method to do it?

What we want is a method `nextIntInRange`, say, that has two integer parameters, and returns a random integer in the range given by these parameters. That doesn't seem to be a difficult task. Try it for yourself before reading on.

Here is one possible way of coding a class method (i.e. a static method) to do it:

```
public static int nextIntInRange (int first, int last) {
    int range = last - first + 1;
    return (int)(range*Math.random()) + first;
}
```

(The expression `last - first + 1` evaluates to the number of integers in the range `first` to `last`.)

If this method is in a class `Test` and we want to generate a random integer in the range 1 to 6, say, we can code statements such as

```
...
int nextDieToss;
nextDieToss = nextIntInRange(1, 6);
...
```

anywhere within the class `Test`.

The trouble here is that we don't want to have to include the `nextIntInRange` method within every class that requires a random integer to be generated. What we would like to do instead is have the method `nextIntInRange` placed in just one class but be available to every other class that needs it. Inheritance offers us a convenient mechanism to do just that.

The class `Random` comes with Java and can be found in the package *java.util*. This class implements a random number generator for use in any application needing random numbers. (For example, an object of this class is created and used by the method `random()` in the class `Math`, as you will see if you browse the code for this class).

[*An aside*: the class `Random` actually implements what is known as a pseudo random number generator. The number generated is not random in the strict meaning of the word because the process the class uses to generate the next random number is quite determined. However, to all intents and purposes we can take the numbers generated as random because they display properties similar to those exhibited by truly random numbers. *End aside*]

If you like, you can browse the code for the class `Random` in the *java.util* package to discover the various methods it contains, but what is of interest to us here is that this class has an instance method `nextInt` which has no parameters and returns a random integer in the range

$$-2,147,483,648 \quad \text{to} \quad 2,147,483,647.$$

That is, the value returned is of type `int` and is randomly selected from within the entire `int` range. The method `nextInt` is an instance, not a class, method and so can only be invoked if the corresponding message is sent to an object of the class `Random`.

Here is a typical way we can use the method `nextInt` in the class `Random`. The following code generates a random integer in the range 1 to 6:

```
...
Random rand = new Random();
int next;
next = rand.nextInt();
next = Math.abs(next) % 6 + 1;
...
```

Notice that first we need to create an object of the class `Random`. This object (`rand` in the above code) can be thought of as an object that generates random numbers in response to receiving the appropriate message. In this case, we send it the message `nextInt()` to generate a random integer. We need to ensure the random integer is not negative; then modular division by 6 gives a random integer in the range 0 to 5. Adding 1 gives us the required random integer.

Now, here is the trick. If we add an instance method `nextIntInRange` to the class `Random`, we could invoke this method every time we required a random integer within some range. Here is the code for such a method:

```
public int nextIntInRange (int first, int last) {
    // returns a random integer >= first and <= last
    int range = last - first + 1;
    int next = nextInt();
    return Math.abs(next) % range + first;
}
```

But there is a problem: `Random` is a class provided with Java, and if everyone were to add extra methods whenever they felt like it, soon there would be chaos. So instead, we use the mechanism of inheritance to create a new class which we shall call, somewhat unimaginatively, `RandomPlus`. The class `RandomPlus` will have all the features of the class `Random` but in addition will have the new method `nextIntInRange`. Here is how we code such a class:

```
package genesis;

import java.util.*;

public class RandomPlus extends Random {

    /*
    Extend the class Random so that a random integer
    in a given range can be generated.
    */

    public int nextIntInRange (int first, int last) {
        // returns a random integer
        // >= first and <= last
        int range = last - first + 1;
        int next = nextInt();
        return Math.abs(next) % range + first;
    }
}
```

The `extends` declaration

Notice the use of the key word `extends` within the class declaration. This ensures that all the features of the class `Random` are available to this class. In particular, in the code for the method `nextIntInRange`, direct use is made of the method `nextInt` inherited from the class `Random`. We could have similarly used any of the other methods from the class `Random` if we had wished.

We say that `RandomPlus` is a *subclass* of `Random`, or alternatively, that `Random` is a *superclass* of `RandomPlus`. (The terms *child* and *parent* class are sometimes used to refer to a subclass and superclass respectively.) To use our new subclass to simulate, for example, the tossing of a die, we code

```
...
RandomPlus rand = new RandomPlus();
int next;
next = rand.nextIntInRange(1, 6);
...
```

Of course, we can also send to the object `rand` in the code above any message that an object of the class `Random` would understand. In effect, we have an object with all the functionality of an object of the class `Random`, plus more!

The package statement

To use the class `RandomPlus` in this way, we need to ensure that it is visible to our application. We can either place it together with its compiled code in the same folder as our application, or add it to a package such as *genesis* and place it together with its compiled code in the folder containing the *genesis* package (which is what we have done).

Notice that to ensure the class `RandomPlus` becomes part of the *genesis* package the code for the class needs to begin with the statement:

```
package genesis;
```

Then any class that wants to make use of the `RandomPlus` class needs to begin with the statement

```
import genesis.*;
```

to ensure the *genesis* package is imported.

Supplying a default constructor

One further point. In the code fragment above that simulates the tossing of a die, we created a new object of the class `RandomPlus` with the statement

```
RandomPlus rand = new RandomPlus();
```

which invoked the constructor method `RandomPlus()`. But no such constructor method is defined in the class `RandomPlus`, so where has it come from and what does it do?

As we observed in Chapter 7, if a class has no constructor method explicitly defined, the Java system supplies a so-called default constructor (i.e. a constructor method with an empty parameter list). This is exactly what has happened with the class `RandomPlus` because it has no explicit constructor method.

Hence the constructor method `RandomPlus()` is supplied for us by Java. Without going into details here, this default constructor method will, when invoked, automatically invoke the code for the constructor method `Random()`, the default constructor in the superclass `Random`. Invoking the method `Random()` in the superclass creates a new random number generator object (as you can confirm by looking at its code in the class `Random`) and this is exactly what we want.

If all this seems rather complicated, you're right! The relationship between constructor methods and inheritance is a topic in its own right and will be considered in detail in Section 8.3.

PROBLEM 1: testing the class `RandomPlus`

Construct the code for a class `TestRandomPlus` which when compiled and run generates and outputs to the Transcript window 100 random integers in the range 25 to 36. Your code should make use of the method `nextIntInRange` in the class `RandomPlus`.

For help with this problem see Hints.

□

While we are on the topic of generating random integers, you may find the following problem an interesting challenge.

PROBLEM 2: detecting repetitions

Making use of the method `nextIntInRange` in the class `RandomPlus`, construct a class `Consec4Sevens` that repeatedly generates and displays in the Transcript window random integers in the range 5 to 8 until 4 consecutive sevens are generated.

Now construct a class `Consec4Any` that repeatedly generates and displays random integers in the range 4 to 9 until 4 consecutive integers are the same.

For help with this problem see Hints.

□

PROBLEM 3: extending `SquareFigure`

The class `SquareFigure` was introduced in Section 2.4. In fact, we haven't actually studied in any detail the code for this class, being content simply to understand the various messages that can be sent to this class. (All messages are sent to the class SquareFigure itself, not to objects of this class. The methods invoked as a consequence are therefore all class (i.e. static) methods.) The aim of this problem is to use inheritance to extend this class by adding a new method to the class. As you shall see, we can do this by using existing methods without any need to know how those methods were themselves coded.

Construct a class SquarePlus which inherits the class SquareFigure and has the additional class method

```
public static void moveNorthEast (int d)
```

which moves the square in the north-east diagonal direction by moving it d pixels right and d pixels up. Your code for this method should make direct use of the methods moveRight and moveUp inherited from SquareFigure.

Construct a class TestSquarePlus to test this new subclass.

For help with this problem see Hints.

□

8.2 Inheritance as class specialisation

In Section 8.1 we saw how inheritance can be used to create a new class (the subclass) that extends an existing class (the superclass). But inheritance also allows us to create a subclass that redefines some of the methods that would otherwise have been inherited from the superclass. This enables us to customise these methods to the particular special needs of the subclass.

Example: silver credit cards

Revisit the class CreditCard introduced in Section 7.4. The diagram at the top of the next page summarises this class. In this diagram, variable names are placed within sharp-cornered rectangles while method names are placed within round-cornered rectangles. The solid rectangles contain the instance variables and methods, while the dashed rectangles contain the class (static) variables and methods.

Suppose the bank has a deluxe version of the credit card for their special (i.e. rich) customers. This so-called silver credit card is like the ordinary credit card, except

- no interest is payable on the first \$1,000 overdrawn, e.g. if the account is overdrawn by \$1,600, only interest on \$600 is payable;
- a special management fee, currently \$80, is levied from time to time; this management fee is the same for all silver credit card accounts.

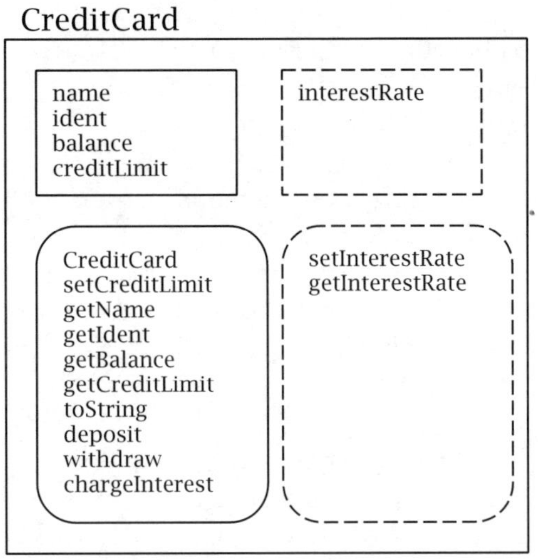

Our task is to construct a class `SilverCreditCard` whose objects are silver credit card accounts.

We could construct the class `SilverCreditCard` from scratch, but as silver credit cards are much like ordinary credit cards, a better approach is to define the class `SilverCreditCard` as a subclass of `CreditCard` so that it inherits all the required features of this superclass. All we then need do is construct the code for those features that are new and, if necessary, write new code for any existing methods that require specialisation.

Without beating around the bush, here is the complete code for the class `SilverCreditCard`:

```
import genesis.*;

public class SilverCreditCard extends CreditCard {

    /* Objects of this class are
    silver credit card accounts. */

    // new class variable
    protected static int fee = 80;

    // constructors
    public SilverCreditCard
                (String aName, String id, int aLimit) {
        super(aName, id, aLimit);
    }
```

```
    public SilverCreditCard ( ) {
        super();
    }

    // redefined instance methods
    public String toString ( ) {
        // silver credit card information;
        // redefines the CreditCard method
        return super.toString()+"\n  management fee: "+fee;
    }

    public void chargeInterest ( ) {
        // charge interest on amount overdrawn above
        // $1,000; redefines the CreditCard method
        if (balance < -1000)
            balance = balance +
                (int)((balance+1000)*(interestRate/100));
    }

    // new instance method
    public void chargeFee ( ) {
        // the management fee is charged
        balance = balance - fee;
    }

    // new class methods
    public static void setFee (int newFee) {
        // set the management fee
        fee = newFee;
    }

    public static int getFee ( ) {
        // get the management fee
        return fee;
    }
}
```

The code for this class raises several issues which we will discuss shortly, but first let's test this new class. We have placed the classes `SilverCreditCard` and `CreditCard` in the *Silver Credit Card* folder.

PROBLEM 4: testing the class `SilverCreditCard`

Open the folder *Silver Credit Card* and run the class `TestSilverCreditCard` whose code is given below:

```
import genesis.*;

public class TestSilverCreditCard {

    /*
    Test the class SilverCreditCard.
    */

    public static void main (String [] args) {
        CreditCard cc = new CreditCard("Bill", "34", 1000);
        cc.withdraw(600);
        cc.chargeInterest();
        SilverCreditCard scc =
                new SilverCreditCard("Jo", "999", 2000);
        scc.withdraw(1600);
        scc.chargeInterest();
        Transcript.println(cc);
        Transcript.println(scc);
        scc.chargeFee();
        SilverCreditCard.setInterestRate(5.25);
        SilverCreditCard.setFee(90);
        Transcript.println(cc);
        Transcript.println(scc);
    }
}
```

Modify the code for this class to test other features of the `SilverCreditCard` class.

Notice that any message that an ordinary credit card object can understand can also be sent to a silver credit card object, although the effect may be different. In addition, silver credit card objects understand new messages such as `chargeFee` that involve the new management fee. These messages cannot be sent to an ordinary credit card object — try it and see what happens: you will get a compiler error.

□

Discussion

The class SilverCreditCard inherits all the instance and class variables and, with the exception of the methods toString and chargeInterest, all the instance and class methods of the class CreditCard. To these features are added

- the class variable fee (this is declared as a class variable as its value is shared by all silver credit card objects);
- two constructor methods;
- the instance method chargeFee that models the charging of the management fee to a particular object; and
- the setter and getter class methods setFee and getFee that set and get respectively the class variable fee.

In addition, the methods toString and chargeInterest are not inherited from the class CreditCard but are redefined to suit the particular needs of the subclass. This is summarised in the diagram below.

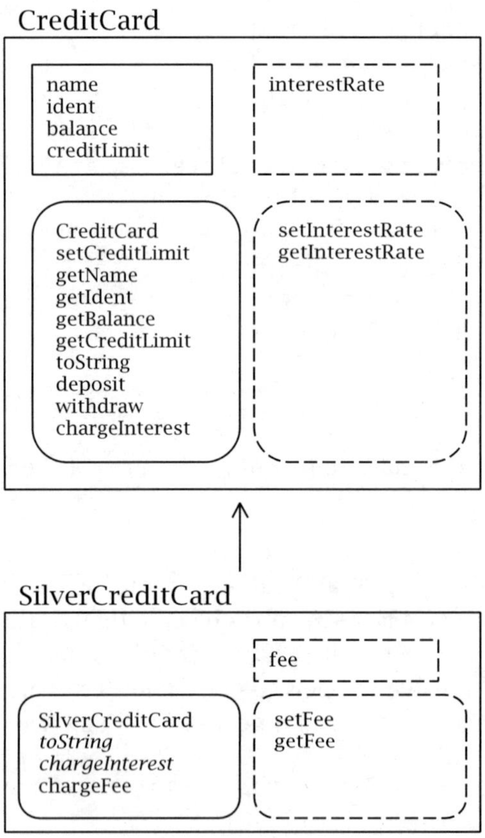

In this diagram only the new variables and the new and redefined methods are shown for the `SilverCreditCard` subclass. The remaining variables and methods are inherited. Redefined methods are shown in italics.

The addition of the variable `fee` and the methods `chargeFee`, `setFee` and `getFee` are straightforward and correspond to class extension as discussed in Section 8.1 so we shall not discuss them further. The two new constructor methods are discussed in detail later in Section 8.3 so we shall say no more about them here.

That leaves us with what is of particular interest in this section: the redefined methods `toString` and `chargeInterest`.

Redefining methods

In general, any method in the superclass can be redefined in a subclass. Each redefined method must have the same name and parameter types in the subclass as the original method in the superclass, and must have the same return type. In such a case, the redefined method takes precedence and the original method is not inherited from the superclass. This mechanism enables us to specialise in the subclass methods that would otherwise have been inherited from the superclass.

[*An aside*: It is permitted to define a method in a subclass which has the same name as a method in the superclass but has different parameter types. In this case the new method becomes an extra feature added to the subclass, in addition to the superclass method of the same name which is inherited. That is, we end up with two methods in the subclass with the same name but distinguished by their different parameter lists. Hence a method in the superclass is only redefined in the subclass by a method that has the same name and parameter types. *End aside*]

The method `toString` needs to be redefined to ensure that the value of the management fee is output when a silver credit card object is passed as an argument to the `println` method. We could have alternatively coded this redefined method as

```
public String toString ( ) {
    // credit card information
    return "credit card account details:\n"
        +"  name:  "+name+"\n"
        +"  identification:  "+ident+"\n"
        +"  balance:  "+balance+"\n"
        +"  credit limit:  "+creditLimit+"\n"
        +"  interest rate:  "+interestRate+"\n"
        +"  management fee:  "+fee;
}
```

without in any way altering the result of invoking the method. However, as the first part of this code is identical to the code for the method toString in the superclass CreditCard, we can make direct use of this superclass method by applying the expression super.toString(). This invokes the toString method in the superclass which returns a string that can be concatenated with the extra information required:

```
super.toString()+"\n  management fee: "+fee;
```

This is now the string we want returned by our redefined toString method.

Using super

As a general rule, if a message to invoke an instance method is sent to the key word super, the compiler will look in the superclass to find the instance method to invoke. This is a very useful ploy because it means we can make use of the code of a superclass instance method even though this method is itself not being inherited from the superclass but rather is being redefined (i.e. coded afresh) in the subclass.

Note however, that the key word super can only be used in this way if the message sent to it invokes an instance method in the superclass. If a class (static) method is redefined in the subclass and we want to invoke the original class method in the superclass, we cannot use the word super. Instead, we simply send the appropriate message to the name of the superclass itself (because that is how we invoke class methods!). For an example of this, see Problem 5 later in this section.

The method chargeInterest also needs to be redefined, as interest is payable only on amounts overdrawn beyond $1,000. In this case, the code for the method in the superclass is unhelpful, so we don't make use of the key word super. Notice how in this code we can refer directly to the instance variable balance and the class variable interestRate. We can do this because they were declared as *protected* variables, making them publicly available to any class in the same package or to any subclass, but private to all other classes.

Inheriting class variables

Before looking at the constructor methods in Section 8.3, consider the following important issues about inheritance raised by the TestSilverCreditCard class.

When the statement

```
SilverCreditCard.setInterestRate(5.25);
```

in the main method in the class TestSilverCreditCard is executed, it results in the interest rate changing not just for all silver credit card objects, but for all ordinary credit card objects as well. This is because the class variable `interestRate` is inherited from the class `CreditCard` and, unlike instance variables which take unique values for each object, its value is therefore shared by all ordinary credit card and silver credit card objects alike. So care must be taken when working with inherited class variables; any change to such a variable performed by the subclass will change the value of the variable in the superclass as well. **Be warned!!**

Finding the method to invoke

Any message that can be sent to an ordinary credit card object can also be sent to a silver credit card object. When a silver credit card object receives a message, it looks in its class `SilverCreditCard` to find the method to invoke. If it finds it there, fine; if not, it looks instead in the superclass `CreditCard`. Hence, if a silver credit card object is sent a message that an ordinary credit card object can understand, the method corresponding to the message is

- either redefined in the `SilverCreditCard` class and hence this new method is invoked,
- or has not been redefined and the original method in the class `CreditCard` is invoked.

PROBLEM 5: redefining `SquareFigure`

Consider again the class `SquareFigure` introduced in Section 2.4. Construct a class `NewSquare` which inherits the class `SquareFigure` and redefines the methods `moveRight`, `moveLeft`, `moveUp` and `moveDown` so that when these messages are sent to the class `NewSquare`, we get the following effects (in each case *x* denotes a positive integer):

- `moveRight(`*x*`)` — square moves right *x* pixels and turns blue;
- `moveLeft(`*x*`)` — square moves left *x* pixels and turns green;
- `moveUp(`*x*`)` — square moves up *x* pixels and turns red;
- `moveDown(`*x*`)` — square moves down *x* pixels and turns black.

For help with this problem see Hints.

□

8.3 Constructor methods and inheritance

Look at the two constructor methods in the subclass `SilverCreditCard`. In each case, a constructor method of the superclass `CreditCard` is invoked by use of the key word `super`. However, the syntax here for the use of `super` differs from the way it is used when redefining an instance method (e.g. see the method `toString` in the subclass `SilverCreditCard`). The word `super` is used here not as the receiver of a message but as the message itself (with the argument list attached).

Consider the first constructor method of `SilverCreditCard`:

```
public SilverCreditCard
            (String aName, String id, int aLimit) {
    super(aName, id, aLimit);
}
```

In this method the statement

```
super(aName, id, aLimit);
```

invokes the constructor method in the superclass `CreditCard` that has a parameter list consisting of two `String` types and one `int` type. The values of `aName`, `id` and `aLimit` are passed as arguments to this method. The effect of this super-statement is as if the following statements had been executed:

```
name = aName;
ident = id;
setCreditLimit(aLimit);
```

as can be confirmed by looking at the code for the corresponding constructor in the class `CreditCard` (see Section 7.4).

The default constructor

Now consider the second constructor method in the class `SilverCreditCard`:

```
public SilverCreditCard ( ) {
    super();
}
```

In this method the statement

```
super();
```

invokes the default constructor method in `CreditCard`, i.e. dialog boxes open requesting that the user supply the name, identification code and initial credit limit for the account.

[*An aside*: The use of the word 'default' to refer to a constructor method with an empty parameter list is rather misleading. It is true that if (and only if) no constructor method whatsoever is explicitly supplied, the Java system will supply a default constructor method and this default constructor will always have an empty parameter list. But if a constructor method with an empty parameter list is explicitly supplied, this method is still known as the default constructor. *End aside*]

There are some general rules that must be understood when using and inheriting constructor methods.

- The **first** thing that always happens when a constructor method in a subclass is invoked is that a constructor method in the superclass is invoked.
  - Either this is done explicitly using a super-statement, as was done in the class `SilverCreditCard` above, in which case the super-statement **must** be the first statement in the constructor,
  - or, if there is no explicit super-statement, the default constructor of the superclass will be **automatically** invoked (in which case it is an error if the superclass does not have a default constructor).
- If (and only if) no constructor method is explicitly defined in a subclass, the Java system will allocate a default constructor which, when invoked, will in turn automatically invoke the default constructor of the superclass.

Example: silver credit card revisited

To help clarify all this, look again at the class `SilverCreditCard`. The second (default) constructor method could have been coded as

```
public SilverCreditCard ( ) {  }
```

That is, the statement-block of the method could have been completely empty! This is because the default constructor of the superclass `CreditCard` is automatically invoked if the subclass constructor has no super-statement. However, although the above code works, good coding practice dictates that the super-statement should always be added explicitly and not just left to the Java system to add implicitly. Leaving it to the system is risky and makes the code difficult to understand.

For example, suppose we had coded the first constructor method of the class `SilverCreditCard` as

```
public SilverCreditCard
                (String aName, String id, int aLimit) {
    name = aName;
    ident = id;
    setCreditLimit(aLimit);
}
```

What would happen when this method is invoked?

Because this code has no explicit super-statement, when the method is invoked the Java system will automatically include the statement `super()` as the first statement to be executed with the result that the default constructor in the superclass `CreditCard` is invoked. As a consequence, dialog boxes would open requesting values for the name, identification code and initial credit limit!

Beware!! At the risk of being boring, we repeat: when a constructor method in a subclass is invoked, it always begins by invoking a constructor method from the superclass. If this is not explicitly indicated with an appropriate super statement, the default constructor of the superclass will be invoked, whether you like it or not.

Whew! We warned you it was complicated!

Good-practice guidelines

Here are guidelines to good practice when coding constructor methods.

- Always include your own default constructor method (i.e. a constructor with an empty parameter list). Don't leave it up to the Java system to supply one, and in any case, the system will only do so if there are no other constructor methods defined.
- In a subclass, always start the code for a constructor method with an appropriate and explicit super-statement to invoke the required constructor method of the superclass. Don't leave it up to the Java system to invoke the default constructor.

Of course, guidelines are often ignored! To give an example, revisit the class `RandomPlus` introduced in Section 8.1. That class does not contain any explicit constructor method; instead it is left to the Java system to supply a default constructor. We were happy to do that because we knew that the default constructor supplied by the system would be just the same as if we had explicitly coded the constructor method

```
public RandomPlus ( ) {
    super();
}
```

and this is exactly what we wanted. The moral of this story? We leave it to the system to provide its own default constructor only if we are very confident that this default is exactly what we want.

To finish this section, here is a problem that involves first creating a class and then creating a subclass. No single part of this problem is difficult, but overall you may find it challenging as it involves the coding of quite a few methods. However, it is typical of the coding required when constructing classes using inheritance.

PROBLEM 6: assessing property taxes

A city council keeps records of properties on which taxes are levied, and they need software to help them maintain the system. For example, within the city there are many town houses. As recorded by the city council, every town house has:

- an address
- an owner
- a value

The council has a tax rate which represents the percentage of the value of a property that is levied as tax. Currently the tax rate is 0.85. (So, for example, on a town house valued at $100,000 the tax would be $850). This tax rate is the same for all properties. The tax payable is rounded to the nearest integer (whole dollar).

Construct a class `TownHouse` whose objects record the information listed above. In your class the address and owner of a town house can be taken to be of type `String` and the value can be assumed to be an integer (i.e. whole dollars only; cents are ignored).

As well as the usual getter and setter methods, your class will need to have a method to calculate the tax payable on the town house. There will also need to be a `toString` method so that details of a house's address, owner, value, tax rate and taxes payable can be displayed.

A default constructor method is needed which requests, via dialog boxes, the initial values of the address, owner and value of a town house object.

The council also has a number of special flats it rents to needy families. As far as the council records are concerned, a council flat is like a town house (i.e. it has an address, an owner and a value) but in addition the name of the tenant is recorded, together with the weekly rent. To help these families, a rebate of 30% is given on the property taxes levied on a council flat.

Construct a class `CouncilFlat` as a subclass of `TownHouse`.

For help with this problem see Hints.

□

Discussion

(Read this discussion only after completing Problem 6 and consulting the Hints.)

Our code for the class CouncilFlat (see Hints) contains the default constructor method:

```
public CouncilFlat ( ) {
    super();
    tenant = DialogBox.request("name of tenant:");
    setRent(DialogBox.requestInt("weekly rent:"));
    type = "Council Flat";
}
```

The statement super() invokes the default constructor of the superclass, i.e. the class TownHouse, and can be omitted because if there is no explicit super-statement the default constructor of the superclass is automatically invoked. However, as we remarked above, it is good practice to include it.

8.4 Subclasses of subclasses

We have seen that inheritance allows us to create a subclass that is like its superclass but extends the features and/or redefines the methods of the superclass. Suppose now we want to construct a class that is like its subclass, except that it extends and/or redefines aspects of the subclass? No problem! We just create a subclass of this subclass!

Example: gold credit cards

Consider again the CreditCard class and its subclass SilverCreditCard introduced in Section 8.2. Suppose the bank has an even more deluxe version of a credit card account for its very special (i.e. very rich) customers. This so-called gold credit card account is like a silver credit card account, except that no interest is payable on the first \$2,000 overdrawn, and a credit limit of \$20,000 is permitted. (Recall that the standard permitted credit limits are \$1,000, \$2,000, \$5,000 and \$10,000.)

Our task this time is to construct a class GoldCreditCard whose objects are gold credit card accounts. This is done in a straightforward way by inheriting the class SilverCreditCard. The class SilverCreditCard now plays a dual role: it is a subclass of CreditCard and a superclass of GoldCreditCard.

Here is its code for the class GoldCreditCard:

```
import genesis.*;

public class GoldCreditCard extends SilverCreditCard {

    /* Objects of class are gold credit card accounts. */

    // constructors

    public GoldCreditCard
                (String aName, String id, int aLimit) {
        super(aName, id, aLimit);
    }

    public GoldCreditCard ( ) {
        super();
    }

    // redefined instance methods

    public void chargeInterest ( ) {
        // charge interest on amount overdrawn above
        // $2,000; redefines the SilverCreditCard method
        if (balance < -2000)
            balance = balance +
                (int)((balance+2000)*(interestRate/100));
    }

    public void setCreditLimit (int limit) {
        // set the credit limit: $20,000 now permitted;
        // redefines the SilverCreditCard method
        if (limit == 20000) creditLimit = limit;
        else super.setCreditLimit(limit);
    }
}
```

PROBLEM 7: testing the class `GoldCreditCard`

Open the folder *Gold Credit Card*. There you will find the class `GoldCreditCard` as well as the classes `CreditCard` and `SilverCreditCard`. Construct a class `TestGoldCreditCard` to test the features of the `GoldCreditCard` class.

For help with this problem see Hints.

□

Discussion

A diagram summarising the inheritance hierarchy for the classes `CreditCard`, `SilverCreditCard` and `GoldCreditCard` is given below. This diagram is in the same style as those given earlier in this unit. In particular, only the new variables and the new and redefined methods are shown for the subclasses `SilverCreditCard` and `GoldCreditCard`. The remaining variables and methods are inherited. Redefined methods are shown in italics.

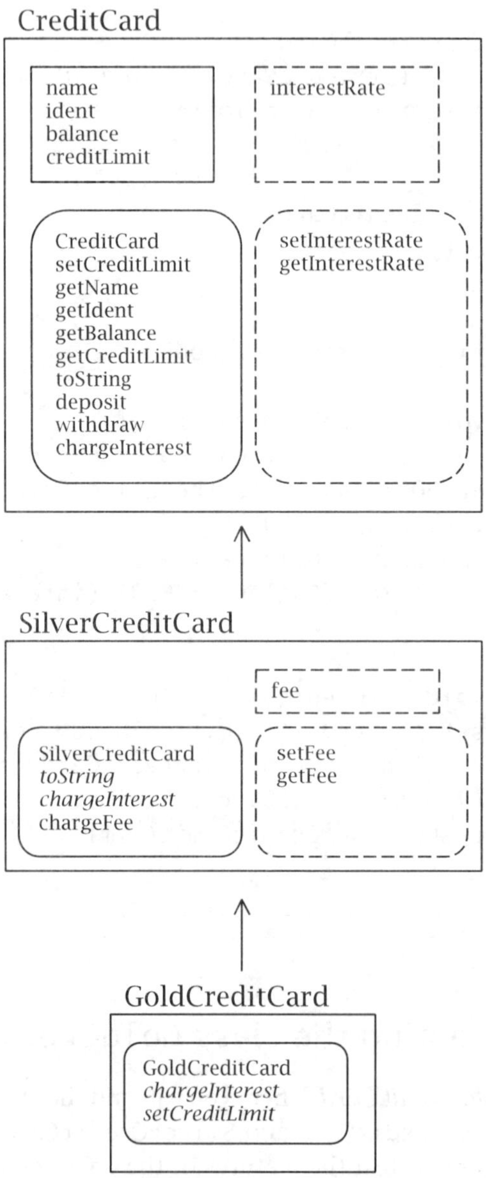

You will need to consult this diagram and have the code for the classes handy in order to closely follow the discussion that follows.

Invoking methods

Consider what happens if we were to execute the following code fragment:

```
GoldCreditCard gcc = new GoldCreditCard();
gcc.setCreditLimit(3000);
```

First, the default constructor method

```
public GoldCreditCard ( ) {
    super();
}
```

of the class GoldCreditCard is invoked. As a consequence the statement super() is executed, with the result that the default constructor method in the superclass SilverCreditCard is invoked. As we have already seen, the default constructor method in SilverCreditCard invokes the default constructor method in its superclass CreditCard.

Once the object gcc has been created and initialised, it is sent the message setCreditLimit(3000). The corresponding method has been redefined in the class GoldCreditCard, so this redefined method is invoked. As a consequence, the statement

```
else super.setCreditLimit(3000);
```

is executed (because 3000 is not equal to 20000: see the code for the method setCreditLimit in the class GoldCreditCard earlier in this section).

Hence, the message setCreditLimit(3000) is sent to the pseudo-object super of the superclass SilverCreditCard. The class SilverCreditCard has not redefined the method setCreditLimit, so it invokes instead the code for the method setCreditLimit in its superclass, CreditCard.

If you look at the code for the method setCreditLimit in the class CreditCard (see Section 7.4), you will notice that, because 3000 is not one of the permitted credit limits, the statement

```
else setCreditLimit(DialogBox.requestInt
            ("Invalid creditlimit. Try again:"));
```

is executed. What happens is a dialog box opens requesting an alternative credit limit. Suppose, for argument sake, that an integer *k* is supplied by the user. Then the message setCreditLimit(*k*) is now sent recursively to the object gcc (of type GoldCreditCard) i.e. to the object that received the original message right at the beginning, and the process begins all over again.

Notice that if k is 20000, then this will result in the variable `creditLimit` being set to this value. This happens even though the code responsible for opening the dialog box requesting the alternative value was buried with the `setCreditLimit` method of the class `CreditLimit` (where 20000 is an invalid limit).

As this example illustrates, careful analysis may be needed to deduce precisely what will happen when a method in a subclass invokes in its turn a method in a superclass. **Be warned!!** Inheritance is a powerful mechanism.

8.5 Polymorphism, subtyping and casting

Because of the way inheritance extends and/or redefines the features of a superclass, any message that can be sent to an object of a class C, say, can also be sent to, and understood by, an object of any subclass of C. As a method can be redefined in a subclass, the actual method that is invoked as a consequence will depend on the class of the object. This idea, that the same message can be sent to objects of different classes, and that the method invoked depends on the class of the object, is known as *polymorphism*.

There is one particularly useful consequence of inheritance that follows from the polymorphic way messages are interpreted: *subtyping*. The idea behind subtyping is that if we have an object of a subclass, we can take a 'blinkered' view of the object and treat it as if it were an object of its superclass.

Subtyping enables us to weaken Java's strong typing system. In Java, we need to state precisely the type of every variable. However, if a variable v, say, is declared to be an object of some class C, at run-time we can assign to v not just an object of the class C, but of any subclass of C. The compiler checks every statement of the form *v.message* to ensure that *message* can invoke some method in the class C (if not, the compiler will signal an error). But if v is in fact referencing an object of a subclass of C, *message* will still be understood, even if it invokes a method in the subclass of C rather than in C itself (when the method has been redefined). This is known as *dynamic binding*.

Example: complex numbers

To illustrate these ideas, let's revisit the class `PlanarPoint` introduced in Section 7.1. Recall that objects of the class `PlanarPoint` model points in the plane, i.e. ordered pairs of real numbers. The class `PlanarPoint` contains methods to perform simple arithmetic with such points, e.g. we can translate a point or add two points.

Complex numbers can also be thought of as ordered pairs of real numbers but with special arithmetic operations defined. For example, the addition and multiplication of two complex numbers is defined by

$$(a, b) + (c, d) = (a + c, b + d)$$

and

$$(a, b) * (c, d) = (ac-bd, ad + bc)$$

respectively. Notice that addition of complex numbers is defined in the same way as we defined the addition of planar points in the class `PlanarPoint`. What we are going to do is construct a class `ComplexNumber` that extends (i.e. inherits) the class `PlanarPoint`.

[*An aside*: why the operations of complex numbers are defined in this way, or why such numbers play an important role in physics and mathematics, will not concern us. We will not need to know anything about complex numbers other than the definitions of addition and multiplication above. *End aside*]

Here is the code for the class `ComplexNumber`. It is in the *genesis* package:

```
package genesis;

public class ComplexNumber extends PlanarPoint {

    /*
    Objects of this class model complex numbers.
    */

    public ComplexNumber (double a, double b) {
        // constructor
        super(a, b);
    }

    public ComplexNumber ( ) {
        // constructor
        super();
    }

    public ComplexNumber mult (ComplexNumber c) {
        // returns the complex product
        // of receiver and c
        double xResult = getX()*c.getX() - getY()*c.getY();
        double yResult = getX()*c.getY() + getY()*c.getX();
        return new ComplexNumber(xResult, yResult);
    }
```

```
    public ComplexNumber add (ComplexNumber c) {
        //returns the complex sum of receiver and c
        double xResult = super.add(c).getX();
        double yResult = super.add(c).getY();
        return new ComplexNumber(xResult, yResult);
    }

    public String toString ( ) {
        // returns a string representation of the receiver
        return "C"+super.toString();
    }
}
```

This code introduces some new issues to do with inheritance which are worth discussing now before we get down to the main task of this section, illustrating polymorphism and subtyping.

Private vs protected

Consider the code for the new method `mult`. Because the inherited instance variables `x` and `y` are declared `private` in the superclass `PlanarPoint`, we cannot refer to them directly but are forced to resort to using the appropriate getter methods inherited from the class `PlanarPoint`. If `x` and `y` had been declared `protected` rather than `private` in `PlanarPoint` this would not have been necessary; we could then have referred to them directly. In this case the code for the method `mult` could have been written as:

```
double xResult = x*c.x - y*c.y;
double yResult = x*c.y + y*c.x;
return new ComplexNumber(xResult, yResult);
```

Redefining methods

Next, consider the redefined method `add`. Even though the rule for adding complex numbers is the same as that for adding planar points, we still need to redefine this method. This is because the original method in the superclass `PlanarPoint` returns a *planar point*, i.e. an object of the class `PlanarPoint`, not a complex number object. We can still make use of the original method (via the expression `super.add(c)`) but we need to then convert the planar point object returned into a complex number object by using the appropriate constructor method.

Finally, we have redefined the method `toString` so that when printing out a complex number we precede its ordered pair of real numbers by the prefix 'C' (for 'Complex'). This will help us differentiate between objects of the class `ComplexNumber` and objects of the class `PlanarPoint` when reading output.

Let us now try evaluating a couple of simple expressions involving complex numbers.

PROBLEM 8: testing the class `ComplexNumber`

Here is the code for a class `TestComplexNumber`:

```
import genesis.*;

public class TestComplexNumber {

    /*
    Testing the class Complex Number.
    */

    public static void main (String [] args) {
        ComplexNumber c1 = new ComplexNumber(0.4, 1);
        ComplexNumber c2 = new ComplexNumber(3, -4);
        ComplexNumber c3 = c1.add(c2);
        ComplexNumber c4 = c1.mult(c3);
        ComplexNumber c5 = new ComplexNumber(1, 1);
        c5.translate(c2);
        Transcript.println(c1);
        Transcript.println(c2);
        Transcript.println(c3);
        Transcript.println(c4);
        Transcript.println(c5);
        Transcript.println(c1.rounded());
    }
}
```

Without actually running this class, try to deduce what would be displayed in the Transcript window if the class was run.

The class `TestComplexNumber` is in the *Test Complex Number* folder. Now run this class to test your deductions.

Try modifying the code to evaluate other expressions involving complex numbers.

□

Discussion

The addition and multiplication of complex numbers as illustrated in the code of the class TestComplexNumber is straightforward. Of more interest is the statement

```
c5.translate(c2);
```

which invokes the translate method in the superclass PlanarPoint. If you look at the code for that method (see Section 7.1) you will notice that its parameter is declared to be of type PlanarPoint. Yet here we are sending it an argument c2 which is of type ComplexNumber, and Java does not complain!

This is our first example of subtyping: although an object of a certain class (PlanarPoint in this case) is expected, Java will in fact accept an object of any subclass (ComplexNumber in this case).

Notice also that the expression

```
c1.rounded()
```

returns a planar point object (of the class PlanarPoint) even though c1 is a complex number object. No surprise here, as returning something of type PlanarPoint is what the method rounded is coded to do!

Subtyped collections

The notion of subtyping allows us to treat a collection (e.g. an array) of objects of a subclass as if it was a collection of objects of a superclass. This concept is applied in the following problem.

PROBLEM 9: spiraling away

Open the folder *Spiral* and run the class Spiral whose code in given at the top of the next page.

A window opens containing a red 'spiraling' polygon. Experiment with different values for the complex number start, and different numbers of vertices in the spiral (the code above has 200 vertices), until you have a good idea of what the code is doing.

For further information, see the discussion following the code for the Spiral class.

□

```
import genesis.*;

public class Spiral {

    /*
    Create a spiral polygon.
    */

    public static void main (String [] args) {
        ComplexNumber centre = new ComplexNumber(195,135);
        ComplexNumber start = new ComplexNumber(0.75,0.6985);
        ComplexNumber [] vertices = new ComplexNumber [200];
        vertices[0] = start;
        for (int i=1; i<200; i++)
            vertices[i] =   start.mult(vertices[i-1]);
        for (int i=0; i<200; i++)
            vertices[i] =   vertices[i].add(centre);
        PolyFigure.create();
        PolyFigure.draw(vertices);
    }
}
```

Discussion

The code for the class `Spiral` makes use of the fact that rotation in the plane can be modelled by the multiplication of complex numbers (we won't attempt to explain why here; if you are not familiar with the mathematics of complex numbers just ignore this detail). We take a complex number *start* whose distance from the origin is only slightly greater than 1 and calculate the complex numbers

$$start * start, start * start * start, \ldots \text{ and so on}$$

where '*' in this case denotes multiplication of complex numbers. These complex numbers form a sequence that spirals out around the origin. We then shift this spiral to the window's centre and draw a polygon (using the class `PolyFigure` introduced in Section 7.2) whose vertices are these complex numbers.

The mathematical details are not important. The point we want to make here is that the method `draw` in the class `PolyFigure` is expecting, via the first argument of the invoking message, an array of planar point objects of the class `PlanarPoint`. But in the statement

```
PolyFigure.draw(vertices);
```

we have passed as argument, not an array of planar points, but an array of complex number objects instead! This succeeds because `ComplexNumber` is a subclass of `PlanarPoint`. Although the class `PolyFigure` is coded to expect an array of planar point objects of the class `PlanarPoint`, it will in fact accept an array of objects of any subclass of `PlanarPoint`. Being able to do this is very useful because complex numbers have precisely the extra mathematical features that make the construction of a figure such as the spiral straightforward.

[*An aside*: Because complex multiplication can be applied to model rotation, the rotating square in Section 7.2 could have been very elegantly coded using complex numbers rather than planar points. If you are familiar with complex numbers you may like to try this as a challenge problem. *End aside*]

Type casting

Suppose we have an array of three planar points, e.g.

```
PlanarPoint [] points = new PlanarPoint [3];
```

Then because of the subtyping allowed by Java, we can populate this array with objects of the class `PlanarPoint` or of any of its subclasses, e.g.

```
points[0] = new ComplexNumber(3, 4);
points[1] = new PlanarPoint(5, 1);
points[2] = new ComplexNumber(-1, 2);
```

Suppose we try to do arithmetic with the complex numbers in this array, e.g.

```
ComplexNumber c;
c = points[0].mult(points[2]);
```

What happens?

PROBLEM 10: type-casting demonstration

The code above has been placed in the class `CastingDemo` whose code is given at the top of the next page. Open the folder *Casting Demo* and try to compile the class `CastingDemo`. Why does this give a compiler error message and how can this error be corrected?

Spend some time thinking about this before reading the discussion following the code for the `CastingDemo` class.

□

```
import genesis.*;

public class CastingDemo{

    /*
    Demonstrating the need for object casting
    */

    public static void main (String [] args) {
        PlanarPoint [] points = new PlanarPoint [3];
        points[0] = new ComplexNumber(3, 4);
        points[1] = new PlanarPoint(5, 1);
        points[2] = new ComplexNumber(-1, 2);
        ComplexNumber c;
        c = points[0].mult(points[2]);
        System.out.println(c);
    }
}
```

Discussion

The problem is that the compiler views the objects referenced by `points[0]` and `points[2]` as planar point objects of the class `PlanarPoint`, not as complex number objects, because `points` is declared to be an array whose elements are of type `PlanarPoint`. Hence, when trying to compile the statement

```
c = points[0].mult(points[2]);
```

the compiler looks in the class `PlanarPoint` to find a method `mult` to invoke. As it cannot find one, it produces the following error message:

```
CastingDemo.java:15: Method mult(genesis.PlanarPoint)
not found in class genesis.PlanarPoint.
        c = points[0].mult(points[2]);
```

What we need to do is tell the compiler that the objects referenced by `points[0]` and `points[2]` are currently complex number objects masquerading as planar point objects! We can do this by casting these objects to the type `ComplexNumber`. To do it we replace the statement

```
c = points[0].mult(points[2]);
```

by the statement

```
c = ((ComplexNumber)points[0]).mult((ComplexNumber)points[2]);
```

Try this yourself. Replace the original statement in the class `CastingDemo` by the statement above, recompile and run.

The syntax for type casting is similar to that for the casting of primitive types we met in Section 3.1. For objects, it takes the form

(*ClassName*) *exp*

where *ClassName* is the name of some class, and *exp* is an expression that evaluates to some object. The compiler will only accept this statement if *ClassName* is a subclass of the (class) type associated by the compiler with the object to which the expression *exp* evaluates. So, for example, in the case of the class `CastingDemo`, an expression such as

```
(ComplexNumber) points[2]
```

is accepted by the compiler because the compiler associates type `PlanarPoint` with the array `points` (and hence with the object `points[2]`) and the class `ComplexNumber` is a subclass of `PlanarPoint`.

Important note about type casting

A statement of the form

(*ClassName*) *exp*

does not change the declared type of the object to which *exp* evaluates. This type cannot change! It simply tells the compiler to treat the object *exp* as if it were an object of the class *ClassName*.

For example, suppose *exp* evaluates to an object *ob*, say, of a class C, and suppose v is a variable of declared type B, where B is a superclass of C. Now, because of subtyping, the Java compiler will allow us to assign the object *ob* to the variable v. That is, an assignment statement of the form

$v = exp$;

would be accepted by the compiler, with the result that v references the object *ob*. In this case, *ob* will be treated as if it were an object of the class B. Then for any statement in which a type cast of the form

$(C)v$

occurs, the compiler will instead treat the object currently referenced by the variable v, i.e. *ob*, as an object of the class C.

Notice in particular, that in the class `CastingDemo` it would *not* be a compiler error to write

```
(ComplexNumber)points[1]
```

because `points` is an array of type `PlanarPoint` and `ComplexNumber` is a subclass of `PlanarPoint`. However, because in this case the object currently referenced by `points[1]` is not a complex number object, but a planar point object of the class `PlanarPoint`, a statement such as

```
((ComplexNumber)points[1]).mult(...)
```

would result in a run-time error. The Java system checks at run-time that every object can invoke a method in response to any message it receives. But type casting does not change the actual type of an object, so in this case as `points[1]` has type `PlanarPoint` and this class does not have a `mult` method to invoke when it receives the message `mult(..)`, an error occurs. **Be warned!!**

To reiterate this important point — every object, when created, has the type given by its class, and this type can never change. However, an object can masquerade as an object of one of its superclasses. Type casting enables the compiler to treat an object as if it has the type named in the brackets; it cannot change the actual type of the object.

One of the most common applications of type casting is when an object is being retrieved from a collection (such as an array) whose base type is a superclass of the actual class of the object.

Whew! Clearly, type casting is fraught with difficulties, and should be used with great care.

The `instanceof` operator

Because type casting may lead to serious run-time errors, Java has supplied an extremely useful operator, `instanceof`, to enable the type of an object to be tested. This operator returns a Boolean value.

To illustrate the operator `instanceof`, within the class `CastingDemo` the expression

```
point[2] instanceof ComplexNumber
```

will evaluate to *true*, while the expression

```
point[1] instanceof ComplexNumber
```

will evaluate to *false*. The general rule is

exp `instanceof` *ClassName*

will evaluate to *true* if and only if *ClassName* is either the actual type of the object to which the expression *exp* currently evaluates, or a superclass of its actual type.

To test your understanding of the `instanceof` operator, what will be printed in the Output window if the following code fragment is executed?

```
CreditCard cc = new CreditCard();
SilverCreditCard scc = new SilverCreditCard();
GoldCreditCard gcc = new GoldCreditCard();
CreditCard [] cards = new CreditCard [3];
cards[0] = cc;
cards[1] = scc;
cards[2] = gcc;
for (int i=0; i<3; i++)
    if (cards[i] instanceof SilverCreditCard)
        System.out.println(i);
```

Answer:

```
1
2
```

The reason 0 is not printed is because only the objects referenced by `cards[1]` and `cards[2]` are currently instances of the class `SilverCreditCard` or one of its subclasses.

The operator `instanceof` can help us when retrieving objects from a collection such as an array. We can test to ensure that an object has the required type before performing any type cast.

PROBLEM 11: making use of casting

Consider the (incomplete) code for the class `UsingCasting` given at the top of the next page. The aim of this problem is to complete the code for the `multComplexNumbers` method which takes an array of type `PlanarPoint` as parameter, and returns the complex number object obtained by multiplying together all the complex number objects (if any) in that array. If there are no complex numbers in the array, your method should return the complex number (0, 0).

The `main` method in the class `UsingCasting` is there just so that you can test your `multComplexNumbers` method. Modify `main` as you please so as to test the various aspects of your method. In particular, you should test that your method returns the complex number `(0,0)` when the array passed to the method contains no complex numbers.

```
import genesis.*;

public class UsingCasting {

    /*
    Uses casting to extract and operate on complex
    numbers within an array of type PlanarPoint.
    */

    public static void main (String [] args) {
        PlanarPoint [] points = new PlanarPoint [3];
        points[0] = new ComplexNumber(3, 4);
        points[1] = new PlanarPoint(5, 1);
        points[2] = new ComplexNumber(-1, 2);
        System.out.println(multComplexNumbers(points));
    }

    public static ComplexNumber multComplexNumbers
                            (PlanarPoint [] pointArray) {
        // returns the complex product of the
        // complex numbers in the array pointArray;
        // if there are no such numbers, returns (0, 0)

        // ADD YOUR CODE HERE

    }
}
```

You will find the above code for the class `UsingCasting` in the folder *Using Casting*.

For help with this problem see Hints.

□

8.6 Inheritance hierarchies

In Chapter 7 we introduced the class `CreditCard` (Section 7.4) and the class `SavingsAccount` (Problem 10 in Section 7.5). In this chapter we derived the class `SilverCreditCard` as a subclass of `CreditCard` (Section 8.2) and the class `GoldCreditCard` as a subclass of `SilverCreditCard` (Section 8.4). This is illustrated in the diagram below in which the arrow denotes 'is a subclass of'.

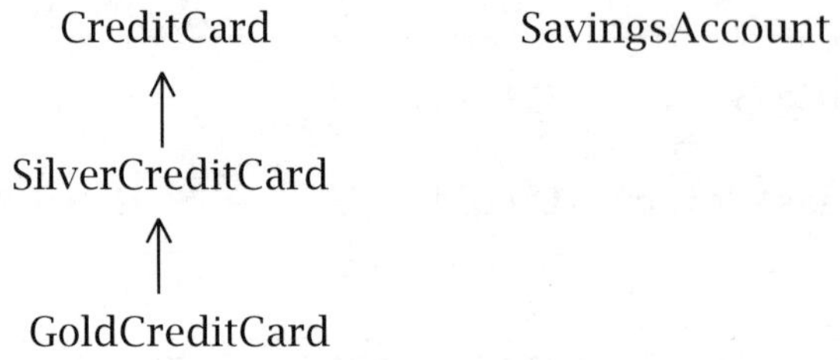

Consider the two classes `CreditCard` and `SavingsAccount` at the top of this hierarchy. Currently they are completely unrelated, i.e. they were derived quite independently. Yet objects of these two classes have much in common. For example, both classes have instance variables to capture the name, identification code and current balance of an object. Furthermore, in addition to the setter and getter methods, both classes have methods for depositing and withdrawing money, as well as a `toString` method. Of course, the actual code for these methods may be different in the different classes, but each method declaration in terms of its parameters and return type is similar.

With so much similarity between the classes, why not 'extract' the commonality and create a class `BankAccount` ,say, where the common features can reside? Then both `CreditCard` and `SavingsAccount` can be coded as subclasses of `BankAccount`! If we were to do this, we would get the inheritance hierarchy in the diagram below.

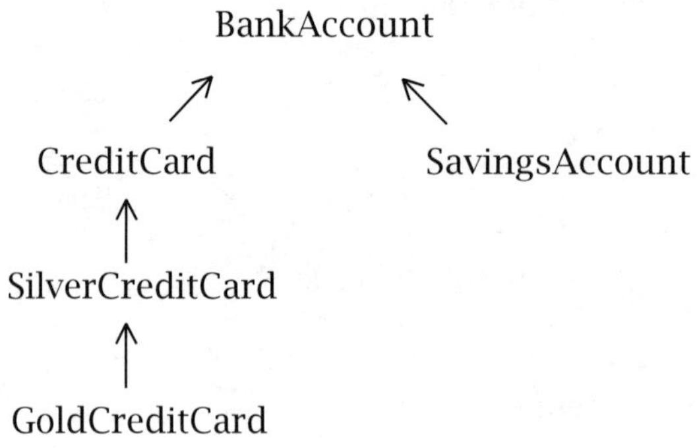

We'll create this hierarchy in just a moment, but first, let's make a few philosophical observations.

Abstract classes

The class `BankAccount` will enable us to structure bank account classes in, hopefully, a coherent way. It will create an architecture where the relationship between classes can be readily seen and exploited. Once common code has been extracted into the `BankAccount` class, the mechanism of inheritance will enable us to share this code. In particular, this common code will not need to be repeated in the subclasses; rather, the design of each subclass can instead concentrate on how it *differs* from its superclass. A well designed inheritance hierarchy can significantly improve the overall comprehensibility of a collection of related classes, making them easier to use, maintain and extend.

As the role of the class BankAccount will be to act as a repository for common code and to help define the overall architectural structure of our hierarchy of classes, we would not expect to create actual objects of this class. Any object within the banking system will be either a credit card object (or a silver or gold specialisation of this) or a savings account object. In this sense, the class BankAccount will be 'abstract', existing only to give structural organisation to our system, and having a different role from the other 'concrete' classes in the hierarchy.

OK. Enough of the philosophy! Now down to details.

Here is our code for the class BankAccount:

```
import genesis.*;

public abstract class BankAccount {

    /*
    Abstract class as root class of Bank Account
    inheritance hierarchy.
    */

    // instance variables
    protected String name;
    protected String ident;
    protected int balance = 0;

    // constructors
    public BankAccount (String aName, String anIdent) {
        name = aName;
        ident = anIdent;
    }

    public BankAccount ( ) {
        name = DialogBox.request
                    ("Name of account holder:");
        ident = DialogBox.request
                    ("Account Identification:");
    }
```

```
    // instance methods
    public String getName ( ) {
        // get name
        return name;
    }

    public String getIdent ( ) {
        // get ident
        return ident;
    }

    public int getBalance ( ) {
        // get balance
        return balance;
    }

    public String toString ( ) {
        // account information
        return "  name:  "+name+"\n"
            +"  identification:  "+ident+"\n"
            +"  balance:  "+balance+"\n";
    }

    public void deposit (int amount) {
        // deposit amount
        if (amount > 0) balance = balance + amount;
        else DialogBox.warn
                ("Must deposit a positive amount.");
    }

    public abstract void withdraw (int amount);
}
```

Discussion

The class BankAccount is much like any other class we have met so far, except in two important respects.

First, the key word abstract is included as part of the declaration of the class. This indicates that no objects of the class can be created; the Java compiler will prevent constructor methods being invoked to instantiate objects of this class. The key word abstract confirms that the role of this class is to help determine the structure of the inheritance hierarchy. The class exists so it can be inherited by other classes.

Well, if it is the case that objects of the class BankAccount cannot be instantiated, why does the class bother to have constructor methods since they would appear to be useless? As we shall see when we look at the subclasses of BankAccount, the constructor methods of the BankAccount class are invoked when instantiating an object of a subclass.

Second, the method withdraw also has the key word abstract included as part of its declaration. This indicates that the method contains only its declaration; it has no associated block of statements. It is placed in the class BankAccount to indicate to all concrete subclasses that this is a method whose statement-block needs to be supplied. The code is not included here because each concrete subclass will have its own distinct version of this method. It would be pointless to include code for this method in the class BankAccount because every subclass completely redefines it anyhow. However, the declaration of withdraw in BankAccount guarantees that at least the parameter list and return type of the method will be the same in each subclass.

Here is a general rule:

> *if a class contains an abstract method, then the class must also be declared abstract.*

Notice that the converse is not true: not all methods (or indeed any of the methods) in an abstract class have to be declared as abstract.

Here is the code for the class SavingsAccount expressed as a subclass of BankAccount (see Prolem 10 in Section 7.5 for a specification of the class SavingsAccount):

```
import genesis.*;

public class SavingsAccount extends BankAccount {

    /* Objects of this class are savings accounts */

    // class variable
    protected static int withdrawCharge = 2;

    // constructors
    public SavingsAccount (String aName, String anIdent) {
        super(aName, anIdent);
    }

    public SavingsAccount ( ) {
        super();
    }
```

```
        // instance methods
        public String toString ( ) {
            // savings account information
            return "savings account details:\n"
                + super.toString() +"\n"
                +"  withdraw charge:  "+withdrawCharge;
        }

        public void withdraw (int amount) {
            // withdraw amount
            if (amount >= 50) {
                int newBalance =
                    balance - amount - withdrawCharge;
                if (newBalance >= 0) balance = newBalance;
                else DialogBox.warn
                    ("Insufficient funds for the withdraw.");
            }
            else DialogBox.warn
                        ("Must withdraw at least $50.");
        }

        // class methods
        public static void setWithdrawCharge (int newCharge) {
            // set withdraw charge
            if (newCharge >= 0) withdrawCharge = newCharge;
        }

        public static double getWithdrawCharge ( ) {
            // get withdraw charge
            return withdrawCharge;
        }
    }
```

Notice how the constructor methods of the class invoke the corresponding constructor methods of the superclass BankAccount by using the super-statement. The other use of the word super to invoke the same-named method in the superclass is demonstrated in the method toString.

PROBLEM 12: CreditCard as a subclass of BankAccount

Construct the class CreditCard (see Section 7.4) as a subclass of BankAccount. For help with this problem see Hints.

□

The remaining two classes, `SilverCreditCard` and `GoldCreditCard`, can be placed unaltered into the inheritance hierarchy as they are already defined as subclasses of `CreditCard`. This inheritance hierarchy is summarised in the diagram below.

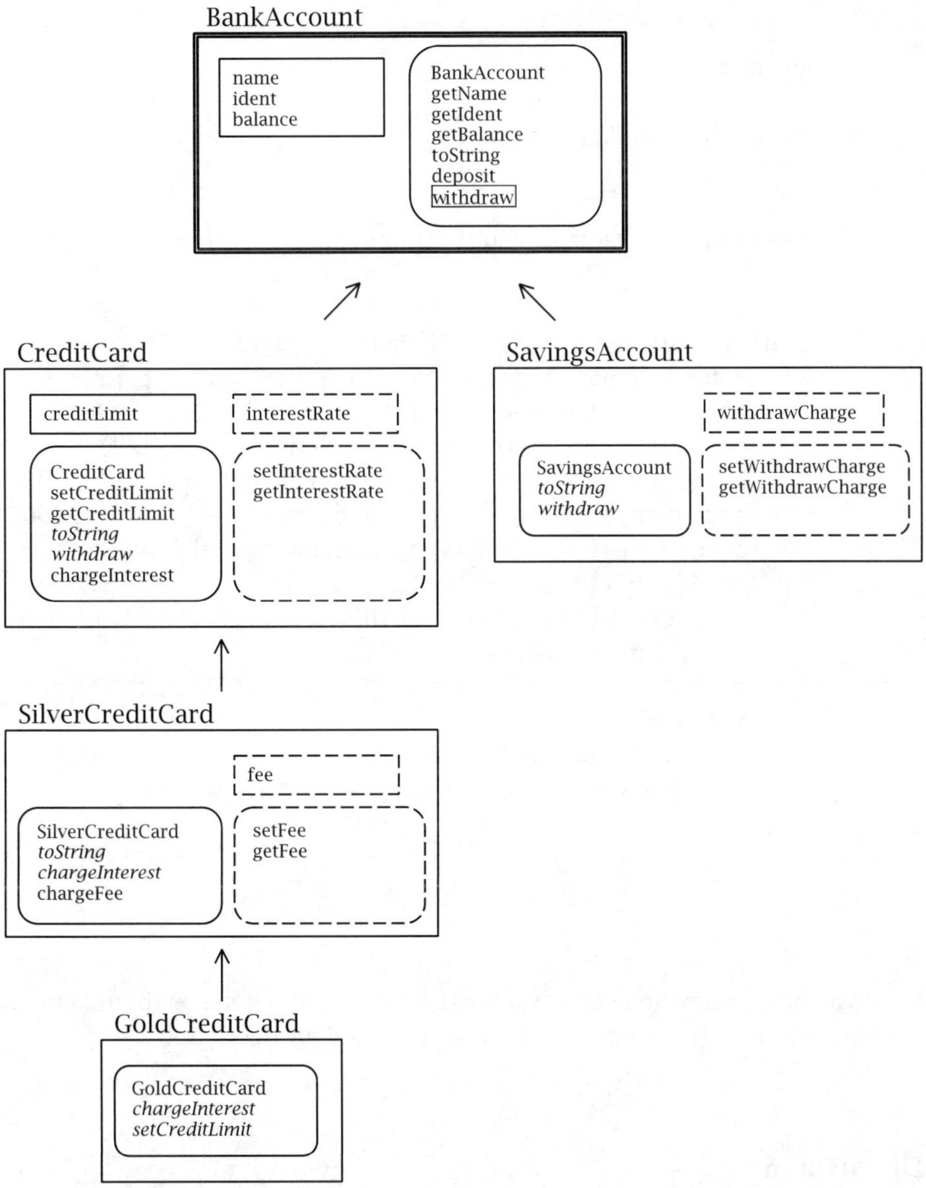

In this diagram the double border for `BankAccount` indicates that it is an abstract class. Similarly, the box for `withdraw` in this class indicates it is an abstract method.

PROBLEM 13: testing the bank-account hierarchy

Open the folder *Bank Account*. In this folder you will find all the classes in the bank-account inheritance hierarchy. Also in this folder is the class `TestBankAccount` whose code is given by:

```
import genesis.*;

public class TestBankAccount {

    /*
    Testing the Bank Account inheritance hierarchy.
    */

    public static void main (String [] args) {
        BankAccount [] accounts = new BankAccount [5];
        accounts[0] = new CreditCard("Tom", "1", 1000);
        accounts[1] = new SavingsAccount("Ann", "2");
        accounts[2] = new SilverCreditCard("Jo", "3", 2000);
        accounts[3] = new GoldCreditCard("Jim", "4", 20000);
        accounts[4] = new SavingsAccount("Yin", "5");
        for (int i=0; i<5; i++) {
            accounts[i].deposit(100*(i+1));
            accounts[i].withdraw(50);
        }
        int sum = 0;
        for (int i=0; i<5; i++)
            sum = sum + accounts[i].getBalance();
        System.out.println (sum);
    }
}
```

What will be output when this class is run? Try to deduce this without actually running the class. Then run the class to confirm your deductions.

□

Discussion

The amazing thing about the code for the `main` method of the `TestBankAccount` class in Problem 13 is that even though objects of the class `BankAccount` cannot be created because the class is abstract, nevertheless, an array `accounts` of type `BankAccount` can be declared! This is fine so long as the array is populated with objects of the concrete subclasses of `BankAccount` as is the case with the code in the class `TestBankAccount`.

The message `deposit(..)` can be sent to each account object as each concrete class in the hierarchy inherits the method `deposit` from the abstract class `BankAccount`. Similarly, as each concrete class in the hierarchy redefines the method `withdraw`, the message `withdraw(..)` can be sent to each account object. Here we have polymorphism at work as different account objects respond differently to this message depending on the actual class of the account object.

The value printed in the Output window is the total balance of the five accounts.

PROBLEM 14: working with abstract classes

Code a method `countSilver` whose declaration is

```
public static int countSilver (BankAccount [] accountArray)
```

which, when invoked and passed an array of type `BankAccount`, returns the number of elements of the array that are objects of the class `SilverCreditCard`.

(Recall that a statement of the form

```
accountArray[i] instanceof SilverCreditCard
```

will return *true* if the array element is an object of the class `SilverCreditCard` or its subclass. Hence such a statement, by itself, will not determine which array elements are precisely of type `SilverCreditCard`.)

For help with this problem see Hints.

□

Chapter 8 self-check

Can you use inheritance to create

- a class that extends the features of a given class?
- a class that redefines some of the methods of a given class?
- a hierarchy of classes?

Do you understand the terms

- subclass and superclass?
- method redefinition?
- polymorphism?
- subtype?

- type casting?
- abstract class?

How do you

- use type casting to re-establish the type of an object masquerading as an object of its superclass?
- use the operator `instanceof` to determine the type of an object?

Can you explain

- the distinction between the way the key word `super` is used in the superclass
  - to invoke a constructor method?
  - to invoke an instance method?
- the circumstances under which Java provides a default constructor method?
- the rules that determine how a constructor method in the superclass is invoked when executing a constructor method in a subclass?
- how to invoke a static method in a superclass?

Graphics and event handling 9

Prerequisites

Chapter 9 assumes you are familiar with the general notion of class inheritance, in particular:

- how a subclass of a given class can be constructed;
- how methods in a superclass can be redefined in a subclass.

If you are unsure of these issues, revise the appropriate sections of Chapter 8.

Overview

In earlier chapters of *Java Genesis* we frequently opened windows to display and animate various shapes and figures. In all cases this has been achieved by sending appropriate messages to classes that have been specially created and placed in the *genesis* package. We have made use of these classes while remaining blissfully ignorant of the details of their code. Indeed, this has demonstrated one of the great strengths of object-oriented programming: to use a class we need only be aware of the messages that can be sent to the class and its objects and understand how the class and its objects will respond to these messages. The actual details of the underlying code of the class can often be ignored.

The classes in the *genesis* package that display graphical shapes have been constructed by applying Java's Swing components that are part of the Java Foundation Classes (JFC), together with Java's Abstract Windowing Toolkit (AWT). The Swing classes are found in the *javax.swing* package. (Note the '*x*' attached to the '*java*'. This package was added as an extension to early versions of Java. It is now a core Java package but its original name survives.) The AWT classes are in the *java.awt* package.

If we want to build applications that make full use of the powerful graphics facilities that come with Java, we need to look in detail at how to use the Swing and AWT classes to construct and manipulate graphical components. This is the task we begin in this chapter. In particular, we look at how actions such as pressing the mouse button or hitting a key on the keyboard can be associated with a graphical component so as to enable us to interact directly with that component.

In this chapter we concentrate on two particular types of graphical components, frames and panels. A frame is the name Java gives to the top-level window not contained inside another window. To display graphics in a frame we

- create a panel and place the graphical objects in the panel;
- add the panel to the window frame.

Each window frame is informed by the underlying operating system whenever certain events occur. For example, the mouse may be moved into the window, or a mouse's button may be pressed while the mouse is positioned in the window, or a key on the keyboard may be pressed, or the window may be turned into an icon or even closed altogether. In all, there are many such events that involve a window and which the window may need to know about.

In this chapter we look at how to associate 'listener' objects with windows and window components. These objects listen for specific events and can, when informed that one of the events they are listening for has occurred, invoke some appropriate response.

With regard to one of the basic principles underlying *Java Genesis*, namely, that it is through solving problems that ideas are best assimilated and understood, we have deliberately included many problems in this chapter. We find graphics programming both challenging and fun and believe you will find these problems enjoyable and rewarding. Explore the ideas introduced in the problems and experiment with coding your own applications.

In Chapter 10 we will extend our understanding of graphics programming to construct graphical components such as buttons and text boxes, enabling us to build graphical user interfaces (GUIs) for our applications.

9.1 Window frames

We look at how a window can be sized, positioned and opened on the computer's screen, and how various graphical shapes and figures can be positioned and displayed in the window.

Problems:

1 opening a blank window
2 centring a window
3 drawing in a window
4 displaying Donald
5 creating patterns with ovals
6 getting the display area's size

9.2 Anonymous inner classes

We introduce the idea of an anonymous inner class, enabling us to create a subclass of a given class entirely within the code of another class. The subclass so constructed remains anonymous as it is not given a name. The anonymous inner class construct is applied to event handling in the following sections.

9.3 Introducing event handling

It is not uncommon at first to find Java's event handling mechanism difficult to follow. However, there is a well-defined process that underlies all event handling in Java. In this section we look at this process in order to motivate and reveal the common features of the mechanism, features that will be repeatedly applied in each of the specific examples of event handling developed in the following sections.

9.4 Window events

We look at how Java handles top-level window events, such as opening or closing a window.

Problems:

7 detecting the window-iconified event
8 using the `ExitFrame` class

9.5 Mouse events

We look at how Java handles some of the events that involve the mouse, such as pressing or releasing the mouse button in a window.

Problems:

9 toggling the square
10 detecting the mouse position
11 displaying the mouse position

12 exploring other mouse events

13 placing small squares

14 Janet and Jim

9.6 Mouse motion events

We look at how Java handles other mouse events, such as moving the mouse in a window.

Problems:

15 following the mouse

16 escaping the mouse

17 dynamically dimensioned oval

9.7 Keyboard events

We look at how Java handles keyboard events, such as pressing a key on the keyboard.

Problems:

18 steering the square

19 carpet snake

Learning outcomes

At the conclusion of Chapter 9 you will understand:

- how to open a window with a given size and in a given position;
- how to position and display various graphical objects in a window;
- how to create an anonymous inner class;
- how to associate listener objects with windows and their components; these objects are informed when events such as pressing the mouse button or pressing a key on the keyboard occur;
- how to invoke an action in response to some specified event occurring;
- how Java classifies and distinguishes between the various kinds of events that involve a window.

9.1 Window frames

When we use Java's Swing to construct a graphical application, the outer-most window in which all the various graphical objects we wish to display are ultimately embedded is known as a *frame*. A frame is constructed as an object of some appropriate subclass of the class `JFrame` (the class `JFrame` is in the *javax.swing* package). To be more precise, a window frame is typically an object of some class that has been explicitly designed to extend the class `JFrame` by adding code to determine the specific size and position of the window on the screen and to display within this window specific graphical objects.

As a first very simple example, consider the code for a class `BlankFrame` that extends the class `JFrame`:

```
import javax.swing.*;

public class BlankFrame extends JFrame {
    /*
    An empty window.
    */

    // constructor
    public BlankFrame ( ) {
        setTitle("A Blank Window");
        setBounds(100, 50, 400, 300);
    }
}
```

The class `Main` has a `main` method that instantiates an object of the class `BlankFrame` and displays it on the screen:

```
public class Main {

    public static void main (String [ ] args) {
        BlankFrame blankWin = new BlankFrame();
        blankWin.setVisible(true);
    }
}
```

PROBLEM 1: opening a blank window

The folder *Blank Window* contains the code for the above two classes. Open this folder and run the class `Main`.

Modify the class `BlankFrame` so that the window is drawn in a different position on the screen, or has a different size, or has a different title.

□

Discussion

Notice that clicking with the mouse on the 'X' in the upper-right corner of the window frame hides the window but does not terminate the underlying Java program; the program must be terminated manually. This is rather unsatisfactory. In Section 9.4 we will see how to extend the `JFrame` class so that clicking on the 'X' does terminate the underlying program.

[*An aside*: If a Java program is launched from a console window it can be terminated by pressing CTRL+C. If launched from Windows it can be terminated by pressing CTRL+ALT+DEL, selecting the Java program from the list of options, and selecting the 'End Task' button. If launched from an IDE such as Kawa it can be terminated by selecting the 'Stop Java' button or equivalent. *End aside*]

Referring to Problem 1, the `main` method in the class `Main` first instantiates an object `blankWin` of the class `BlankFrame`:

```
BlankFrame blankWin = new BlankFrame();
```

and then displays this window frame on the screen by executing the statement

```
blankWin.setVisible(true);
```

The window that opens as a consequence

- has the title 'A Blank Window';
- is positioned so that its upper-left corner is 100 pixels right and 50 pixels down from the upper-left corner of the screen;
- is 400 pixels wide and 300 pixels high.

These features are established when the constructor method of the class `BlankFrame` is invoked in response to the instantiation of the object `blankWin`.

There are many methods that the class `BlankFrame` inherits from `JFrame`. Here is a description of those instance methods that are invoked explicitly in the above code:

- `void setBounds (int x, int y, int w, int h)`

  positions the frame so that its upper-left corner is `x` pixels right and `y` pixels down from the upper-left corner of the screen; sizes the frame to be `w` pixels wide and `h` pixels high

- `void setTitle (String s)`

  sets the title of the frame to be the string `s`

- `void setVisible (boolean b)`

  displays or hides the frame on the screen as `b` is respectively *true* or *false*

The window that opens in this case is not very sophisticated. We haven't displayed anything inside the window, and we cannot even close the application by clicking on the 'X' in the upper-right corner. We shall see later in this chapter how to write code to achieve both.

Notice that we have adopted here the convention of placing the `main` method in a class called `Main`. When executed, this method instantiates the underlying frame object required to run the application. This coding convention enables us to clearly distinguish between the class responsible for starting an application (i.e. the class `Main` containing the `main` method) and the other class(es) that define and control the graphical components in that application (e.g. classes such as `BlankFrame` that are derived from the Swing library classes). We shall follow this simple convention throughout this and the next chapter.

By placing the files *Main.java* and *BlankFrame.java* in the same folder, we ensure that upon compilation the reference to the class `BlankFrame` in the class `Main` can be understood. The compiler will automatically look in the current folder when searching for any class.

Positioning a window frame

To position a window frame we set the x- and y-coordinates of the upper-left corner of the window using the method `setBounds`. But suppose we wish to open our window in the centre of the screen regardless of the actual size of the screen? In this case the x- and y-coordinates of the upper-left corner of the window cannot be given in advance as fixed integers, but will need to be determined at run-time and will take values relative to the actual size of the screen.

To help us do this, Java has a class `Toolkit` that can be found in the *java.awt* package. This class enables us to extract information about the underlying system on which the Java application is running.

Here is the code for a class `CentredFrame` which makes use of the class `Toolkit` to position a window frame in the centre of the screen:

```
import javax.swing.*;
import java.awt.*;

public class CentredFrame extends JFrame {
    /*
    Opens a window in the centre of the screen.
    */

    // constructor
    public CentredFrame ( ) {
        setTitle("A Centred Window");
        Toolkit tk = Toolkit.getDefaultToolkit();
        int screenWidth = tk.getScreenSize().width;
        int screenHeight = tk.getScreenSize().height;
        setBounds
            ((screenWidth-400)/2, (screenHeight-300)/2,
                                                    400, 300);
    }
}
```

The Main class to start the application is similar to what we had before:

```
public class Main {

    public static void main (String [ ] args) {
        CentredFrame centWin = new CentredFrame();
        centWin.setVisible(true);
    }
}
```

PROBLEM 2: centring a window

The folder *Centred Window* contains the code for the above two classes. Open this folder and run the class Main.

Modify the class CentredFrame so that a window is opened positioned in the centre of the screen and having an area one quarter of the area of the screen.

For help with this problem see Hints.

□

Discussion

To use the class Toolkit to extract information about the underlying system, we first create an object of the class Toolkit using the static (class) method getDefaultToolkit. For example, in the class CentredFrame we have the declaration

```
Toolkit tk = Toolkit.getDefaultToolkit();
```

The toolkit object tk contains information about the screen size. For example, the width and height of the screen is given respectively by the expressions:

```
tk.getScreenSize().width;
tk.getScreenSize().height;
```

Once we have this information it is a simple matter to use the setBounds method to centre the window.

Drawing in a window frame

Opening a blank window is not very exciting. We want to be able to display various graphical objects in the window. The classes DisplayFrame and DisplayPanel (together with a Main class similar to what we had before) do just that:

```
import javax.swing.*;
import java.awt.*;

public class DisplayFrame extends JFrame {
    /*
    Display various graphical objects in a window.
    */

    // constructor
    public DisplayFrame ( ) {
        setTitle("Drawing in a Window");
        setBounds(50, 50, 500, 500);
        Container c = getContentPane();
        DisplayPanel dp = new DisplayPanel();
        c.add(dp);
    }
}
```

```
import javax.swing.*;
import java.awt.*;

public class DisplayPanel extends JPanel {

    // constructor
    public DisplayPanel ( ) {
        setBackground(Color.white);
    }

    public void paintComponent (Graphics g) {
        // draw various graphical objects
        super.paintComponent(g);
        g.setColor(Color.red);
        g.fillRect(320, 335, 100, 75);
        g.setColor(new Color(44, 128, 95));
        g.fillOval(50, 200, 150, 200);
        g.drawRect(50, 200, 150, 200);
        g.setColor(Color.blue);
        Font f = new Font("SansSerif", Font.BOLD, 25);
        g.setFont(f);
        g.drawString("Graphics is fun!!", 250, 300);
        g.drawOval(325, 125, 100, 100);
        g.drawOval(330, 130, 90, 90);
        Toolkit tk = Toolkit.getDefaultToolkit();
        Image im = tk.getImage("JavaJim.gif");
        g.drawImage(im, 150, 40, this);
    }
}
```

```
public class Main {

    public static void main (String [ ] args) {
        DisplayFrame dispWin = new DisplayFrame();
        dispWin.setVisible(true);
    }
}
```

PROBLEM 3: drawing in a window

The folder *Display Window* contains the code for the above three classes. Open this folder and run the class `Main`.

Modify the class `DisplayPanel` so as to display other graphical objects in different positions and using different colours.

Experiment and see if you can figure out the code structure before reading the discussion below.

□

Discussion

As well as some specific detail which we will discuss shortly, Problem 3 illustrates Java's general strategy for displaying graphical objects in windows using the Swing classes. Notice that we did not paint directly onto the window frame but instead painted onto a panel and then added that panel to the window. Let's look at the details.

Painting a panel

A panel is a component designed to contain graphical objects. The Swing class `JPanel` is responsible for constructing panels, but invariably we need to extend this class to customise our panels. In our example it is the class `DisplayPanel` that extends `JPanel` and contains the code to create our specific panel.

Setting the background colour

The class `DisplayPanel` begins with a simple default constructor method that sets the background colour of the panel by invoking the following instance method (inherited from the `JComponent` class):

- `void setBackground (Color c)`

  sets the background colour to be `c`

Any colour can be used. In particular, the class `Color` (in the *java.awt* package) comes with the colour constants

```
black      blue    cyan    darkGray    gray    green
lightGray  magenta orange  pink  red   white   yellow
```

which can be extracted by expressions such as `Color.black`, `Color.blue`, etc.

Try modifying the code for the class `DisplayPanel` to set the background to some colour other than white. Go one step further and remove the constructor method of `DisplayPanel` altogether to discover the default background colour of a panel.

The paintComponent method

To place graphical objects in a panel we use the paintComponent method. This instance method is automatically invoked not only when the window frame is drawn on the screen for the first time but each time the window is redrawn for whatever reason. You will not need to invoke the method paintComponent yourself — leave it to be done automatically by the system.

The paintComponent method is inherited from the superclass JFrame, but we need to redefine it in our subclass if we want to display something other than a blank window. To ensure the full functionality of this method is available to us, we begin the code by invoking the paintComponent method in the superclass JPanel,

```
super.paintComponent(g);
```

where g is the object of the class Graphics passed as parameter to our redefined paintComponent method (see below).

The Graphics class

The paintComponent method takes one parameter, an object of the class Graphics, where Graphics is a class in the *java.awt* package. All drawing in Java must be done in a Graphics object. To be specific, Java automatically associates an object of the class Graphics with each panel, and it is this Graphics object that is passed as argument when the paintComponent method is invoked. All the various graphical components that we want to display in the window are then drawn in this Graphics object.

The class Graphics has a variety of instance methods for drawing various graphical objects. Here is a description of those that are invoked explicitly in the paintComponent method of the class DisplayPanel above:

- `void setColor (Color c)`

  sets the current colour to be c; all subsequent graphical objects take this colour until it is changed

- `void fillRect (int x, int y, int w, int h)`

  draws a solid rectangle whose upper-left corner is x pixels right and y pixels down from the upper-left corner of the graphics' container; the rectangle is w pixels wide and h pixels high

- `void drawRect (int x, int y, int w, int h)`

  draws the outline of a rectangle; the parameters are interpreted as for the method fillRect above

- `void fillOval (int x, int y, int w, int h)`

  draws a solid ellipse where the upper-left corner of the bordering rectangle is `x` pixels right and `y` pixels down from the upper-left corner of the graphics' container; the bordering rectangle is `w` pixels wide and `h` pixels high

- `void drawOval (int x, int y, int w, int h)`

  draws the outline of an oval; the parameters are interpreted as for the method `fillOval` above

- `void setFont (Font f)`

  sets the current font style to be `f`; all subsequent strings will be displayed in this font style until it is changed

- `void drawString (String s, int x, int y)`

  draws the string `s` where the start of the baseline of the string is `x` pixels right and `y` pixels down from the upper-left corner of the window's display area

- `void drawImage (Image im, int x, int y, ImageObserver ob)`

  draws the image `im` where the upper-left corner of the image is `x` pixels right and `y` pixels down from the upper-left corner of the graphics' container; the object `ob` is notified of the progress of the drawing process

With these methods described, let us now look at the various issues raised by the code for the `paintComponent` method of the class `DisplayPanel`.

Drawing rectangles and ovals

The statement

```
g.fillRect(320, 335, 100, 75);
```

draws a solid rectangle where the coordinates of the upper-left corner of the rectangle are $(320, 335)$. In this case these coordinates are measured from the upper-left corner of the window frame's display area. To see what we mean, replace the above statement in the `paintComponent` method by the statement

```
g.fillRect(0, 0, 100, 75);
```

and you will see that the top part of the rectangle fits snugly into the top left corner of the window's display area.

Notice that the statements

```
g.fillOval(50, 200, 150, 200);
g.drawRect(50, 200, 150, 200);
```

take the same values for the arguments of their respective messages. The result is that we get a solid oval (ellipse) together with its bounding rectangle.

Setting the colour

Consider the argument of the `setColor` message in the statement

```
g.setColor(new Color(44, 128, 95));
```

The argument needs to be an object of the class `Color`. Previously we have selected a colour by making use of the constants associated with the `Color` class. This time however, we have used a constructor of the `Color` class to create a new `Color` object (in effect to create a new colour). The constructor method used here is

```
Color (int r, int g, int b)
```

where `r`, `g` and `b` are integers in the range 0 to 255 denoting respectively the redness, greenness and blueness of the colour being created. With this constructor, colours of virtually any hue can be created. Experiment with this for yourself. Have fun!

Setting the font

The statement

```
Font f = new Font("SansSerif", Font.BOLD, 25);
```

declares a variable `f` to be of type `Font` and assigns to this variable an object of the class `Font` denoting a particular font style. The constructor method used here is

```
Font (String name, int style, int size)
```

where

- `name` is a string giving the name of the font style, e.g. `"SansSerif"` or `"Monospaced"`;
- `style` is an integer in the range 0 to 3, where 0 denotes 'plain' style, 1 denotes 'bold' style, 2 denotes 'italic' style and 3 denotes 'bold and italic' style. Fortunately we don't need to remember these numbers because the class `Font` has constants `PLAIN`, `BOLD` and `ITALIC` to denote respectively the numbers 0, 1 and 2. Hence to select bold style, for example, we simply send the argument `Font.BOLD`.
- `size` is the font size, e.g. 25.

Displaying an image

The final graphical object displayed by the `paintComponent` method of the class `DisplayPanel` is the image of *Java Jim*. To display an image in a frame we first need to convert the image into an appropriate format, and to do this we make use of an object of the class `Toolkit` (recall we met this class earlier in this section when we wanted to know the dimensions of the screen). We create a default toolkit object by the declaration:

```
Toolkit tk = Toolkit.getDefaultToolkit();
```

With the toolkit object `tk` created, we can now convert our image into a format that can be drawn into the window's graphics component. We do this by invoking the instance method `getImage` of the class `Toolkit`. This method returns an object of the class `Image` (this class is also found in the *java.awt* package). So we can refer to it later, we declare a variable `im` of the class `Image` to store the converted image:

```
Image im = tk.getImage("JavaJim.gif");
```

The argument of the `getImage` method is a string giving the path name of the image file we want to convert (this image file must be either *gif* or *jpeg*). As the image of *Java Jim* is a file located in the same folder as the `DisplayPanel` class, this path name reduces to just the name of the file.

Now that we have the converted image object `im`, we can add it to the graphics component of the window frame by the statement

```
g.drawImage(im, 150, 40, this);
```

The second and third arguments supplied with the message `drawImage` give the x- and y-coordinates of the upper-left corner of the image.

The fourth argument is the object that needs to be informed of the progress in displaying the image. The `this` used here refers (as always) to the object that is invoking the `paintComponent` method. In our case it is the panel object itself. This final argument is needed particularly when we are displaying images obtained directly over the internet. In such situations, delays in transmission may occur and the panel needs to be kept informed of progress.

Adding a panel to a frame

The class `DisplayPanel` has extended the class `JPanel` by adding the code needed to paint the graphical objects we require. To display our graphical objects in the window frame we now have to:

- create an object of the `DisplayPanel` class;
- add that object to the window frame.

The content pane

Each window frame comes with a special component known as a *content pane*. In the class `DisplayFrame` this pane is extracted by the statement:

```
Container c = getContentPane();
```

To display our graphical objects we first create a panel object of the class `DisplayPanel`

```
DisplayPanel dp = new DisplayPanel();
```

and then add this panel object to the content pane:

```
c.add(dp);
```

Creating the window frame

All that remains now is to create and open the window frame itself. This is precisely the role of the `main` method in the `Main` class.

Whew! There are certainly a lot of new ideas in this graphics example. Here are a couple of interesting problems to challenge you and enable you to further explore the ideas for yourself.

PROBLEM 4: displaying Donald

Open the folder *Donald Demo* and run the class `Main`.

The files *DonaldFrame.java* and *DonaldPanel.java* are empty. They have been compiled and then their contents deleted but the compiled *.class* files remain in the folder.

Try to construct classes `DonaldFrame` and `DonaldPanel` so that when these classes are compiled and the `Main` class run, a window opens similar to the one opened in the above demonstration. You will find the image file *Donald.gif* in the *Donald Demo* folder.

Don't be concerned if the widow that opens when the `Main` class is run with your *.java* files does not look exactly the same as the demonstration. It will be a lucky guess if you get the colours of the border of the image of Donald to be the same as ours. Concentrate on experimenting and exploring the effect of different `paintComponent` methods.

For help with this problem see Hints.

□

PROBLEM 5: creating patterns with ovals

Open the folder *Oval Pattern Demo* and run the class `Main`. The *OvalFrame.java* and *OvalPanel.java* files are empty. They have been compiled and then their contents deleted but the compiled *.class* files remain in the folder.

Try to construct classes `OvalFrame` and `OvalPanel` so that when these classes are compiled and the `Main` class run, a window opens similar to the one opened in the above demonstration.

The pattern shown in the demonstration was constructed by drawing ovals. For help with this problem see Hints.

□

Dimensions of the display area

As we have remarked several times, the dimensions of the display area of a window are less than those of the window itself because of the border that surrounds the window. We can now determine the actual dimensions of the display area.

PROBLEM 6: getting the display area's size

Open the folder *Blank Window* containing the classes `BlankFrame` and `Main`. We saw in Problem 1 that when the `Main` class is run a window 400 pixels wide and 300 pixels high is opened. Replace the code for the `Main` class in that folder by the following code:

```
import java.awt.*;
public class Main {

    public static void main (String [ ] args) {
        BlankFrame blankWin = new BlankFrame();
        blankWin.setVisible(true);
        Container c = blankWin.getContentPane();
        Dimension d = c.getSize();
        System.out.println("width is "+d.width);
        System.out.println("height is "+d.height);
    }
}
```

Compile and run this `Main` class. The width and height of the display area of the window frame is printed in the Output window.

□

Discussion

Notice that the dimensions of a window can only be extracted once the window has been set visible. The dimensions of the display area of a window frame are given by the dimensions of the content pane associated with that window. First we get the content pane:

```
Container c = blankWin.getContentPane();
```

Then we extract the dimensions of this pane by sending it the `getSize()` message:

```
Dimension d = c.getSize();
```

The method `getSize` returns an object of type `Dimension`. All we need to know about such an object is that it has public instance variables `width` and `height` whose values we extract to get the size of the pane:

```
System.out.println("width is "+d.width);
System.out.println("height is "+d.height);
```

When we executed the above `Main` class on a computer running Windows95 the following was printed in the Output window:

```
width is 392
height is 268
```

That is, the left and right borders were together 8 pixels wide, while the top and bottom borders were together 32 pixels wide. Executing the code on a computer running Windows98 gave the width of the display area as 390 pixels and its height as 266 pixels. You may well get different values on your computer.

Summary

Here is a summary of the Swing and AWT classes we met in this section.

The class `JFrame` and its instance methods:

- `setTitle (String s)`
- `setBounds (int x, int y, int w, int h)`
- `setVisible (boolean b)`
- `getContentPane()`

The class `JPanel` and its instance methods:

- `setBackground (Color c)`
- `paintComponent (Graphics g)`

The class `Graphics` **and its instance methods:**

- `setColor (Color c)`
- `fillRect (int x, int y, int w, int h)`
- `drawRect (int x, int y, int w, int h)`
- `fillOval (int x, int y, int w, int h)`
- `drawOval (int x, int y, int w, int h)`
- `setFont (Font font)`
- `drawString (String s, int x, int y)`
- `drawImage (Image im, int x, int y, ImageObserver ob)`

The class `Color` **and its constructor method**

- `Color (int r, int g, int b)`

and its class constants `red`, `blue`, etc.

The class `Toolkit` **and its class method**

- `getDefaultToolkit()`

and its instance methods:

- `getScreenSize()`
- `getImage (String s)`

The class `Font` **and its constructor method**

- `Font (String name, int style, int size)`

and its class constants `PLAIN`, `BOLD` and `ITALIC`.

The class `Container` **and its instance methods:**

- `getSize()`
- `add(Component p)`

The class `Dimension` **and its public instance variables** `width` **and** `height`**.**

The class `Image`**.**

9.2 Anonymous inner classes

Now that we know how to display a variety of graphical objects within a window frame, the next thing we would like to do is listen for and react to various events such as clicking the mouse or pressing a key on the keyboard. This will enable us to interact directly with the window and its graphical components.

The approach to event handling taken in *Java Genesis* is based on a special Java construct known as an *anonymous inner class*. In this section we introduce this concept through a simple example.

Consider the code for the class SumRounded:

```
import genesis.*;

public class SumRounded {

    public static void main (String [ ] args) {
        PlanarPoint [ ] p = new PlanarPoint [3];
        p[0] = new PlanarPoint(2.2, 1.3);
        p[1] = new PlanarPoint(0.7, 0.4);
        p[2] = new PlanarPoint(1.9, 2.1);
        PlanarPoint sum = new PlanarPoint(0, 0);
        for (int i=0; i<3; i++)
            sum = sum.add(p[i].rounded());
        System.out.println(sum);
    }
}
```

When executed, this code invokes the add and rounded methods of the class PlanarPoint (see Section 7.1) to:

- round each of the three planar points $(2.2, 1.3)$, $(0.7, 0.4)$ and $(1.9, 2.1)$ to the nearest grid position (i.e. the nearest point with both coordinates a whole number);
- add these rounded points.;
- print out the resulting sum.

The class SumRounded is in the folder *Sum Rounded.* If you run this class you will get the output $(5.0, 3.0)$, namely,

$$(2.0, 1.0) + (1.0, 0.0) + (2.0, 2.0).$$

Now suppose that for the final point $(1.9, 2.1)$ in the code above we want instead to round using the rule whereby we simply truncate each number to the corresponding whole number. That is, we want (1.9, 2.1) to be rounded to the point (1.0, 2.0).

Using a defined subclass

One way to do this would be to construct a subclass FunnyPlanarPoint of PlanarPoint that redefines the rounded method:

```
import genesis.*;

public class FunnyPlanarPoint extends PlanarPoint {

    public FunnyPlanarPoint (double a, double b) {
        super(a, b);
    }

    public PlanarPoint rounded ( ) {
        return new PlanarPoint((int)getX(), (int)getY());
    }
}
```

The class SumRounded is now modified to give the class FunnySumRounded:

```
import genesis.*;

public class FunnySumRounded {

    public static void main (String [ ] args) {
        PlanarPoint [ ] p = new PlanarPoint [3];
        p[0] = new PlanarPoint(2.2, 1.3);
        p[1] = new PlanarPoint(0.7, 0.4);
        p[2] = new FunnyPlanarPoint(1.9, 2.1);
        PlanarPoint sum = new PlanarPoint(0, 0);
        for (int i=0; i<3; i++)
            sum = sum.add(p[i].rounded());
        System.out.println(sum);
    }
}
```

This time the final point (1.9, 2.1) is declared to be an object of the subclass FunnyPlanarPoint, and consequently the redefined rounded method is invoked by the expression

```
p[i].rounded()
```

when `i` takes the value 2.

The class FunnySumRounded is in the folder *Funny Sum Rounded.* If you run this class you will get the output (4.0, 3.0).

The trouble here is that we had to go to all the effort of defining the subclass `FunnyPlanarPoint` to be applied just once!

Using an anonymous inner class

The anonymous inner class construct is designed to deal with just this situation. It enables us to effectively create a subclass at the point it is needed. The subclass does not need to be created in advance and, as we shall see, it does not even need to be given a name. The anonymous inner class construct is particularly useful when we want to create just one instance (object) of a subclass.

Here is the code for a class AnonSumRounded that uses the anonymous inner class construct to achieve the same outcome as the class FunnySumRounded:

```
import genesis.*;

public class AnonSumRounded {

    public static void main (String [ ] args) {
        PlanarPoint [ ] p = new PlanarPoint [3];
        p[0] = new PlanarPoint(2.2, 1.3);
        p[1] = new PlanarPoint(0.7, 0.4);
        p[2] = new PlanarPoint(1.9, 2.1) {
            public PlanarPoint rounded ( ) {
              return new PlanarPoint((int)getX(),(int)getY());
            }
        };
        PlanarPoint sum = new PlanarPoint(0, 0);
        for (int i=0; i<3; i++)
            sum = sum.add(p[i].rounded());
        System.out.println(sum);
    }
}
```

The class AnonSumRounded is in the folder *Anon Sum Rounded.* If you run this class you will again get the output (4.0, 3.0).

Discussion

Let's look closely at the anonymous inner class construct in this code:

```
new PlanarPoint(1.9, 2.1) {
    public PlanarPoint rounded ( ) {
        return new PlanarPoint((int)getX(), (int)getY());
    }
};
```

We start by declaring a new planar point object using a constructor method of the class `PlanarPoint` but then append in braces the required redefinition of the `rounded` method. As a consequence, the new object created is not of the class `PlanarPoint` but of a subclass of `PlanarPoint` in which the `rounded` method has been redefined as given.

What we have done with this construct is effectively create a subclass of the class `PlanarPoint`. This creation has taken place within the `AnonSumRounded` class (hence it is called an *inner* class construction) and the subclass of the class `PlanarPoint` so constructed remains unnamed (hence it is called an *anonymous* inner class).

The end result is the same as if we had created an explicit subclass as we did for the `FunnySumRounded` class. As before, the redefined `rounded` method is invoked by the expression

```
p[i].rounded()
```

when `i` takes the value 2.

Of course, the anonymous inner class construction is only worthwhile if, as in the case above, we want to declare a single instance of the resulting subclass. If we had wanted to have several planar points to which the redefined `rounded` method was to apply, then it would have been better to define and use the explicit subclass `FunnyPlanarPoint`.

9.3 Introducing event handling

In the following sections we will discover, through looking at some typical examples, how Java handles events such as pressing a mouse button or hitting a key on the keyboard. We will see that the anonymous inner class construct introduced in the last section is particularly useful when we come to write code that can respond to such events.

The basic idea is that we first associate *event listeners* with a graphical component. The listener responsible is then informed whenever specific events occur within the graphical component. As a consequence, the listener is able to instigate appropriate actions in response to the event.

An analogy

The Java mechanism for event handling may at first appear complicated. However, all event handling in Java follows a very well defined process. To help us understand this process, consider a simple analogy based on a house and some house-related events.

Many events occur within a house. In our analogy we shall consider just four:

- the telephone rings
- the fire alarm sounds
- a mouse runs across the floor
- the washing machine completes its cycle

The first thing to observe is that these events can occur even if there is nothing to listen for them. The telephone can ring in an empty house; a empty house can burn down; mice just love it when there is no one at home; the washing machine can operate unattended.

To handle these events we need to add *listeners* to the house. For example, a person could be designated to listen for the telephone and the fire alarm, while a cat could have the responsibility to listen for the mouse. Perhaps nobody is listening for the washing machine. This illustrates the following ideas:

- listeners are needed if we want to be able to react to events;
- the one listener can listen for several events;
- each listener listens only for those events for which they have been given responsibility (the cat ignores the telephone; the person ignores the mouse);
- some events may have no designated listener.

When an event occurs, an appropriate message identifying the type of the event is sent to the listener responsible. So, for example, when a telephone rings the person listening knows immediately it's a telephone and not the fire alarm because the message they receive (i.e. the sound that reaches their ears) identifies the event. Clearly, it is important that the telephone and fire alarm events are not confused.

In addition, more detailed information about the event that has occurred is sent with the identifying message. For example, the message received (i.e. the sound heard) may identify the event as a ringing telephone and also identify which telephone in the case when the house has more than one. Similarly, the cat will receive the message 'mouse moved' but in addition will receive information about the current position of the mouse, its speed and direction, etc. This information will be needed if the cat is to react appropriately.

Taking an object-oriented approach, we can think of the name of the message sent by the event as identifying the type of the event, and the argument passed with the message as giving specific detailed information about the event.

When a message is received that a specific event has occurred, it is the responsibility of the listener to invoke some appropriate action. For example, if the telephone rings, the person picks up the receiver; if the fire alarm sounds, the person jumps out the window; if the mouse moves, the cat pounces. Taking again an object-oriented approach, when the listener receives a message that a specific event has occurred, the listener invokes the corresponding method.

Notice that it is up to the listener to decide what action to take in response to receiving a message that a particular event has occurred. Rather than answering a ringing telephone, the person can chose to ignore it; rather than jumping out the window when the fire alarm sounds, the person can instead grab the fire extinguisher or even completely ignore the peril and continue sleeping. If the cat has just had a large dinner it may decide to ignore the mouse. What happens will be at the discretion of the listener and will be determined by the method invoked by the listener in response to the message received.

So what does this analogy tell us about how events are handled in Java? Each graphical component has events associated with it. Typical events would be that the window is closed, or a mouse button is pressed, or a key is pressed, or the mouse is moved. To respond to these events we need to add event listeners to the graphical component. Indeed, we may need to add several event listeners: one will listen for mouse-related events, one will listen for key-related events, and so on. When an event occurs, a message is sent to the listener responsible. (Of course, it is possible no listener has been added to the graphical component to listen for that particular event. In this case the event is just ignored.)

The message sent to the listener is such that

- the message name identifies the type of event that has occurred;
- the message argument gives specific information about the event.

In all cases, the argument sent with the message will be a specially constructed event object whose instance variables capture relevant details about the event. When the listener object receives the message, it invokes its corresponding method making use, if required, of the information about the event passed as the argument to the message. As a consequence some appropriate action will be undertaken.

One final observation. Event handling is non-sequential in that events can occur in any order. Indeed, one event may occur several times while another event may not occur at all. Generally, the order in which the events occur is unpredictable. Consequently our programs must be ready to invoke event handlers as the need arises.

Let us now look at some specific examples.

9.4 Window events

Consider the problem of terminating the underlying Java program when we close a window frame. In the examples we considered in Section 9.1, closing the window frames in the usual way by clicking with the mouse on the 'X' in the window's upper-right corner left the underlying Java program still running. To terminate the program as a consequence of closing a window we need to add a *window listener* to our window frame.

Termination on closing a window

Here is the code for a class `TerminatorFrame`, together with an associated `Main` class, which when run opens a blank window that when closed in the usual way terminates the underlying program:

```
import javax.swing.*;
import java.awt.event.*;

public class TerminatorFrame extends JFrame {

    /* Closing the window terminates the Java program. */

    // constructor
    public TerminatorFrame ( ) {
        setTitle("A Blank Window");
        setBounds(100, 50, 400, 300);
        WindowAdapter winLisnr = new WindowAdapter() {
            public void windowClosing(WindowEvent e) {
                System.exit(0);
            }
        };
        addWindowListener(winLisnr);
    }
}
```

```
public class Main {

    public static void main (String [ ] args) {
        TerminatorFrame termWin = new TerminatorFrame();
        termWin.setVisible(true);
    }
}
```

The code for the above classes is in the folder *Terminator Window.* Open this folder and run the `Main` class. Notice that the application can be terminated by clicking with the mouse on the 'X' in the window's upper-right corner.

Discussion

The code for the `TerminatorFrame` class is like the code for the `BlankFrame` class we met in Section 9.1 except for the extra import statement

```
import java.awt.event.*;
```

at the beginning of the class, and the following additional statements in the constructor method which we will consider in detail:

```
WindowAdapter winLisnr = new WindowAdapter() {
    public void windowClosing(WindowEvent e) {
        System.exit(0);
    }
};
addWindowListener(winLisnr);
```

Adding a window listener

The last statement, namely,

```
addWindowListener(winLisnr);
```

is a message sent to the window frame object being constructed. (In our case, the window frame object is assigned to the variable `termWin` when the `Main` class is run.) The message's argument `winLisnr` is an object of an anonymous subclass of the class `WindowAdapter` in which the method `windowClosing` has been redefined. (The `WindowAdapter` class will be discussed in detail shortly.)

When the window frame receives the `addWindowListener(winLisnr)` message, it invokes its `addWindowListener` method inherited from the `JFrame` class. As a direct consequence of invoking this method, the object `winLisnr` becomes a listener for window events and is informed when any one of seven distinct window events associated with the window frame occurs. What happens is that when one of these window events occurs, an appropriate message is sent to the listener object `winLisnr`.

The window events

The seven window events, and the corresponding message sent to the window listener object when the event occurs, are as follows:

- the window has been opened;

  message sent to window listener: `windowOpened(evt)`
- an attempt has been made to close the window (e.g. by clicking with the mouse on the 'X' in the window's upper-right corner);

  message sent to window listener: `windowClosing(evt)`
- the window has been closed;

  message sent to window listener: `windowClosed(evt)`
- the window has been iconified, i.e. minimized as an icon;

  message sent to window listener: `windowIconified(evt)`
- the window has been de-iconified, i.e. expanded from its icon;

  message sent to window listener: `windowDeiconified(evt)`
- the window has been activated;

  message sent to window listener: `windowActivated(evt)`
- the window has been de-activated;

  message sent to window listener: `windowDeactivated(evt)`

In all cases, the argument `evt` passed with the message is an object of the class `WindowEvent`. The details are not important here; suffice it to say that the listener can interrogate the object `evt` if further information about the event is required. For example, information about which window passed the message can be extracted from the object `evt`. This information may be useful when a listener object has the task of listening for window events from several windows.

Creating the window listener

Let us now turn our attention to the listener object `winLisnr` defined by:

```
WindowAdapter winLisnr = new WindowAdapter() {
    public void windowClosing(WindowEvent e) {
        System.exit(0);
    }
};
```

As any one of the above seven window events can occur in the window frame, then any of the above seven associated messages can be sent to the listener object `winLisnr`. Consequently, it is essential that `winLisnr`'s class have seven instance methods that can be invoked in response to these messages. By declaring `winLisnr` to be an object of an (anonymous inner) subclass of the class `WindowAdapter` this is guaranteed, as the class `WindowAdapter` does indeed implement seven appropriate instance methods.

The `WindowAdapter` class

The class `WindowAdapter` is in the *java.awt.event* package. (This package contains all the event handling Java classes. When creating applications that handle events we will need to import the *java.awt* and *java.awt.event* packages.) `WindowAdapter` is an abstract class that has no instance or class variables and consists of only seven instance methods, namely

```
public void windowOpened (WindowEvent e) {
    // invoked when a window has been opened
}

public void windowClosing (WindowEvent e) {
    // invoked when the 'X' in the upper-right
    // corner of the window is selected
}

public void windowClosed (WindowEvent e) {
    // invoked when a window has been closed
}

public void windowIconified (WindowEvent e) {
    // invoked when a window is iconified
}

public void windowDeiconified (WindowEvent e) {
    // invoked when a window is de-iconified
}

public void windowActivated (WindowEvent e) {
    // invoked when a window is activated
}

public void windowDeactivated (WindowEvent e) {
    // invoked when a window is de-activated
}
```

As can be seen from the code above, none of the seven methods in the class `WindowAdapter` actually does anything. Hence the default is that no further actions are undertaken as a consequence of the corresponding window event occurring. By constructing a subclass of the class `WindowAdapter` we are able to redefine any of these methods so that some specific action actually happens when the corresponding window event occurs.

This is precisely what we did in the class `TerminatorFrame` where an anonymous subclass of `WindowAdapter` was constructed to redefine the method `windowClosing`. When this method is invoked (by clicking with the mouse on the 'X' in the window's upper-right corner) the statement `System.exit(0)` is executed. As a consequence, the active Java application terminates. That is, not only does the window close, but the Java application itself ends. This is because sending the message `exit(0)` to the class `System` will always immediately terminate execution of the current Java program.

One final observation. Each method of the class `WindowAdapter` has as a parameter an object of the class `WindowEvent`. As explained earlier, the object of the class `WindowEvent` passed as the argument contains further information about the event, such as the window in which the event occurred. In the examples in this section there is no need to be concerned about the nature of this method parameter as it is not referred to directly in our redefined methods' code.

PROBLEM 7: detecting the window-iconified event

Construct a class `IconifiedFrame` which modifies the class `TerminatorFrame` so that every time the window frame is reduced to an icon the message 'Window iconified!' is printed in the Output window. The application still terminates when the window is closed in the usual way.

For help with this problem see Hints.

□

The class `ExitFrame`

Because we almost always want the running application to terminate when we close our window frames, we have created a class `ExitFrame` and placed it in the *genesis* package. Its code is given at the top of the next page.

From now on, every time we create a window frame application we will import the *genesis* package and extend the class `ExitFrame` rather than the class `JFrame` itself. The underlying application will then terminate when any such open window is closed by clicking with the mouse on the 'X' in the window's upper-right corner.

```
package genesis;

import javax.swing.*;
import java.awt.*;
import java.awt.event.*;

public class ExitFrame extends JFrame {

    /*
    Creates a window which when closed
    terminates the underlying Java program.
    */

    public ExitFrame ( ) {
        // set the icon for the window
        Toolkit tk = Toolkit.getDefaultToolkit();
        Image im = tk.getImage
                ("c:\\genesis\\packages\\genesis\\jim.gif");
        setIconImage(im);

        // add listener to respond to the window closing
        addWindowListener(new WindowAdapter ( ) {
            public void windowClosing(WindowEvent e) {
                System.exit(0);
            }
        });
    }
}
```

Notice that in the class `ExitFrame` the window listener has been created as an object of an (anonymous inner) subclass of `WindowAdapter` and added to the window frame all in the one statement:

```
addWindowListener(new WindowAdapter ( ) {
    public void windowClosing(WindowEvent e) {
        System.exit(0);
    }
});
```

From now on this will be the usual way we will do it.

[*An aside*: The class `ExitFrame` uses a `Toolkit` object to set the icon associated with the window frame. Notice the '\\' used when defining the path for the image *jim.gif* to be used as the icon. The path needs to be supplied as a string argument to the `getImage` message, but the backslash '\' character by itself has a special meaning within a string. To overcome this, two backslashes within a string are interpreted as a single backslash. *End aside*]

PROBLEM 8: using the `ExitFrame` class

Open the folder *Display Window* (see Problem 3) and modify the `DisplayFrame` class by replacing the heading of the class by:

```
import genesis.*;
import java.awt.*;

public class DisplayFrame extends ExitFrame {
```

Recompile and run the application. You will notice that when the window is closed in the usual way the underlying application terminates.

□

9.5 Mouse events

Consider the problem of drawing a square in a window so that whenever the mouse is positioned in the window and the (left) mouse button pressed, the square toggles between solid and hollow. Here is the code for classes `ToggleSquareFrame` and `ToggleSquarePanel` together with an associated `Main` class which when run implements this application:

```
import genesis.*;
import java.awt.*;

public class ToggleSquareFrame extends ExitFrame {

    // constructor
    public ToggleSquareFrame ( ) {
        setTitle("Toggle the Square");
        setBounds(100, 50, 400, 400);
        Container c = getContentPane();
        ToggleSquarePanel p = new ToggleSquarePanel();
        c.add(p);
    }
}
```

```
import javax.swing.*;
import java.awt.*;
import java.awt.event.*;

public class ToggleSquarePanel extends JPanel {
    /*
    Paints a square which is toggled between hollow
    and solid when the mouse button is pressed.
    */

    // instance variables
    private boolean filled = true;

    // constructor
    public ToggleSquarePanel ( ) {
        setBackground(Color.white);
        MouseAdapter mouseLisnr = new MouseAdapter() {
            public void mousePressed(MouseEvent evt) {
                filled = !filled;
                repaint();
            }
        };
        addMouseListener(mouseLisnr);
    }

    public void paintComponent (Graphics g) {
        // paint square in the window
        super.paintComponent(g);
        g.setColor (Color.red);
        if (filled) g.fillRect(150, 150, 100, 100);
        else g.drawRect(150, 150, 100, 100);
    }
}
```

```
public class Main {

    public static void main (String [ ] args) {
        ToggleSquareFrame togWin = new ToggleSquareFrame();
        togWin.setVisible(true);
    }
}
```

PROBLEM 9: toggling the square

The code for the above classes is in the folder *Toggle Square*. Open this folder and run the `Main` class. Move the mouse so it is positioned in the window and observe what happens when the (left) mouse button is pressed.

Modify the code for the class `ToggleSquarePanel` so that when the mouse button is pressed in the window the square toggles between solid red and solid blue.

Use your imagination to construct interesting effects when the mouse button is pressed. For example, the size of the square could toggle between large and small, or with every mouse click the square could be drawn in a new random position, or the shape could toggle between square and circle.

For help with this problem see Hints.

□

Discussion

The classes `ToggleSquareFrame` and `Main` have the same structure as the applications we met earlier in this chapter. `ToggleSquareFrame` extends the `ExitFrame` class (which, you will recall from Section 9.4, extends the `JFrame` class by adding a window listener so that the underlying application is terminated when the window is closed). The class `ToggleSquareFrame` itself instantiates the panel object in which the graphical objects are painted and adds this panel to the frame's content pane. The `Main` class contains the `main` method and is responsible for instantiating the window frame object and opening it.

Adding a mouse listener

The code of interest to us in this section is in the `ToggleSquarePanel` class. Consider the statements

```
MouseAdapter mouseLisnr = new MouseAdapter() {
    public void mousePressed(MouseEvent evt) {
        filled = !filled;
        repaint();
    }
};
addMouseListener(mouseLisnr);
```

in the constructor method of the class `ToggleSquarePanel`. With the experience of window events that we gained in Section 9.4, we can probably make some intuitive guesses as to what is going on here.

Consider first the statement:

```
addMouseListener(mouseLisnr);
```

It is a message sent to the panel object. The message argument `mouseLisnr` is an object of an anonymous subclass of the class `MouseAdapter` in which the method `mousePressed` has been redefined.

As a direct consequence of sending this message, the object `mouseLisnr` becomes a listener for mouse events and is informed when any one of five distinct mouse events associated with the window occur. What happens is that when one of these mouse events occurs, an appropriate message is sent to the listener object `mouseLisnr`.

The mouse events

The five mouse events, and the corresponding message sent to the mouse listener object when the event occurs, are as follows:

- the mouse button has been pressed;

  message sent to mouse listener: `mousePressed(evt)`
- the mouse button has been released;

  message sent to mouse listener: `mouseReleased(evt)`
- the mouse has entered the window;

  message sent to mouse listener: `mouseEntered(evt)`
- the mouse has exited the window;

  message sent to mouse listener: `mouseExited(evt)`
- the mouse button has been pressed and released without being moved;

  message sent to mouse listener: `mouseClicked(evt)`

In all cases, the argument `evt` passed with the message is an object of the class `MouseEvent`. As we shall see in Problem 10 below, the mouse listener can interrogate the object `evt` if further information about the mouse event is required. For example, information about the position of the mouse when the event occurred can be extracted from the object `evt`. This information is often useful when deciding on the action to take in response to the event.

Let us now turn our attention to the mouse listener object `mouseLisnr` defined by

```
MouseAdapter mouseLisnr = new MouseAdapter() {
    public void mousePressed(MouseEvent evt) {
        filled = !filled;
        repaint();
    }
};
```

The MouseAdapter class

The class MouseAdapter is an abstract class in the *java.awt.event* package that has no instance or class variables and implements five instance methods corresponding to the five messages that a mouse listener can receive. To be specific, these methods are:

```
public void mousePressed (MouseEvent e) {
    // invoked when the mouse button has been pressed
}

public void mouseReleased (MouseEvent e) {
    // invoked when the mouse button has been released
}

public void mouseEntered (MouseEvent e) {
    // invoked when the mouse enters the window
}

public void mouseExited (MouseEvent e) {
    // invoked when the mouse exits the window
}

public void mouseClicked (MouseEvent e) {
    // invoked when the mouse button is pressed
    // and released without being moved
}
```

Just as for the class WindowAdapter we met earlier in this section, none of the five methods in the class MouseAdapter actually do anything. Hence the default is that no further actions are undertaken as a consequence of the corresponding mouse event occurring. By constructing a subclass of the class MouseAdapter we are able to redefine any of these methods so that some specific action actually happens when the corresponding mouse event occurs.

This is precisely what we did in the class ToggleSquarePanel where an anonymous subclass of MouseAdapter was constructed to redefine the mousePressed method. When this method is invoked (by pressing the mouse button when the mouse is positioned in the window) the statements

```
filled = !filled;
repaint();
```

are executed. The first thing that happens is that the Boolean instance variable filled has its value negated (if *true* it becomes *false*, if *false* it becomes *true*). By itself, however, this would not result in any change to the square.

The statement

```
repaint();
```

is then executed and this affects the change.

The `repaint` method

The `repaint` message is sent to the panel. When it receives this message the display area of the window frame is redrawn. What actually happens is that everything is removed from the display area and it is then redrawn afresh by invoking the panel's `paintComponent` method. As the `paintComponent` method makes use of the value of `filled` when drawing the square (as you can confirm by looking at the code), the change in the value of `filled` results in the appearance of the square changing between solid and hollow.

Extracting the position of the mouse

Each method of the class `MouseAdapter` has as a parameter an object of the class `MouseEvent`. As indicated earlier, the object of the `MouseEvent` class passed as the argument when the method is invoked contains further information about the event, such as the position of the mouse when the event occurs. This information can be extracted and used as illustrated in the example that follows.

Consider the code for classes `DetectMouseFrame` and `DetectMousePanel`, together with an associated `Main` class:

```
import genesis.*;
import java.awt.*;

public class DetectMouseFrame extends ExitFrame {

    // constructor
    public DetectMouseFrame ( ) {
        setTitle("Detect the Mouse");
        setBounds(50, 100, 400, 400);
        Container c = getContentPane();
        DetectMousePanel p = new DetectMousePanel();
        c.add(p);
    }
}
```

```
import javax.swing.*;
import java.awt.*;
import java.awt.event.*;

public class DetectMousePanel extends JPanel {
    /*
    Paints a circle at the mouse's position
    when the mouse button is pressed.
    */

    // instance variables
    private int xCentre = 200, yCentre = 200;

    // constructor
    public DetectMousePanel ( ) {
        setBackground(Color.white);
        addMouseListener(new MouseAdapter() {
            public void mousePressed(MouseEvent evt) {
                xCentre = evt.getX();
                yCentre = evt.getY();
                repaint();
            }
        });
    }

    public void paintComponent (Graphics g) {
        // draw circle on the board
        super.paintComponent(g);
        g.setColor(Color.red);
        g.fillOval(xCentre-25, yCentre-25, 50, 50);
    }
}
```

```
public class Main {

    public static void main (String [] args) {
        DetectMouseFrame detectWin = new DetectMouseFrame();
        detectWin.setVisible(true);
    }
}
```

When the `Main` class is run a window opens with a circle drawn at the window's centre. If the mouse is positioned in the window, whenever the (left) mouse button is pressed the circle moves so that its centre is now at the new position of the mouse.

PROBLEM 10: detecting the mouse position

The code for the above classes is in the folder *Detect Mouse*. Open this folder and run the `Main` class to confirm that the behaviour is as described above.

Modify the class `DetectMousePanel` so that when the mouse button is pressed

- if both the x- and y-coordinates of the mouse's position are less than 200 the circle is coloured blue;
- if both the x- and y-coordinates of the mouse's position are greater than 200 the circle is coloured green;
- otherwise the circle is coloured red.

For help with this problem see Hints.

□

Discussion

Notice particularly the assignment statements

```
xCentre = evt.getX();
yCentre = evt.getY();
```

in the code for the method `mousePressed` in the anonymouse inner class defining the mouse listener in the class `DetectMousePanel`. The messages `getX()` and `getY()` are sent to the `MouseEvent` object `evt`. As we have remarked before, the object `evt` exists only to convey information about the mouse event that has occurred (in this case, the event that the mouse button was pressed). In particular, the object `evt` contains information about the mouse's position when the button was pressed, and the instance methods `getX` and `getY` in the class `MouseEvent` extract this information by returning the x- and y-coordinates of that position respectively.

PROBLEM 11: displaying the mouse position

Open the folder *Mouse Position Demo* and run the `Main` class. When the mouse is positioned in the window and the button pressed, the current position of the mouse is displayed in the window.

In this folder the classes `MousePositionFrame` and `MousePositionPanel` have been compiled and the code in the *.java* files removed.

Construct classes `MousePositionFrame` and `MousePositionPanel` so that when the `Main` class is run with your classes the application exhibits the same behaviour as the demonstration.

For help with this problem see Hints.

□

So far we have made use of the mouse-pressed event and ignored the other four mouse events. The next problem rectifies this situation.

PROBLEM 12: exploring other mouse events

Once again open the folder *Toggle Square* (see Problem 9). Modify the class `ToggleSquarePanel` by replacing the name `mousePressed` within the anonymous inner class in the constructor method by:

- `mouseReleased`
- `mouseEntered`
- `mouseExited`
- `mouseClicked`

In each case recompile the class and run the `Main` class to discover how the modification has changed the behaviour of the application.

□

Discussion

In Problem 12:

- if we use `mouseReleased`: the square toggles whenever the mouse button is released while positioned in the window;
- if we use `mouseEntered`: the square toggles whenever the mouse is moved into the window from outside;
- if we use `mouseExited`: the square toggles whenever the mouse is moved from inside the window to outside;
- if we use `mouseClicked`: the square toggles whenever the mouse is pressed and released while positioned in the window; the mouse must not move after the button has been pushed and before it is released.

Here are a couple of problems that are both interesting and fun. They are not difficult but you may find them a bit of a challenge.

PROBLEM 13: placing small squares

Open the folder *Small Squares Demo* and run the `Main` class. Each time the mouse button is pressed in the window a small square is added to the window at the mouse's current position.

In this folder the classes `SmallSquaresFrame` and `SmallSquaresPanel` have been compiled and the code in the *.java* files removed.

Construct classes `SmallSquaresFrame` and `SmallSquaresPanel` so that when the `Main` class is run with your classes the application exhibits the same behaviour as the demonstration.

For help with this problem see Hints.

□

PROBLEM 14: Janet and Jim

Open the folder *Janet Jim Demo* and run the `Main` class. A window opens displaying an image of *Java Janet*. If the mouse is moved into the window the image displayed changes to *Java Jim*. If then the mouse exits the window, the window reverts to displaying the original image. The whole process can be repeated as often as required.

In this folder the classes `JanetJimFrame` and `JanetJimPanel` have been compiled and the code in the *.java* files removed.

Construct classes `JanetJimFrame` and `JanetJimPanel` so that when the `Main` class is run with your classes the application exhibits the same behaviour as the demonstration.

The images *JavaJanet.gif* and *JavaJim.gif* are in the folder *Janet Jim Demo*.

For help with this problem see Hints.

□

9.6 Mouse motion events

In addition to the five mouse events to which mouse listeners can respond, there are two other mouse-related events. These events are concerned with the movement of the mouse within a graphical component and occur when

- the mouse is moved (while no button is being held down);
- the mouse is dragged (moved while the (left) button is held down).

Java treats these two mouse events differently from the other mouse events. To listen and respond to these two events we need to add a mouse motion listener object.

As an illustration, consider the problem of displaying a circle which follows the mouse as the mouse is moved within the window. The code for classes `FollowMouseFrame` and `FollowMousePanel` and an associated `Main` class that implement this application is given below.

This code is very similar to the code for the classes `DetectMouseFrame` and `DetectMousePanel` that we met in Section 9.5. The only essential difference is that in the `FollowMousePanel` class we have added a mouse motion listener (rather than a mouse listener) and have redefined the `mouseMoved` method (rather than the `mousePressed` method) of that listener so as to move the circle to the mouse's position whenever the mouse is moved (rather than only when the mouse's button is pressed).

PROBLEM 15: following the mouse

The code below for the classes `FollowMouseFrame` and `FollowMousePanel` is in the folder *Follow Mouse.* Open this folder and run the `Main` class. Move the mouse in the window that opens and observe what happens.

Modify the code for the class `FollowMousePanel` by replacing the method name `mouseMoved` within the anonymous inner class in the constructor method by `mouseDragged`. Recompile the class and run the `Main` method.

```
import genesis.*;
import java.awt.*;

public class FollowMouseFrame extends ExitFrame {

    // instance variables
    private int xCentre = 200, yCentre = 200;

    // constructor
    public FollowMouseFrame ( ) {
        setTitle("Follow the Mouse");
        setBounds(50, 100, 400, 400);
        Container c = getContentPane();
        FollowMousePanel p = new FollowMousePanel();
        c.add(p);
    }
}
```

```
import javax.swing.*;
import java.awt.*;
import java.awt.event.*;

public class FollowMousePanel extends JPanel {
    /*
    Draws a circle that follows the mouse as it moves.
    */

    // instance variables
    private int xCentre = 200, yCentre = 200;

    // constructor
    public FollowMousePanel ( ) {
        setBackground(Color.white);
        MouseMotionAdapter motionLisnr =
                                new MouseMotionAdapter() {
            public void mouseMoved(MouseEvent evt) {
                xCentre = evt.getX();
                yCentre = evt.getY();
                repaint();
            }
        };
        addMouseMotionListener(motionLisnr);
    }

    public void paintComponent (Graphics g) {
        // draw circle on the board
        super.paintComponent(g);
        g.setColor(Color.red);
        g.fillOval(xCentre-25, yCentre-25, 50, 50);
    }
}
```

```
public class Main {

    public static void main (String [] args) {
        FollowMouseFrame followWin = new FollowMouseFrame();
        followWin.setVisible(true);
    }
}
```

Compare what happens when the mouse is moved with what happens when the mouse is dragged.

□

Discussion

The classes FollowMouseFrame and Main have the same structure as the applications we met earlier in this chapter so we will say no more about them and concentrate instead on the FollowMousePanel class.

Adding a mouse motion listener

Consider the statements

```
MouseMotionAdapter motionLisnr = new MouseMotionAdapter() {
    public void mouseMoved(MouseEvent evt) {
        xCentre = evt.getX();
        yCentre = evt.getY();
        repaint();
    }
};
addMouseMotionListener(motionLisnr);
```

in the constructor method of the class FollowMousePanel. The statement

```
addMouseMotionListener(motionLisnr);
```

is a message sent to the panel object itself. The message argument motionLisnr is an object of an anonymous subclass of the class MouseMotionAdapter in which the method mouseMoved has been redefined. As a consequence, the object motionLisnr becomes a listener for mouse motion events and is informed when either of the two distinct mouse motion events associated with the window occurs.

The mouse motion events

The two mouse motion events and the corresponding messages sent to the mouse motion listener when either event occurs are as follows:

- the mouse is moved while no button is being held down;

  message sent to mouse motion listener: mouseMoved(evt)
- the mouse is moved while the (left) button is being held down;

  message sent to mouse listener: mouseDragged(evt)

In both cases, the argument evt passed with the message is, just as for the other 5 mouse-related events, an object of the class MouseEvent. Hence we know, for example, information about the position of the mouse when the event occurred can be extracted from the object `evt`.

The mouse motion listener object `motionLisnr` is defined by:

```
MouseMotionAdapter motionLisnr = new MouseMotionAdapter() {
    public void mouseMoved(MouseEvent evt) {
        xCentre = evt.getX();
        yCentre = evt.getY();
        repaint();
    }
};
```

The `MouseMotionAdapter` class

The class `MouseMotionAdapter` is an abstract class in the *java.awt.event* package that has no instance or class variables and implements two instance methods corresponding to the two messages that a mouse motion listener can receive. To be specific, these methods are:

```
public void mouseMoved (MouseEvent e) {
    // invoked when the mouse is moved
}

public void mouseDragged (MouseEvent e) {
    // invoked when the mouse button is held
    // down and the mouse moved
}
```

Just as for the classes `WindowAdapter` and `MouseAdapter` we met earlier in this chapter, the methods in the class `MouseMotionAdapter` don't actually do anything. Hence the default is that no further actions are undertaken as a consequence of the corresponding mouse motion event occurring. By constructing a subclass of the class `MouseMotionAdapter` we are able to redefine any of these methods so that some specific action actually happens when the corresponding mouse motion event occurs.

This is precisely what we did in the class `FollowMousePanel` where an anonymous subclass of `MouseMotionAdapter` was constructed to redefine the method `mouseMoved`. When this method is invoked (by moving the mouse in the window) the statements

```
xCentre = evt.getX();
yCentre = evt.getY();
repaint();
```

are executed. These statements extract the current position of the mouse and then request that the window be redrawn (by sending the message `repaint()`).

The `paintComponent` method that is invoked as a consequence then draws the circle so that its centre is at the current position of the mouse. Hence the circle is redrawn whenever the mouse moves. As a result the circle seems to 'follow' the mouse.

Here are a couple of problems that use a mouse motion listener to handle mouse motion events.

PROBLEM 16: escaping the mouse

Open the folder *Escape Mouse Demo* and run the `Main` class. A window opens with a circle drawn at its centre. If the mouse moves too close to the circle, the circle moves to a random position in the window.

In this folder the classes `EscapeMouseFrame` and `EscapeMousePanel` have been compiled and the code in the *.java* files removed.

Construct classes `EscapeMouseFrame` and `EscapeMousePanel` so that when the `Main` class is run with your classes the application exhibits the same behaviour as the demonstration.

For help with this problem see Hints.

□

The next problem is not difficult but it is trickier than it looks.

PROBLEM 17: dynamically dimensioned oval

Open the folder *Dynamic Oval Demo* and run the `Main` class. A window opens displaying an oval at its centre. As the mouse moves in the window the oval is constantly redrawn so that the mouse's current position determines a corner of the oval's bounding rectangle. The oval is always drawn so that its centre is the centre of the window's display area.

In this folder the classes `DynamicOvalFrame` and `DynamicOvalPanel` have been compiled and the code in the *.java* files removed. Construct classes `DynamicOvalFrame` and `DynamicOvalPanel` so that when the `Main` class is run with your classes the application exhibits the same behaviour as the demonstration.

It will help if you recall that to draw an oval we need to know the coordinates of the upper-left corner of the oval's bounding rectangle and the width and height of that rectangle. If the mouse's position determines the upper-left corner, then it's not so bad. However, if the mouse's position determines one of the other corners (e.g. when the mouse is in the right or bottom half of the window) then we need to calculate the coordinates of the upper-left corner from the coordinates of the corner determined by the mouse.

Assume the window is 400 pixels wide and high and the display area is 392 pixels wide and 368 pixels high.

For further help with this problem see Hints.

□

9.7 Keyboard events

Consider the problem of drawing a square in a window so that whenever one of the arrow key on the keyboard is pressed, the square moves by 10 pixels in the direction indicated on the key (i.e. right, left, up or down). Here is the code for classes SteerSquareFrame and SteerSquarePanel together with an associated Main class that when run implements this application:

```
import genesis.*;
import java.awt.*;

public class SteerSquareFrame extends ExitFrame {

    // constructor
    public SteerSquareFrame ( ) {
        setTitle("Steer the Square");
        setBounds(100, 50, 400, 400);
        Container c = getContentPane();
        SteerSquarePanel p = new SteerSquarePanel();
        c.add(p);
    }
}
```

```
import javax.swing.*;
import java.awt.*;
import java.awt.event.*;

public class SteerSquarePanel extends JPanel {

    /* Steer a square with the arrow keys.*/

    // instance variables
    private int xCorner = 175, yCorner = 175;
```

```
    // constructor
    public SteerSquarePanel ( ) {
        setBackground(Color.white);
        KeyAdapter keyLisnr = new KeyAdapter() {
            public void keyPressed(KeyEvent evt) {
                moveSquare(evt);
            }
        };
        addKeyListener(keyLisnr);
    }

    public void paintComponent (Graphics g) {
        // draw square
        super.paintComponent(g);
        requestFocus();
        g.setColor(Color.red);
        g.fillRect(xCorner, yCorner, 50, 50);
    }

    public void moveSquare (KeyEvent e) {
        // move the square
        int keyCode = e.getKeyCode();
        switch (keyCode) {
            case KeyEvent.VK_RIGHT:
                    xCorner = xCorner + 10; break;
            case KeyEvent.VK_LEFT:
                    xCorner = xCorner - 10; break;
            case KeyEvent.VK_UP:
                    yCorner = yCorner - 10; break;
            case KeyEvent.VK_DOWN:
                    yCorner = yCorner + 10; break;
        }
        repaint();
    }
}
```

```
public class Main {

    public static void main (String [] args) {
        SteerSquareFrame steerWin = new SteerSquareFrame();
        steerWin.setVisible(true);
    }
}
```

PROBLEM 18: steering the square

The code for the above classes is in the folder *Steer Square*. Open this folder and run the `Main` class. Investigate how the arrow keys can be used to move the square about the window.

Modify the class `SteerSquarePanel` so that rather than the arrow keys, the keys K, J, I and M can be used instead to move the square right, left, up and down respectively. (The class `KeyEvent` has integer constants VK_A, VK_B, etc. to represent the keys A, B and so on.)

□

Discussion

The classes `SteerSquareFrame` and `Main` have the same structure as the applications we met earlier in this chapter so we will say no more about them and concentrate instead on the `SteerSquarePanel` class.

Adding a keyboard listener

Consider the statements

```
KeyAdapter keyLisnr = new KeyAdapter() {
    public void keyPressed(KeyEvent evt) {
        moveSquare(evt);
    }
};
addKeyListener(keyLisnr);
```

in the constructor method of the class `SteerSquarePanel`. The statement

```
addKeyListener(keyLisnr);
```

is a message sent to the panel object. The message argument `keyLisnr` is an object of an anonymous subclass of the class `KeyAdapter` in which the method `keyPressed` has been redefined. As a consequence, the object `keyLisnr` becomes a listener for keyboard events and is informed when any of the three distinct keyboard events associated with the window frame occurs.

The keyboard events

The three keyboard events and the corresponding message sent to the keyboard listener when the event occurs are as follows:

- a key on the keyboard is pressed;

  message sent to keyboard listener: `keyPressed(evt)`

- a key on the keyboard is released;

  message sent to mouse listener: `keyReleased(evt)`
- a character is returned from the keyboard;

  message sent to the keyboard listener: `keyTyped(evt)`

In each case, the argument `evt` passed with the message is an object of the class `KeyEvent`. For the first two messages, the argument `evt` captures information about the key that was pressed. For the last message, the argument `evt` captures information about the character that is returned from the keyboard. For example, if we press and release the 'A' key the lower-case character 'a' is returned by the keyboard; if we press the 'shift' key and the 'A' key together and then release both, the upper-case character 'A' is returned by the keyboard. We shall say no more about this event.

The keyboard listener object `keyLisnr` is defined by:

```
KeyAdapter keyLisnr = new KeyAdapter() {
    public void keyPressed(KeyEvent evt) {
        moveSquare(evt);
    }
};
```

The `KeyAdapter` class

The class `KeyAdapter` is an abstract class in the *java.awt.event* package that has no instance or class variables and implements three instance methods corresponding to the three messages that a keyboard listener can receive. To be specific, these methods are:

```
public void keyPresed (KeyEvent e) {
    // invoked when a key on the keyboard is pressed
}

public void keyReleased (KeyEvent e) {
    // invoked when a key on the keyboard is released
}

public void keyTyped (KeyEvent e) {
    // invoked when a character is
    // returned by the keyboard
}
```

Just as for the other adapter classes we met earlier, the methods in the class `KeyAdapter` don't actually do anything. By constructing a subclass of the class `KeyAdapter` we are able to redefine any of these methods so that some specific action actually happens when the corresponding mouse motion event occurs.

Keyboard codes

In the class SteerSquarePanel an anonymous subclass of KeyAdapter was constructed to redefine the method keyPressed. When this method is invoked (by pressing a key on the keyboard) the statement

```
moveSquare(evt);
```

is executed. That is, the message moveSquare(evt) is sent to the panel object, and hence the method moveSquare in SteerSquarePanel is invoked.

Consider the code for the method moveSquare:

```
public void moveSquare(KeyEvent e) {
    // move the square
    int keyCode = e.getKeyCode();
    switch (keyCode) {
        case KeyEvent.VK_RIGHT: xCorner = xCorner+10; break;
        case KeyEvent.VK_LEFT: xCorner = xCorner-10; break;
        case KeyEvent.VK_UP: yCorner = yCorner-10; break;
        case KeyEvent.VK_DOWN: yCorner = yCorner+10; break;
    }
    repaint();
}
```

When the message getKeyCode() is sent to an object of type KeyEvent, an integer identifying the key that has been pressed is returned. We can then use this information to decide on the appropriate action to take. The integer codes identifying each key on the keyboard are defined as class constants in the class KeyEvent. Hence we don't need to know the actual values of these integers. For example, the integer representing the up-arrow key is the constant VK_UP of the class KeyEvent and can be referred to by the expression KeyEvent.VK_UP. We shall not go into further details.

In the method moveSquare, we use a switch-statement to decide on the appropriate action to take depending upon which of the arrow keys has been pressed. For example, if the up-arrow key is pressed we decrease by 10 the value of the variable yCorner. As this variable represents the y-coordinate of the upper- left corner of the square in the window, when the window is redrawn the square is displayed 10 pixels higher in the window. The result of pressing the other arrow keys can be described similarly.

Requesting focus

In order for a panel to detect keystrokes it needs to be have the *focus*. Without having the focus a panel will not be able to react to any keystroke. This focus is not given to a panel automatically but must be requested explicitly.

This is done by including the statement

```
requestFocus();
```

in the code for the `paintComponent` method.

We complete this section with a problem you should find an interesting challenge.

PROBLEM 19: carpet snake

Open the folder *Carpet Snake Demo* and run the `Main` class. A window opens displaying part of a carpet snake. By pressing the arrow keys, the snake will move around the window.

In this folder the classes `CarpetSnakeFrame` and `CarpetSnakePanel` have been compiled and the code in the *.java* files removed.

Construct classes `CarpetSnakeFrame` and `CarpetSnakePanel` so that when the `Main` class is run with your classes the application exhibits the same behaviour as the demonstration.

For help with this problem see Hints.

□

Chapter 9 self-check

Can you

- open a window with a given size and at a given position on the screen?
- open a window centred on the screen?
- display and position in a window
  - rectangles, squares, ovals and circles?
  - strings?
  - an image?

Do you understand

- how to determine the dimensions of the display area of a window?
- how to create an anonymous inner class?
- how to add event listeners to a window frame?
- how to add a panel to a window's content pane?

What is the similarity, and what is the distinction, between

- window events?
- mouse events?
- mouse motion events?
- keyboard events?

Do you understand the role played by, and the arguments required, when invoking the instance methods

- `setTitle`
- `setBounds`
- `setVisible`
- `getContentPane`
- `add`

Do you understand the role played by, and the arguments required, when invoking the instance methods

- `setBackground`
- `paintComponent`
- `repaint`

Do you understand the role played by, and the arguments required, when invoking the instance methods

- `addWindowListener`
- `addMouseListener`
- `addMouseMotionListener`
- `addKeyListener`

Do you understand the role played by, and the arguments required, when invoking the instance methods

- `setColor`
- `fillRect`
- `drawRect`
- `fillOval`
- `drawOval`
- `setFont`

- `drawString`
- `drawImage`

Do you understand how to listen for and respond to

- window events such as attempting to close a window?
- mouse events such as pressing or releasing the (left) mouse button?
- mouse motion events such as moving or dragging the mouse?
- keyboard events such as pressing the arrow keys?

Do you understand the role played by and the distinction between

- the adapter classes `WindowAdapter`, `MouseAdapter`, `MouseMotionAdapter` and `KeyAdapter`?
- the event classes `WindowEvent`, `MouseEvent`, `MouseMotionEvent` and `KeyEvent`?

Graphical components 10

Prerequisites

Chapter 10 follows on closely from Chapter 9. In particular, you will need to know how to:

- instantiate and open a window frame;
- paint graphical objects onto a panel and how to add the panel to a window frame's content pane;
- add event listeners to windows and panels.

Overview

In Chapter 9 we saw how to paint shapes and figures on a panel and then add that panel to the content pane of a window frame. We also saw how to add event listeners to handle the various events associated with the window. In this chapter we look at how to add multiple panels to a window, and consider other graphical components, namely:

- action buttons
- text fields
- labels

These components enable us to create applications where the main interaction with the user is through a graphical interface.

As with chapter 9, the emphasis in this chapter is on exploration and experimentation. The approach is to study, emulate and modify working code in order to create new applications.

10.1 Multiple panels

A panel in Java plays a role similar to an artist's canvas in the real world. It is a component upon which graphical shapes and figures can be drawn before being displayed in a window frame. We look at how we can paint on multiple panels, position and size them, and then add them to a window.

Problems:

1 a window with two panels

2 local mouse position

10.2 Case study: toggle-neighbours puzzle

We make use of panels to construct a simple puzzle based on toggling squares. This puzzle illustrates the role of a mediator object in facilitating inter-object communication.

Problems:

3 the puzzle demonstrated

4 a 5 by 5 puzzle

5 the puzzle revisited

10.3 Action buttons

Action buttons enable a user to readily pass a specific message directly to an underlying application. We see how an action button can be created and how, by adding an associated action listener, the application can respond in some appropriate way to the button being pressed. A button is first added to a panel and the panel is then added to the window's content pane. We look at how the default layout managers arrange buttons within a panel and panels within a window pane.

Problems:

6 temperature conversion

7 a button to toggle a square

8 a GUI to toss a die

9 exploring the flow layout

10 comparing flow and border layouts

11 creating buttons and placing panels

12 selecting colours by button

13 Janet and Jim buttons

10.4 Text fields and labels

A text field is used to display textual information between the user and the application. We see how such fields can be created and applied. Labels enable us to display a short piece of text. We see how a label can be used to indicate the role of a component, as well as to distinguish one component from another.

Problems:

14 temperature conversion revisited

15 moving a circle to a given position

16 mixing colours

10.5 Interfaces

An interface is much like an abstract class. No instances of an interface can be instantiated but classes that implement an interface can be constructed and objects of these classes can be instantiated. In this section we look at how and why interfaces are used in Java, and observe that we have been using them already without necessarily realising it.

Problem:

17 implementing an interface

Learning outcomes

At the conclusion of Chapter 10 you will understand:

- how to position and size a panel in a window;
- how to arrange several panels within a window;
- how objects can communicate via a mediator;
- how to create GUIs that make use of action buttons, text fields and labels;
- how to associate an action listener with an action button;
- how to get and set text in a text field;
- the default flow layout used to position components in a panel;
- the default border layout used to position panels in a window;
- the role played by interfaces in Java, and how an interface can be implemented.

10.1 Multiple panels

In Chapter 9 we painted graphical shapes on one panel and then added that panel to a window's content pane. Although this is perfectly adequate in many cases, there are often situations where we want to first paint our graphical objects on separate panels, and then position the panels in different parts of the window for displaying.

As an analogy, think of a window on the screen as something like a wall in a room. We can create one entire fresco for the wall and, indeed, there are many famous examples of this. But more commonly, as we usually want to display several paintings, we first get the artists to paint on their own panel, and then separately size, position and hang the panels on the wall.

We can follow the same approach when designing our windows. We can paint on separate panels and when the figures are arranged on each panel to our satisfaction, size and position (i.e. 'hang') the panels in the window in order to display them.

There are several advantages to this. We can size the panels and position them anywhere in the window, just as we can arrange paintings on a wall. Effectively, the panels sub-divide the window into areas that can be dealt with as if they were separate sub-windows. Furthermore, we can add event listeners to the individual panels, enabling us to handle events within a panel rather than just within the window as a whole.

To illustrate this, consider the following example.

Example: a window with two panels

Here is the code for a class `SeekMousePanel` that extends the JPanel class:

```
import javax.swing.*;
import java.awt.*;
import java.awt.event.*;

public class SeekMousePanel extends JPanel {

    /*
     Circle will seek the mouse.
    */

    // instance variables
    private int xCentre = 200, yCentre = 200;
```

```
    // constructor
    public SeekMousePanel ( ) {
        setBackground(Color.yellow);
        addMouseMotionListener(new MouseMotionAdapter() {
            public void mouseMoved(MouseEvent evt) {
                seekMouse(evt);
            }
        });
    }

    public void paintComponent (Graphics g) {
        // draw circle on the panel
        super.paintComponent(g);
        g.setColor(Color.red);
        g.fillOval(xCentre-50, yCentre-50, 100, 100);
    }

    public void seekMouse(MouseEvent e) {
        // move circle towards the mouse
        int xDist = e.getX() - xCentre;
        int yDist = e.getY() - yCentre;
        if (xDist > 0) xCentre = xCentre + 3;
        if (xDist < 0) xCentre = xCentre - 3;
        if (yDist > 0) yCentre = yCentre + 3;
        if (yDist < 0) yCentre = yCentre - 3;
        repaint();
    }
}
```

As we shall see when we add an object of this class to a window frame, a red circle is displayed. When the mouse is moved in the panel the circle moves towards the mouse. To be specific, when the method `seekMouse` is invoked, the x- and y-coordinates of the common centre of the circle are both adjusted by 3 pixels whenever that will bring the circle closer to the mouse's position. This shifting of the circle ceases whenever the mouse is not moving.

Consider now the code for a class `ToggleSeekFrame` given on the next page. This class extends `ExitFrame` and is much like the `JFrame` subclasses that we met in Chapter 9, except that *two* panel objects, `tsp` of the `ToggleSquarePanel` class that we met in Section 9.5 and `smp` of the `SeekMousePanel` class above, are added to the frame's content pane `c`. Notice that these panel objects are separately sized and positioned:

```
tsp.setBounds(25, 25, 400, 400);
smp.setBounds(450, 25, 400, 400);
```

```
import genesis.*;
import java.awt.*;

public class ToggleSeekFrame extends ExitFrame {

    // constructor
    public ToggleSeekFrame ( ) {
        setTitle("Toggle and Seek");
        setBounds(50, 100, 875, 480);
        Container c = getContentPane();
        c.setLayout(null);
        c.setBackground(Color.blue);
        ToggleSquarePanel tsp = new ToggleSquarePanel();
        SeekMousePanel smp = new SeekMousePanel();
        tsp.setBounds(25, 25, 400, 400);
        smp.setBounds(450, 25, 400, 400);
        c.add(tsp);
        c.add(smp);
    }
}
```

Notice also that the content pane `c` is sent a message to set its layout manager to `null`:

```
c.setLayout(null);
```

We shall discuss why we need this statement later in this section. For now just accept that it is included to override the default way in which panels are arranged in a content pane so as to allow the panels to be sized and positioned as requested by their `setBounds` statements.

Finally, here is the code for a `Main` class that has a `main` method that instantiates and sets visible an object `togWin` of the `ToggleSeekFrame` class:

```
public class Main {

    public static void main (String [ ] args) {
        ToggleSeekFrame togWin = new ToggleSeekFrame();
        togWin.setVisible (true);
    }
}
```

PROBLEM 1: a window with two panels

The code for the above classes is in the folder *Toggle And Seek*. Open this folder and run the `Main` class. A window with blue background opens containing two panels, one on the left with white background and the other on the right with yellow background.

If the mouse is positioned in the left panel, the square toggles between solid and hollow when the mouse button is pressed; if the mouse is positioned in the right panel, the circle follows the mouse as it moves.

Modify the code for the classes so that:

- the square toggles whenever the mouse enters the panel on the left;
- the circle jumps to the mouse's position when the mouse is positioned in the panel on the right and the mouse's button pressed.

Try adjusting the position and size of the panels in the window. What happens if the areas occupied by the two panels overlap? Try it and see.

For help with this problem see Hints.

□

Discussion

Notice that the mouse event handlers associated with the two panels created in the `ToggleSeekFrame` class are quite distinct. Each event handler responds only when an event occurs within its associated panel. The panels act like sub-windows within the main window.

In this example we have deliberately coloured the backgrounds of the panels and window so that they are clearly delineated. If the `setBackground(..)` statements are removed from the classes, the boundary between the panels and the window will no longer be visible. The boundary will still be in the same place, however, and the mouse events will still be detected only when the mouse is positioned in the corresponding panel. Try it for yourself and see!

Border layout of the content pane

Consider the problem of laying out panels in a window frame's content pane. We saw that in the class `ToggleSeekFrame` we needed to add the statement

```
c.setLayout(null);
```

to override the default layout. A window frame's content pane has a default *border layout manager* which allows components to be added to the top (north), bottom (south), left (east), right (west) or centre of the pane. To illustrate this, consider the class BorderLayoutFrame:

```
import javax.swing.*;
import genesis.*;
import java.awt.*;

public class BorderLayoutFrame extends ExitFrame {

    // constructor
    public BorderLayoutFrame ( ) {
        setTitle("Border Layout");
        setBounds(300, 100, 200, 200);
        Container c = getContentPane();
        JPanel p1 = new JPanel();
        p1.setBackground(Color.red);
        c.add(p1, "North");
        JPanel p2 = new JPanel();
        p2.setBackground(Color.green);
        c.add(p2, "West");
        JPanel p3 = new JPanel();
        p3.setBackground(Color.yellow);
        c.add(p3, "Center");
        JPanel p4 = new JPanel();
        p4.setBackground(Color.magenta);
        c.add(p4, "East");
        JPanel p5 = new JPanel();
        p5.setBackground(Color.pink);
        c.add(p5, "South");
    }
}
```

In this class we have added five panels to a window, one in each of the five positions. Notice the syntax for doing this: we send to the content pane c the message

add(*panel*, *position*)

where *panel* is the panel we want to add and *position* is one of the strings

"North" "South" "West" "East" "Center"

(Note the American spelling.) In this example the five panels contain no graphical objects but each has its background colour set uniquely.

The class `BorderLayoutFrame` is in the folder *Border Layout*. Open this folder and run the `Main` class to discover how the five panels are arranged in the window frame.

If we simply use the `add(`*panel*`)` message as we have done so far, *panel* is added by default to the centre of the pane. This is fine for the applications we met in Chapter 9 but if we add more than one panel in this way they will all be added to the centre. In this case not only will they obscure each other, but each will expand to take up the entire frame. Sending the message `setLayout(null)` removes the default border layout manager from the content pane, with the result that panels can be positioned 'by hand' using the `setBounds` message as we did in the class `ToggleSeekFrame`.

Often however, the default border layout is exactly what we want. In these cases we would not send the `setLayout(null)` message but instead layout our panels in the window using `add(.., "North")`, `add(.., "South")`, etc. We will see examples of this in Section 10.3.

PROBLEM 2: local mouse position

Open the folder *Local Position Demo*. Explore what happens as the mouse is moved within the window that opens when the `Main` class is run.

The classes in this folder have been compiled and the code removed from the *.java* files. Your task is to code the following three classes which when compiled and executed create an application with the same behaviour as the demonstration:

- `LocalPositionFrame`: This class extends the class `ExitFrame`. An object of this class (i.e. a window frame) instantiates, positions and sizes two panel objects of the class `MousePosnPanel` and adds them to the content pane.
- `MousePosnPanel`: This class extend the class `JPanel`. An object of this class displays the current position of the mouse whenever the mouse is within the panel (see Problem 11 in Chapter 9).
- `Main`: This class contains only a `main` method to instantiate and set visible an object of the class `LocalPositionFrame`.

For help with this problem see Hints.

□

Discussion

Notice that in the class `LocalPositionFrame`, two panel objects are instantiated, just as with the class `ToggleSeekFrame` in Problem 1. However, in Problem 2 the two panel objects belong to the same class (the `MousePosnPanel` class). We can display several panels of the same type in a window and each can come with its own event handlers. This idea is explored further in the next section.

10.2 Case study: toggle-neighbours puzzle

In this section we are going to make use of panels to construct a simple toggle-neighbours puzzle. In the process we will discover how to use a mediator to facilitate inter-object communication.

PROBLEM 3: the puzzle demonstrated

To get some idea of where we are heading, open the folder *Tog Neigh Puzzle* and run the Main class. Dialog boxes open requesting first a number for the width of the puzzle and then a number for the height of the puzzle. Suppose the integers n and m are supplied by the user. A window then opens displaying an n by m grid of hollow squares.

If the mouse is positioned in any square and the button pressed, that square together with its immediate horizontal and vertical neighbours toggle between hollow and solid.

The aim of the puzzle is, by clicking with the mouse on the appropriate squares, to reach a stage where each square in the grid is solid.

Supply various values for the puzzle's width and height and see if you can solve it.

□

In this case study we will investigate how the classes that created this puzzle were constructed.

A simple toggle puzzle

Consider the problem of creating a 5 by 5 grid of squares where each square can be toggled by the mouse. We have already seen in the class `ToggleSquarePanel` (see Section 9.5) how we can create a panel that contains a square that can be toggled by the mouse. Here is a class `SimpleSquarePanel` that is quite similar:

```
import javax.swing.*;
import java.awt.*;
import java.awt.event.*;

public class SimpleSquarePanel extends JPanel {

    /*
    Paints a square which is toggled between hollow
    and solid when the mouse button is pressed.
    */

    // instance variables
    private boolean filled = false;

    // constructor
    public SimpleSquarePanel ( ) {
        setBackground(Color.white);
        addMouseListener(new MouseAdapter() {
            public void mousePressed(MouseEvent evt) {
                toggle();
            }
        });
    }

    public void paintComponent (Graphics g) {
        // paint square in the window
        super.paintComponent(g);
        g.setColor (Color.red);
        if (filled) g.fillRect(1, 1, 48, 48);
        else g.drawRect(1, 1, 48, 48);
    }

    public void toggle ( ) {
        filled = !filled;
        repaint();
    }
}
```

The main difference between this class and the class ToggleSquareCanvas is the position and size of the square. In this case $(1, 1)$ are the coordinates of the square's upper-left corner, and it is 48 pixels wide.

The class Tog5by5Frame instantiates 25 objects of the class SimpleSquarePanel and positions them into a 5 by 5 grid:

```
import genesis.*;
import java.awt.*;

public class Tog5by5Frame extends ExitFrame {

    /* Toggle square and neighbours. */

    // instance variables
    private int numWide, numHigh, totNum;
    private SimpleSquarePanel [] panels;

    // constructor
    public Tog5by5Frame ( ) {
        numWide = 5;
        numHigh = 5;
        totNum = numWide*numHigh;
        setTitle(numWide+" by "+numHigh+" Toggle Puzzle");
        setBounds(100, 50, 100+50*numWide, 140+50*numHigh);
        Container c = getContentPane();
        c.setLayout(null);
        panels = new SimpleSquarePanel [totNum];
        for (int i=0; i<totNum; i++) {
            panels[i] = new SimpleSquarePanel();
            panels[i].setBounds
              (50*(i%numWide)+50, 50*(i/numWide)+50, 50, 50);
            c.add(panels[i]);
        }
    }
}
```

Consider some of the detail of this code. An instance variable `panels` denoting an array of `SimpleSquarePanel` objects is declared by the statement:

```
private SimpleSquarePanel [] panels;
```

In the constructor method the code

```
panels = new SimpleSquarePanel [totNum];
for (int i=0; i<totNum; i++) {
    panels[i] = new SimpleSquarePanel();
    panels[i].setBounds
            (50*(i%numWide)+50, 50*(i/numWide)+50, 50, 50);
    c.add(panels[i]);
}
```

creates this array to have length 25 (as `totNum` is `numWide*numHigh`). For each `i` between 0 and 24,

- a new panel object of the class `SimpleSquarePanel` is instantiated and assigned to that index position in the array;
- the position and size of the panel is determined;
- the panel is added to the content pane of the object of the `Tog5by5Frame` class being instantiated by the constructor method.

Determining the position and size of each panel is the trickiest part of the whole code. We would like the x- and y-coordinates of the upper-left corner of each of the 25 panels to be given by:

(50, 50)	(100, 50)	(150, 50)	(200, 50)	(250, 50)
(50, 100)	(100, 100)	(150, 100)	(200, 100)	(250, 100)
(50, 150)	(100, 150)	(150, 150)	(200, 150)	(250, 150)
(50, 200)	(100, 200)	(150, 200)	(200, 200)	(250, 200)
(50, 250)	(100, 250)	(150, 250)	(200, 250)	(250, 250)

These 25 panels are indexed from 0 to 24 using the following correspondence:

0	1	2	3	4
5	6	7	8	9
10	11	12	13	14
15	16	17	18	19
20	21	22	23	24

For each `i` in the range 0 to 24, the x- and y-coordinate of square `i` with respect to the above correspondence is given by the expressions

`50*(i%numWide)+50` and `50*(i/numWide)+50`

respectively. Convince yourself that these calculations are correct by checking them by hand. The upper-left corners of the panels are 50 pixels apart in both the horizontal and vertical direction. By making the panels each 50 pixels wide and high, they exactly fit together. Furthermore, as each panel contains a square positioned at (1, 1) and 48 pixels wide, each square will be displayed so that it is uniformly 1 pixel from the boundary of its respective panel area.

The overall size of the window to contain these 25 panels is set by the statement:

```
setBounds(100, 50, 100+50*numWide, 140+50*numHigh);
```

That is, the dimension of the grid of panels is taken into account and the window is 100 pixels wider and 140 pixels higher than this grid so as to give the grid an aesthetically pleasing empty border.

All that is now required is an appropriate `Main` class whose `main` method instantiates and sets visible a window frame object of the class `Tog5by5Frame`:

```
public class Main {

    public static void main (String [] args) {
        Tog5by5Frame togWin = new Tog5by5Frame();
        togWin.setVisible(true);
    }
}
```

PROBLEM 4: a 5 by 5 puzzle

The code for the above classes is in the *Tog 5 by 5 Puzzle* folder. Open this folder and run the `Main` class. Notice that if you position the mouse on any square and press the button, that square alone toggles.

Modify the class `Tog5by5Frame` so that instead of getting a 5 by 5 grid of squares, the user is requested via dialog boxes for the number of squares wide and the number of squares high, and the window then opens displaying this requested rectangular grid of squares.

For help with this problem see Hints.

□

Using a mediator

The 5 by 5 toggle puzzle in Problem 4 is fine as far as it goes, but only the square selected by the mouse is toggled when the mouse's button is pressed. How can we get those squares that are the immediate horizontal and vertical neighbours of the selected square to toggle as well?

The problem here is that each mouse-event handler is associated with an individual panel, and there is no mechanism in the above code whereby one panel can pass the `toggle` message to any other panel. The trick is to employ what is known as a *mediator* to facilitate communication between the panels.

In the above application the window frame object of the class `Tog5by5Frame` referenced by the variable `togWin` knows about each panel. This is because each panel is instantiated within the constructor method of the `Tog5by5Frame` class and then stored within the array denoted by the instance variable `panels`. Therefore, if we want to pass a message to any panel, it would be sensible to tell the window frame object itself about it and let this object pass the message for us, as this object is able, through the array `panels`, to contact any panel in the window.

What we are suggesting is that the window frame object could be a 'mediator' among the panels, acting much like a post office which when sent messages (i.e. letters) sorts and delivers them.

Here is the strategy. If the mouse button is pressed while the mouse is positioned over a panel, not only will the square in that panel toggle, but a message will be sent to the mediator object requesting the mediator send the message `toggle` to the immediate horizontal and vertical neighbours of the selected panel. To do this, each panel will need a reference to the mediator object so the panel can send it messages. (The mediator, through the array `panels`, will already have a reference to every panel. What we will need is a reference in reverse so that every panel references the window frame object in which it resides.)

What we will do is construct classes `TogNeighFrame` and `SquarePanel`, as well as an associated `Main` class, that together implement this 'mediator' strategy in order to create the toggle-neighbours puzzle demonstrated in Problem 3.

To begin, here is the code for the class `TogNeighFrame`:

```
import genesis.*;
import java.awt.*;

public class TogNeighFrame extends ExitFrame {
    /*
    Rectangular grid of squares that each toggle together
    with neighbours when the mouse is positioned in the
    square and the button pressed.
    */

    // instance variables
    private int numWide, numHigh, totNum;
    private SquarePanel [] panels;

    // constructor
    public TogNeighFrame ( ) {
        numWide = DialogBox.requestInt("Number wide:");
        numHigh = DialogBox.requestInt("Number high:");
        totNum = numWide*numHigh;
        setTitle
         (numWide+" by "+numHigh+" Toggle Neighbours Puzzle");
        setBounds(100, 50, 100+50*numWide, 140+50*numHigh);
```

```
        Container c = getContentPane();
        c.setLayout(null);
        panels = new SquarePanel [totNum];
        for (int i=0; i<totNum; i++) {
            panels[i] = new SquarePanel(i, this);
            panels[i].setBounds
              (50*(i%numWide)+50, 50*(i/numWide)+50, 50, 50);
            c.add(panels[i]);
        }
    }

    public void togNeighOf (int index) {
        // toggle the neighbours of tile with given index
        if (index%numWide != numWide-1)
            panels[index+1].toggle();
        if (index%numWide != 0)
            panels[index-1].toggle();
        if (index < totNum-numWide)
            panels[index+numWide].toggle();
        if (index > numWide-1)
            panels[index-numWide].toggle();
    }
}
```

There are only two essential differences between the code for this class and the code for the class Tog5by5Frame we met in Problem 4.

Passing the mediator to the panel

First, there is the code

```
for (int i=0; i<totNum; i++) {
    panels[i] = new SquarePanel(i, this);
    panels[i].setBounds
            (50*(i%numWide)+50, 50*(i/numWide)+50, 50, 50);
    c.add(panels[i]);
}
```

within the constructor method. This code associates a new panel object of the class SquarePanel with each index position in the array panels. Notice this time, however, that two arguments are passed when instantiating a new panel object. The first argument passes the current index value i, while the second passes this denoting the window frame object of the class TogNeighFrame currently being constructed. The first argument is needed so that each panel can record its position in the array panels; the second argument will be the mediator object that the panel needs to know about. The full details will become clear when we look at the code for the class SquarePanel.

Toggling neighbours

Second, the method togNeighOf is new. This method takes as parameter an integer index denoting an index position and sends the message toggle to each panel that is an immediate horizontal or vertical neighbour of the panel with index position index in the array panels. That is, this method toggles the neighbours of a given square, where the given square is identified by its index position in the array panels. The actual arithmetic in this code is a bit tricky. Check it for yourself by hand so that you are convinced that it successfully identifies the neighbours of a panel given the index of that panel in the array panels.

Now consider the code for the class SquarePanel:

```
import javax.swing.*;
import java.awt.*;
import java.awt.event.*;

public class SquarePanel extends JPanel {
    /*
    Paints a square which is toggled between hollow
    and solid when the mouse button is pressed.
    */

    // instance variables
    private boolean filled = false;
    private TogNeighFrame mediator;
    private int indexPosn;

    // constructor
    public SquarePanel (int index, TogNeighFrame med) {
        mediator = med;
        indexPosn = index;
        setBackground(Color.white);
        addMouseListener(new MouseAdapter() {
            public void mousePressed(MouseEvent evt) {
                toggle();
                mediator.togNeighOf(indexPosn);
            }
        });
    }
```

```
        public void paintComponent (Graphics g) {
            // paint square in the window
            super.paintComponent(g);
            g.setColor (Color.red);
            if (filled) g.fillRect(1, 1, 48, 48);
            else g.drawRect(1, 1, 48, 48);
        }

        public void toggle ( ) {
            filled = !filled;
            repaint();
        }
    }
```

There are three differences between the code for this class and the code for the class SimpleSquarePanel we met in Problem 4. First, two new instance variables are declared:

```
private TogNeighFrame mediator;
private int indexPosn;
```

The varible mediator is of type TogNeighFrame and will denote the mediator object through which messages to any other panel object can be passed. The variable indexPosn is an integer recording the index position of the panel object.

Second, the constructor method has two parameters. The first is an integer that is assigned to the variable indexPosn. The second is the mediator object that is assigned to the variable mediator. Both these values are passed by the mediator object itself when it instantiates a panel object. Recall from above that the mediator object is none other than that window frame object of the class TogNeighFrame that instantiates each panel object and places them in the instance variable panels. Consequently, the variable indexPosn takes the index value that that panel object has in the array panels, while mediator becomes the object of the class TogNeighFrame that is doing all this instantiating in the first place and in which the square panels reside.

Third, the code for the mousePressed method in the anonymous inner class within the constructor method now contains the two statements:

```
toggle();
mediator.togNeighOf(indexPosn);
```

The result of executing these statements is that first the square in this panel object will toggle and then the mediator object will invoke its togNeighOf method with the integer `indexPosn` passed as argument. But these statements will be executed only if the mouse is pressed, so the end result is that if the mouse is pressed, the square in the panel corresponding to the current position of the mouse will toggle and the mediator will be instructed to toggle all the neighbouring squares of this panel as well.

All that remains now is to construct the class `Main` whose `main` method instantiates the mediator object itself and sets it visible:

```
public class Main {

    public static void main (String [] args) {
        TogNeighFrame togWin = new TogNeighFrame();
        togWin.setVisible(true);
    }
}
```

The toggle-neighbours puzzle toggles the selected square and each of its neighbours. The following problem considers the construction of related puzzles where the squares to be toggled have a relationship other than 'neighbour of' with the selected square.

PROBLEM 5: the puzzle revisited

The above classes `TogNeighFrame`, `SquarePanel` and `Main` are in the folder *Tog Neigh Puzzle*. Once again open this folder and run the `Main` class.

Modify the code for these classes so that when the mouse is positioned in a square and the button pressed,

- every square except the selected square will toggle;
- every square in the same row and column as the selected square will toggle;
- a square chosen at random from among all the squares other than the selected square will toggle.

Note : In each case you will need to modify only the `togNeighOf` method in the class `TogNeighFrame`. No other code need be changed.

Use your imagination to create other interesting patterns of squares to toggle when a square is selected by the mouse and the button pressed.

For help with this problem see Hints.

□

10.3 Action buttons

In this and the next section we look at some graphical components that are particularly useful when constructing graphical user interfaces (GUIs). Typically, the role of a GUI is to enhance the means of communication between the computer user and the underlying computer application.

To help motivate the ideas and techniques that we will be introducing in this and the next section, consider the following simple example of a GUI.

PROBLEM 6: temperature conversion

Open the folder *Temperature Conversion* and run the `Main` class. A window opens containing

- two components labelled 'deg F' and 'deg C' in which floating point numbers representing respectively temperatures in Fahrenheit and Centigrade can be either inserted by the user or displayed by the underlying application;
- two 'action' buttons which, when pressed, convert the displayed temperature from Fahrenheit to Centigrade, or conversely.

Note: In this and the next section we shall say a graphical component is 'pressed' if the mouse is positioned over the component and the (left) mouse button pressed.

Try inserting various floating point numbers in the display areas and pressing the buttons to observe the result.

□

The graphical components in which the values of the Fahrenheit and Centigrade degrees can be inserted or displayed are examples of text fields; they will be discussed in the next section. In this section we shall concentrate on constructing and using the 'action button' graphical component.

Applying an action button

To illustrate how we can apply the action button graphical component, consider the following code for classes `ButtonToggleFrame` and `SqPanel` together with a `Main` class. These classes implement an application whereby a square can be toggled between solid and hollow by pressing on an action button labelled 'toggle square'.

```
import genesis.*;
import javax.swing.*;
import java.awt.*;
import java.awt.event.*;

public class ButtonToggleFrame extends ExitFrame {
    /*
     A square that toggles when a button is pressed.
    */

    // instance variable
    private SqPanel square = new SqPanel();

    // constructor
    public ButtonToggleFrame ( ) {
        setTitle("Toggle using a Button");
        setBounds(100, 50, 400, 400);
        JButton togBut = new JButton("toggle square");
        togBut.addActionListener(new ActionListener() {
            public void actionPerformed (ActionEvent e) {
                square.toggle();
            }
        });
        Container c = getContentPane();
        JPanel butPanel = new JPanel();
        butPanel.add(togBut);
        butPanel.setBackground(Color.white);
        c.add(butPanel, "South");
        c.add(square, "Center");
    }
}
```

```
import javax.swing.*;
import java.awt.*;

public class SqPanel extends JPanel {
    /*
    Paints a square which can be toggled
    between hollow and solid.
    */

    // instance variables
    private boolean filled = true;
```

```
    // constructor
    public SqPanel ( ) {
        setBackground(Color.white);
    }

    public void paintComponent (Graphics g) {
        // paint square in the window
        super.paintComponent(g);
        g.setColor (Color.red);
        if (filled) g.fillRect(150, 125, 100, 100);
        else g.drawRect(150, 125, 100, 100);
    }

    public void toggle ( ) {
        // toggle square
        filled = !filled;
        repaint();
    }
}
```

```
public class Main {

    public static void main (String [] args) {
        ButtonToggleFrame butWin = new ButtonToggleFrame();
        butWin.setVisible(true);
    }
}
```

Note: `square` is declared as an instance variable in the `ButtonToggleFrame` class rather than as a local variable in the constructor method because it is referenced in the anonymous inner class. An inner class can reference instance variables of the enclosing class but not local variables of the enclosing method.

PROBLEM 7: a button to toggle a square

The above classes are in the folder *Button Toggle*. Open this folder and run the `Main` class. A window opens displaying a solid red square and an action button which when pressed toggles the square. Experiment with modifying the code for the class `ButtonToggleFrame` so that other interesting things happen when the button is pressed.

□

Discussion

The `SqPanel` class paints a square in a panel and is typical of panel classes we have met many times before. It is similar to the class `SimpleSquarePanel` (see Section 10.2) except that no mouse listener has been added. In this example it will be an action button that invokes the `toggle` method, and the code for that is in the `ButtonToggleFrame` class.

The `ButtonToggleFrame` class illustrates the general strategy for installing an action button in a window. First, an action button is instantiated as an object of the class `JButton`. In the example here, the new button is assigned to the variable `togBut`:

```
JButton togBut = new JButton("toggle square");
```

The class `JButton` is in the *javax.swing* package. The string passed as the argument of the `JButton` constructor (in this case the string `"toggle square"`) becomes the label shown on the action button itself when the button is displayed in the window.

Adding an action listener

In order to program a response when the action button is pressed, an *action listener* is associated with the button. In the `ButtonToggleFrame` class, the code to achieve this is:

```
togBut.addActionListener(new ActionListener() {
    public void actionPerformed (ActionEvent e) {
        square.toggle();
    }
});
```

The process for installing an action listener for an action button is similar to the process for installing a window, mouse or key listener (see Chapter 9). The method `addActionListener` is sent to the button object, with the action listener object we want to associate with the button passed as the argument. Just as for the listener objects we installed in Chapter 9, the action listener is defined as an object of an anonymous inner class.

To be more specific, we create an object of an anonymous inner class that implements `ActionListener` by redefining the method `actionPerformed`. This method is the only one in `ActionListener` and is the method automatically invoked when the action listener is informed by the system that the action button has been pressed. `ActionListener` is in the *java.awt.event* package.

[*An aside*: You may recall from Chapter 9 that each listener added to a window was an object of an anonymous subclass of the corresponding 'adapter' class.

For example, a mouse listener was defined as an object of a subclass of the class `MouseAdapter`; a key listener was defined as an object of a subclass of the class `KeyAdapter`. When adding an action listener to an action button, however, the listener is not defined as an object of some 'ActionAdapter' class, but instead is defined as an object of an anonymous inner class that implements `ActionListener`. We shall say more about this distinction in Section 10.5. *End aside*]

In the case of the action listener added to the action button `togBut` in the class `ButtonToggleFrame`, the method `actionPerformed` is redefined so that the message `toggle()` is sent to the object `square` of the class `SqPanel`.

[*An aside*: The method `actionPerformed` has a parameter `e` whose type is the class `ActionEvent`. Just as for the window, mouse and other events we met in Chapter 9, the argument value passed to this parameter when the method is invoked contains detailed information about the actual action event that has occurred. We shall have no need to make use of this information in any of the examples we shall consider here, but see Section 10.5. *End aside*]

Now that the action button has been created and an action listener associated with it, we need to add the button to the window so it can be displayed. This is done by adding the button to a panel and then adding the panel to the window's content pane.

To create a panel, we directly instantiate an object of the class `JPanel`. In the example here, the new panel is assigned to the variable `butPanel`:

```
JPanel butPanel = new JPanel();
```

Next, the action button we have created is added to the panel and the panel's background colour is set to white:

```
butPanel.add(togBut);
butPanel.setBackground(Color.white);
```

Finally the panel is added to the bottom of the window's content pane:

```
c.add(butPanel, "South");
```

The object `square` of the class `SqPanel` containing the square is also added to the window's pane, but this time in its centre:

```
c.add(square, "Center");
```

PROBLEM 8: a GUI to toss a die

Open the folder *Die Toss GUI Demo* and run the Main class. Each time the 'toss die' button is pressed a random integer in the range 1 to 6 is displayed. The colour of the number displayed toggles between red and blue.

The classes in this folder have been compiled and the code removed from the *.java* files. Create classes `DieTossFrame`, `DieTossPanel` and `Main` which when compiled and run give the same behaviour as the demonstration.

For help with this problem see Hints.

□

Flow layout of a panel

The content pane of a window has by default a border layout manager (see Section 10.1). A panel however, has by default a *flow* layout manager. This means that if we add graphical components such as action buttons to a panel, by default those components will be positioned one after the other in the same way words in a text document flow one after the other.

To illustrate this, consider the code for the class `FlowLayoutFrame`:

```
import javax.swing.*;
import genesis.*;
import java.awt.*;

public class FlowLayoutFrame extends ExitFrame {

    // constructor
    public FlowLayoutFrame ( ) {
        setTitle("Flow Layout");
        setBounds(300, 100, 200, 200);
        Container c = getContentPane();
        JPanel p = new JPanel();
        JButton [] buttons = new JButton [10];
        for (int i=0; i<10; i++) {
            buttons[i] = new JButton("button "+i);
            p.add(buttons[i]);
        }
        c.add(p);
    }
}
```

In this code 10 action buttons are created and added to the panel p which is then in turn added to the content pane c. The buttons don't actually do anything because no action listeners have been added — this simply illustrates the way buttons are positioned inside a panel.

PROBLEM 9: exploring the flow layout

The class `FlowLayoutFrame`, together with an appropriate `Main` class, is in the folder *Flow Layout*. Open this folder and run the `Main` class.

Resize the window to various sizes and notice the way the positioning of the buttons changes, at all times maintaining a 'flow' layout within the panel.

□

Compare this with the class `FlowBorderLayoutFrame` below where the 10 buttons are added not to one panel as in Problem 9 but to 5 different panels. These panels are then added to the borders and centre of the window pane.

```
import javax.swing.*;
import genesis.*;
import java.awt.*;

public class FlowBorderLayoutFrame extends ExitFrame {

    // constructor
    public FlowBorderLayoutFrame ( ) {
        setTitle("Flow and Border Layout");
        setBounds(300, 100, 200, 200);
        Container c = getContentPane();
        JPanel [] panels = new JPanel [5];
        for (int i=0; i<5; i++) panels[i] = new JPanel();
        JButton [] buttons = new JButton [10];
        for (int i=0; i<10; i++) {
            buttons[i] = new JButton("button "+i);
            panels[i/2].add(buttons[i]);
        }
        c.add(panels[0], "North");
        c.add(panels[1], "West");
        c.add(panels[2], "Center");
        c.add(panels[3], "East");
        c.add(panels[4], "South");
    }
}
```

PROBLEM 10: comparing flow and border layouts

The class `FlowBorderLayoutFrame`, together with an appropriate `Main` class, is in the folder *Flow And Border Layout*. Open this folder and run the `Main` class.

Resize the window to various sizes and notice the way the positioning of the buttons changes, at all times maintaining a 'flow' layout within each of the five different panels, and a border layout for the panels themselves.

□

Here is the general strategy for laying out graphical components such as action buttons:

- components are first added to panels; within each panel the components are positioned one after the other in conformance with the panel's default flow layout;
- the panels are then added to the north, south, east, west or centre of a window's content pane using the pane's default border layout.

Be warned that if we add two or more panels in the same position of the window pane one panel will obscure the other.

PROBLEM 11: creating buttons and placing panels

Open again the folder *Button Toggle*.

Modify the class `ButtonToggleFrame` so that an additional action button labelled 'close' is created which when pressed has the effect of terminating the application. Add this new button to the same panel as the 'toggle square' button, and experiment with panel positions by adding the panel in turn to the top, bottom, left, right and centre of the window.

Now create a separate panel for the 'close' button and add the two panels to different border locations, e.g. one at the top and one at the bottom of the window.

For help with this problem see Hints.

□

PROBLEM 12: selecting colours by button

Open the folder *Colour By Button Demo* and run the `Main` class. Two windows open; the one on the left contains the four action buttons 'red', 'blue', 'cyan' and 'green', and the one on the right is empty. The background colour of the window on the right can be chosen by pressing the appropriately labelled button in the window on the left.

The classes in this folder have been compiled and the code removed from the *.java* files. Create the class `ColourFrame`, together with a `Main` class which when compiled and run give the same behaviour as in the demonstration.

For help with this problem see Hints.

□

PROBLEM 13: Janet and Jim buttons

In Problem 14 of Chapter 9 a window was opened with the property that whenever the mouse entered the window the image *JavaJanet.gif* was displayed, while whenever the mouse exited the window the image *JavaJim.gif* was displayed instead.

Modify the code for the classes in that problem to place two action buttons 'Janet' and 'Jim' at the bottom of the window with the property that if the 'Janet' button is pressed the image *JavaJanet.gif* is displayed, while if the 'Jim' button is pressed the image of *JavaJim.gif* is displayed instead.

Modify your code so that the action buttons contain icons as well as text. For example, a declaration of the form

```
JButton janetBut =
    new JButton("Janet", new ImageIcon("Janeticon.gif"));
```

will create a button `janetBut` upon which both the string `"Janet"` and the icon image *Janeticon.gif* are displayed. To assist, the images *JavaJanet.gif*, *Janeticon.gif*, *JavaJim.gif* and *Jimicon.gif* have been placed in the folder *Janet Jim Buttons.*

For help with this problem see Hints.

□

10.4 Text fields and labels

Let us return to the GUI example we met at the beginning of Section 10.3 (see Problem 6). This GUI converts temperatures from degrees Fahrenheit to Centigrade and conversely. Here is the code for the class ConversionFrame:

```
import genesis.*;
import javax.swing.*;
import java.awt.*;
import java.awt.event.*;

public class ConversionFrame extends ExitFrame {
    /* Convert Fahrenheit to Centigrade and conversely. */

    // instance variables
    private JTextField fah, cent;

    // constructor
    public ConversionFrame ( ) {
        setTitle("Fahrenheit <-> Centigrade");
        setBounds(100, 100, 350, 250);
        Font f = new Font("SansSerif", Font.BOLD, 30);
        fah = new JTextField("32.0", 9);
        fah.setFont(f);
        cent = new JTextField("0.0", 9);
        cent.setFont(f);
        JLabel fahLabel =
                    new JLabel("deg F:", JLabel.RIGHT);
        fahLabel.setFont(f);
        JLabel centLabel =
                    new JLabel("deg C:", JLabel.RIGHT);
        centLabel.setFont(f);
        JButton fahToCent = new JButton("convert F to C");
        fahToCent.setFont(f);
        JButton centToFah = new JButton("convert C to F");
        centToFah.setFont(f);
        fahToCent.addActionListener(new ActionListener() {
            public void actionPerformed(ActionEvent evt) {
                double fahDegrees =
                  Double.valueOf(fah.getText()).doubleValue();
                double centDegrees =
                  (int)((fahDegrees-32)*5/9*100)/100.0;
                cent.setText(""+centDegrees);
            }
        });
```

```
        centToFah.addActionListener(new ActionListener() {
            public void actionPerformed(ActionEvent evt) {
                double centDegrees =
                  Double.valueOf(cent.getText()).doubleValue();
                double fahDegrees =
                  (int)((centDegrees*9/5+32)*100)/100.0;
                fah.setText(""+fahDegrees);
            }
        });
        JPanel p = new JPanel();
        p.add(fahLabel);
        p.add(fah);
        p.add(centLabel);
        p.add(cent);
        p.add(fahToCent);
        p.add(centToFah);
        Container c = getContentPane();
        p.setBackground(Color.white);
        c.add(p);
    }
}
```

Discussion

Two new graphical components are introduced in this code: *text fields* and *labels*.

Text fields

A *text field* is useful when we want to input, output or display text. Text can either be inserted directly by typing into the text field, or it can be inserted into the text field by the running application.

A text field is instantiated as an object of the class `JTextField`. In the example here, the two text fields are assigned to the variables `fah` and `cent` and the font for the text they display is set to be the new font assigned to the variable `f`:

```
Font f = new Font("SansSerif", Font.BOLD, 30);
fah = new JTextField("32.0", 9);
fah.setFont(f);
cent = new JTextField("0.0", 9);
cent.setFont(f);
```

The class `JTextField` is in the *javax.swing* package. The first argument passed to the `JTextField` constructor is the string to be initially displayed in the text field. The second argument gives the size of the text field by indicating the number of characters that may be displayed. Actually, more characters than this can be entered into the text field but the field will scroll and consequently they may not all be in view. In practice it is wise to set the second argument to be slightly larger than the maximum number of characters you want to display.

Here is how we get and set the text displayed in a text field:

- the current text in a text field is returned by sending the text field object the message `getText()`;
- new text can be displayed in a text field by sending the text field object the message `setText(..)` where the string to be displayed is passed as the argument.

Because only strings are displayed in a text field, we need to do a string-to-number conversion if we want to retrieve a value of type `int` or `double` from a text field. Similarly, we need to do a number-to-string conversion if we want some number to be displayed in a text field. We shall say more about this shortly.

Labels

A *label* is used when we wish to display a short piece of text. Typically, a label is used to identify some other component (e.g. a text field) and distinguish it from other components.

A label is instantiated as an object of the class `JLabel`. In this example, the two labels are assigned to the variables `fahLabel` and `centLabel` and again the font for the text they display is set to be the font `f`:

```
JLabel fahLabel = new JLabel("deg F:", JLabel.RIGHT);
fahLabel.setFont(f);
JLabel centLabel = new JLabel("deg C:", JLabel.RIGHT);
centLabel.setFont(f);
```

The class `JLabel` is also in the *javax.swing* package. The first argument passed to the `JLabel` constructor is the string to be displayed. The second argument determines the position of the label relative to its neighbouring components. The constants of the class `JLabel` that can be used here are `RIGHT`, `CENTER` and `LEFT`, and they respectively position the label close to the component on the right, midway between the components to the right and left, or close to the component on the left.

The action buttons

In the class `ConversionFrame` the two action buttons `fahToCent` and `centToFah` are created; again the font is set to be `f`:

```
JButton fahToCent = new JButton("convert F to C");
fahToCent.setFont(f);
JButton centToFah = new JButton("convert C to F");
centToFah.setFont(f);
```

Consider the action button fahToCent. When this button is pressed, the temperature in Fahrenheit currently displayed in the fah text field is converted into Centigrade and displayed in the cent text field. The code to implement this conversion is contained in the redefined actionPerformed method in the anonymous inner class used to add an action listener to the button (see Section 10.3 for a description of how action buttons are created and installed):

```
public void actionPerformed(ActionEvent evt) {
    double fahDegrees =
        Double.valueOf(fah.getText()).doubleValue();
    double centDegrees =
        (int)((fahDegrees-32)*5/9*100)/100.0;
    cent.setText(""+centDegrees);
}
```

To extract the string displayed in the fah text field and convert it into a floating point number of type double, we need to use the incredibly ugly expression:

```
Double.valueOf(fah.getText()).doubleValue();
```

The sub-expression fah.getText() extracts the string currently being displayed. The rest of the 'noise' in the expression is Java's way of converting the string into a double number. (We need not be too concerned with why; just accept that this is what we need to do! However, if you want to find out why, check out the class Double in the *java.lang* package.)

The expression

```
(int)((fahDegrees-32)*5/9*100)/100.0;
```

converts the temperature into Centigrade. Multiplying by 100, casting to int and then dividing by 100.0 ensures that the temperature is truncated to 2 decimal places.

Finally, the expression

```
cent.setText(""+centDegrees);
```

sets the string displayed in the cent text field to be the calculated Centigrade temperature. Notice that we need to prefix the variable centDegrees of type double with ""+ to covert it into a string. This convoluted expression is one way in Java to convert a non-string type into its string representation. It is needed here as the argument of the setText message must be a string.

The remaining code in the class `ConversionFrame` creates a panel `p`, adds the text field, label and action button components to this panel, and then adds the panel to the window frame's content pane.

PROBLEM 14: temperature conversion revisited

Again open the folder *Temperature Conversion*. Modify the `ConversionFrame` class so that

- the text fields are sized differently and contain different initial values;
- the labels display different text and are aligned differently;
- the components are arranged differently in the window frame.

Resize the window and notice how the components are automatically rearranged. (Recall a flow layout is the default arrangement of components within a panel.)

□

We complete this section with a couple of problems that require the creation of action buttons, labels and text fields.

PROBLEM 15: moving a circle to a given position

Open the folder *Circle Position Demo* and run the `Main` class. A window opens displaying a circle at its centre. At the bottom of the window is an action button labelled 'move' and two text fields displaying respectively the x- and y-coordinates of the circle's centre.

If we press the mouse's button in the window, the circle will move so its centre is at the mouse's current position and the text fields will be updated accordingly. On the other hand, if we enter integers into the text fields and press the 'move' action button, the circle will move so its centre is at the position displayed by the text fields.

The classes in this folder have been compiled and the code removed from the *.java* files. Create classes `CirclePosnFrame` and `CirclePanel`, together with a `Main` class such that when compiled and run the application that results has the same behaviour as the demonstration.

For help with this problem see Hints.

□

PROBLEM 16: mixing colours

Open the folder *Mixing Colours Demo* and run the `Main` class. Two windows appear on the screen. The top window is empty, but the bottom window displays three text fields labelled 'red', 'green' and 'blue' respectively, and an action button labelled 'mix colours'.

If an integer in the range 0 to 255 is inserted into each text field and the action button pressed, the top window has its background coloured according to the colour mix determined by the given integers.

The classes in this folder have been compiled and the code removed from the *.java* files. Create a class `MixingColoursFrame`, together with a `Main` class such that when compiled and run the application that results has the same behaviour as the demonstration.

For help with this problem see Hints.

□

10.5 Interfaces

In this section we look at the concept of an interface and examine the role it plays in Java. The ideas in this section will not be needed elsewhere in *Java Genesis.* However, interfaces are widely used in Java and it is inevitable you will come across the concept if you study other Java sources.

Let us look closely at the code we have been using to add an action listener to an action button. For example, here is the code for a class `RedBlueFrame` which has two action buttons labelled 'red' and 'blue'. When pressed, these buttons set the background colour of the window frame:

```
import genesis.*;
import javax.swing.*;
import java.awt.*;
import java.awt.event.*;

public class RedBlueFrame extends ExitFrame {
    /*
    Background colour selected by button.
    */

    // instance variable
    private Container c;
```

```
        // constructor
        public RedBlueFrame ( ) {
            setBounds(100, 50, 400, 400);
            c = getContentPane();
            JButton redBut = new JButton("red");
            redBut.addActionListener(new ActionListener() {
                public void actionPerformed (ActionEvent e) {
                    c.setBackground(Color.red);
                }
            });
            JButton blueBut = new JButton("blue");
            blueBut.addActionListener(new ActionListener() {
                public void actionPerformed (ActionEvent e) {
                    c.setBackground(Color.blue);
                }
            });
            Panel p= new Panel();
            p.add(redBut);
            p.add(blueBut);
            c.add(p, "South");
        }

    }
```

This class is in the folder *Red Blue.* Open this folder and run the associated `Main` class to confirm that the application has the specified behaviour.

The action listener associated with the 'red' button, for example, is an object of an implementation of `ActionListener` defined using the anonymous inner class construct:

```
    redBut.addActionListener(new ActionListener() {
        public void actionPerformed (ActionEvent e) {
            c.setBackground(Color.red);
        }
    });
```

What is of interest here is the entity `ActionListener`. `ActionListener` is in the *java.awt.event* package and its code is shown at the top of then next page.

If you look at this code you will notice that `ActionListener` is declared to be an *interface.* An interface in Java is much like an abstract class. For example, `ActionListener` has a declared method, `actionPerformed`, which has no associated block of statements, just as would be the case if this were an abstract method defined in an abstract class.

```
package java.awt.event;

import java.util.EventListener;

public interface ActionListener extends EventListener {

    /* Invoked when an action occurs. */

    public void actionPerformed(ActionEvent e);
}
```

Under most circumstances, we can treat an interface as if it were a class. Indeed, this is precisely what we do when we create an implementation of `ActionListener` using the anonymous inner class construct. The fact that `ActionListener` is an interface rather than a class is of no importance as far as the anonymous inner class construct is concerned.

Single vs multiple inheritance

So why does Java have interfaces, and how does an interface differ from a class? The answer to this question lies in the limitation of inheritance. In Java, a class can extend at most one other class. For example, the class `RedBlueFrame` above extends the class `ExitFrame`. That is, `RedBlueFrame` is a subclass of `ExitFrame` and hence an object of the class `RedBlueFrame` can be used whenever an object of the class `ExitFrame` is expected (see Chapter 8 for more on polymorphism and subtyping). But suppose we wanted `RedBlueFrame` to extend some other class as well. In Java this would not be possible.

[*An aside*: A language like Java that allows a class to extend at most one other class is said to allow *single* inheritance. Languages exist that allow a class to extend more than one other class; C++ is an example. Such languages are said to allow *multiple* inheritance. Although multiple inheritance is often a useful language feature, it adds considerable complexity to a language. *End aside*]

Java uses the idea of an interface to partially overcome the restriction of single inheritance. If we want a class to provide the features of an interface, we *implement* (rather than extend) the interface. A class can implement as many interfaces as it wishes without restriction while at the same time extending one other class if required.

Red-blue example revisited

The simplest way to see how this works is with an example. Consider again the class `RedBlueFrame`. The 'red' and 'blue' action buttons have distinct action listener objects associated with them. That is, in this example (and indeed in all the examples we have seen so far in this chapter) we associate a distinct action listener with each action button.

Now this is an entirely reasonable thing to do and we recommend it as a sound approach when creating action buttons. However, there is another approach, and one that you will find commonly adopted in the Java literature.

This alternative approach involves making the window frame itself the action listener associated with each action button! That is, we create just one action listener object to be shared by each action button, and this common action listener will be none other than the window frame itself!

To make this possible, of course, the window frame will need to be an action listener as well as a frame object. That is, the window frame will need to be a subtype of the interface `ActionListener`, or to use the terminology of interfaces, the class of the window frame will need to *implement* the `ActionListener` interface.

Here is the code for a class `RedBlueAgainFrame` that does this:

```
import genesis.*;
import javax.swing.*;
import java.awt.*;
import java.awt.event.*;

public class RedBlueAgainFrame
            extends ExitFrame implements ActionListener {
    /* Background colour selected by button.*/

    // instance variable
    private Container c;

    // constructor
    public RedBlueAgainFrame ( ) {
        setBounds(100, 50, 400, 400);
        c = getContentPane();
        JButton redBut = new JButton("red");
        redBut.addActionListener(this);
        JButton blueBut = new JButton("blue");
        blueBut.addActionListener(this);
        Panel p= new Panel();
        p.add(redBut);
        p.add(blueBut);
        c.add(p, "South");
    }
```

```
        public void actionPerformed (ActionEvent evt) {
            String butLabel = evt.getActionCommand();
            if (butLabel.equals("red"))
                c.setBackground(Color.red);
            else if (butLabel.equals("blue"))
                c.setBackground(Color.blue);
        }
    }
```

Just to be convinced that this code really works, open the folder *Red Blue Again* and run the associated `Main` class.

Let us consider carefully the code for the class `RedBlueAgainFrame`.

First, notice that this class implements the interface `ActionListener`. This requires that the method `actionPerformed` be defined in the body of the class.

Second, to add an action listener to each action button, we now code

```
redBut.addActionListener(this);
```

and

```
blueBut.addActionListener(this);
```

respectively where `this`, of course, is the object of the `RedBlueAgainFrame` class that is currently being instantiated by the constructor method. That is, both action buttons will have the window frame in which they will be displayed as their associated action listener. Notice that the anonymous inner class construct is no longer required.

Finally, consider the code for the method `actionPerformed`:

```
public void actionPerformed (ActionEvent evt) {
    String butLabel = evt.getActionCommand();
    if (butLabel.equals("red"))
        c.setBackground(Color.red);
    else if (butLabel.equals("blue"))
        c.setBackground(Color.blue);
}
```

Previously, the method `actionPerformed` was defined separately within each anonymous inner class so as to invoke the response required when the associated action button was pressed. But now, as the window frame object itself is the action listener for both buttons, we redefine the method just once in the class `RedBlueAgainFrame`. This one method will be invoked regardless of whether the ‘red’ or ‘blue’ button is pressed and hence its code must be able to determine which of the buttons has been pressed in order to respond appropriately.

The way this is done is to make use of the object of type `ActionEvent` that is passed as the argument with the `actionPerformed` message. Previously we had not needed to use this object, but now its use becomes essential. This object contains information about the button that has been pressed. To be precise, it knows the label of the pressed button and this can be extracted by coding:

```
String butLabel = evt.getActionCommand();
```

With this information, we can now test to see which button has been pressed and respond accordingly:

```
if (butLabel.equals("red"))
    c.setBackground(Color.red);
else if (butLabel.equals("blue"))
    c.setBackground(Color.blue);
```

PROBLEM 17: implementing an interface

Again open the folder *Temperature Conversion*. Modify the `ConversionFrame` class so that

- it implements the interface `ActionListener`;
- the method `actionPerformed` is redefined in the class `ConversionFrame` itself and contains the code to first determine which of the two buttons has been pressed and then respond appropriately.

For help with this problem see Hints.

□

Chapter 10 self-check

Can you

- add multiple panels to a window frame’s content pane?
- position and size a panel in a window?
- add graphical components to a panel?
- use a mediator to pass messages between objects?

Can you create and apply

- action buttons?
- text fields?
- labels?

Do you understand how to

- add an action listener to an action button?
- add panels to a window?
- set and get textual data in a text field?
- convert strings into the number types `int` or `double`?

Do you understand

- the default flow layout used to position components in a panel?
- the default border layout used to position panels in a window's content pane?
- the role played by a mediator in facilitating inter-object communication?
- the role played by an interface?
- how to implement an interface?

11 Exceptions and files

Prerequisites

As well as familiarity with the basic Java programming constructs, Chapter 11 assumes an understanding of:

- graphics and event handling as discussed in Chapter 9;
- GUI components as discussed in Chapter 10.

Overview

As you have no doubt often observed, a program that compiles successfully may nevertheless give rise to an error condition when it is executed. The types of errors that can occur during the execution of a program fall into 3 broad categories.

hardware errors
These errors emanate from the hardware of the system. For example, an error will occur if there is insufficient memory to execute the program, or if a print message is sent to a printer whose paper supply is exhausted. These errors are not the responsibility of the programmer in so far as a programmer usually has no control over the state of the system on which the program is to run. We shall ignore these errors and have no more to say about them in *Java Genesis.*

run-time exception
These errors arise because the code attempts to perform an invalid operation. For example, the code may attempt to access an array outside its bounds, or to do integer division by zero, or to cast an object to an incompatible type. These are all serious programming errors and as programmers it is our responsibility to ensure through sound coding that these errors do not occur. We should make sure, for example, that our code

does *not* attempt to access an array outside its bounds. In this chapter we look at the way Java handles these exceptions if they occur.

I/O exceptions
These are the exceptions that arise because the program is not being used as intended. For example, non-numeric data may be supplied as input when a number is expected. As the programmer has no control over the user and cannot force the user to behave in a specified way, there is little a programmer can do to prevent these exceptions from occurring. However, Java has special language features to help us handle such exceptions if they do occur. Java's mechanism for handling these user-generated exceptions will be discussed in this chapter and applied to file input/output (referred to colloquially as I/O).

Before beginning our study of exceptions and how to handle them in Java, consider the following analogy. Most high rise buildings are fitted with a fire escape. This is a flight of stairs providing an alternate route to the same floors that the lifts access. The fire escape is not used in general day-to-day operation. However, exceptions to the normal situation caused by power failure, lift failure or fire will force people to look for an alternative route through the building and the fire escape then comes to the fore. We can think of the fire escape as a mechanism to handle exceptions when they arise. Exception handling in Java is like constructing a fire escape to be used when exceptions arise during the execution of our program.

11.1 Throwing and catching exceptions

Errors in programs give rise to exceptional conditions that can be a nightmare to deal with cleanly. We look at the special language features that Java introduces to handle these exceptions. Our emphasis in this section is on run-time exceptions.

Problems:

1 modular division exception
2 catching all exceptions
3 catching specific exceptions
4 more on specific exceptions
5 passing back exceptions
6 temperature conversion exceptions

11.2 File input and output

As the contents of the central memory of a computer are lost when the machine is turned off, we need to be able to output key information to a file that can be kept on a persistent storage device such as a hard disk. This information can then be read from the disk when required at some later stage. We look at a particular class of file, the *text file*. These files enable us to store information in a text-readable format. When performing I/O, Java insists that we establish mechanisms to handle any I/O exceptions that may arise.

Problems:

7 text file output

8 printing to the Output window

9 appending file output

10 the first 250 primes

11 text file input

12 copying a file

13 using `StringTokenizer`

14 primes between 900 and 1000

15 totaling a shopping list

16 keyboard data input

11.3 Case study: a telephone book

We construct a class to manage a simple telephone book consisting of a collection of names and telephone numbers. The case study develops a GUI enabling names and telephone numbers to be stored in a text file and retrieved from that file as required.

Problems:

17 the telephone book GUI

18 preventing duplicate entries

19 removing entries

11.4 Case study: map making

In this case study an application is developed that enables us to create a map of the coastline of an island. Using the mouse, we click on a sequence of coordinates to represent the island's coast. These coordinates are then saved to a text file. A map of the island can then be re-created by reading the coordinates from the file.

Problems:

20 mapping the coastline

21 improving map making

Learning outcomes

At the conclusion of Chapter 11 you will understand:

- how exceptions can arise when a program is executed;
- the different categories of exceptions that can arise;
- some important Java exceptions;
- how to catch exceptions as they arise;
- how to throw exceptions back to the invoking method;
- how to create and write to a text file that will persist when the program is no longer running;
- how to append text to an existing text file;
- how to input text from a text file;
- how to use delimiter characters to partition a string into tokens;
- how to input text from the keyboard.

11.1 Throwing and catching exceptions

In this section we explore the various ways exceptions can be handled in Java by working through a simple example.

Example: modular division of integers

To illustrate a couple of the exceptions that can be thrown when a program is running, consider the class `ModDivFrame1`:

```
import genesis.*;
import javax.swing.*;
import java.awt.*;
import java.awt.event.*;

public class ModDivFrame1 extends ExitFrame {

    /* Performs mod division. */
```

```
    // instance variables
    private JTextField numerator, denominator, result;
    private String task =
        "Enter integers and press '=' to perform operation.";
    private JLabel message = new JLabel(task, JLabel.CENTER);

    // constructor
    public ModDivFrame1 ( ) {
        setTitle("Performing Mod Division");
        setBounds(100, 100, 550, 125);
        Font f = new Font("SansSerif", Font.BOLD, 20);
        message.setFont(f);
        numerator = new JTextField("0", 10);
        denominator = new JTextField("1", 10);
        result = new JTextField("0", 10);
        JLabel modSign = new JLabel("%", JLabel.CENTER);
        JButton equalBut = new JButton("=");
        equalBut.addActionListener(new ActionListener() {
            public void actionPerformed(ActionEvent evt) {
                performModDivision();
            }
        });
        JPanel p1 = new JPanel();
        p1.add(numerator);
        p1.add(modSign);
        p1.add(denominator);
        p1.add(equalBut);
        p1.add(result);
        JPanel p2 = new JPanel();
        p2.add(message);
        Container c = getContentPane();
        c.add(p1, "Center");
        c.add(p2, "South");
    }

    public void performModDivision ( ) {
        int numValue = Integer.parseInt(numerator.getText());
        int denomValue =
                    Integer.parseInt(denominator.getText());
        int modValue = numValue%denomValue;
        result.setText(""+modValue);
        message.setText(task);
    }
}
```

PROBLEM 1: modular division exceptions

The above class is in the folder *Modular Division 1*. Open this folder and run the `Main` class. A GUI similar to those we met in Chapter 10 opens enabling the user to perform modular division on any two integers input directly into the GUI's first two text fields.

Experiment with supplying various integers and pressing the '=' button. What happens when:

- an input that is not an integer is supplied?
- we attempt to divide by 0?

□

Discussion

If the '=' button is pressed in the Problem 1 GUI, the `performModDivision` method is invoked. Consider the expression

```
Integer.parseInt(numerator.getText())
```

in this method. This expression extracts the text displayed in the text field, i.e.

```
numerator.getText()
```

and converts it to an integer of type `int`. (Compare this with the way Java converts text to a floating point number of type `double` — see Section 10.4.)

Throwing an exception

If non-integer data is contained in the first text field, an error occurs when an attempt is made to evaluate the expression. This is because under these circumstances it would not be possible to parse the string in the text field so as to produce an integer.

What happens is that the Java system 'throws an exception'. The phrase 'throws an exception' is used to indicate that an object of the class `Exception` or one of its subclasses is created and 'thrown' by the Java system. The exception object created contains information about the exception that has occurred, and it is this information that gets printed in the Output window when the '=' button is pressed.

For the above, the exception thrown is an object of the `NumberFormatException` class. This class is a subclass of `IllegalArgumentException` which is a subclass of `RunTimeException` which in turn is a subclass of `Exception`. All these classes are in the *java.lang* package.

When the exception is thrown, execution of the method performModDivision stops and the thrown exception object is passed back to the method invoking performModDivision. This was the actionPerformed method in the anonymous inner class used to add an action listener to the action button equalBut. The method actionPerformed now also ceases execution immediately and the thrown exception object is passed back to the underlying Java system which prints the exception's message in the Output window.

Similarly, if non-numeric data is contained in the second text field, an exception occurs when evaluation of the expression

```
Integer.parseInt(denominator.getText())
```

in the method performModDivision is attempted. As before, under these circumstances it would not be possible to parse the string returned by the expression denominator.getText() so as to produce an integer. Again, the exception thrown is an object of the class NumberFormatException.

In the case when the second text field contains 0, a different type of exception occurs when evaluation of the expression

```
numValue%denomValue
```

in the method performModDivision is attempted. This is because it is not possible to perform integer division when the denominator is zero. In this case the exception thrown is an object of the class ArithmeticException which is also a subclass of RunTimeException.

Catching all exceptions

In the class ModDivFrame1 we left the handling of the thrown exceptions to the underlying Java system. But Java supplies a mechanism that enables us to catch and handle thrown exceptions ourselves. As an illustration, consider the class ModDivFrame2 which is identical to the class ModDivFrame1 except that the method performModDivision is altered to the code given at the top of the next page.

PROBLEM 2: catching all exceptions

The folder *Modular Division 2* contains the class ModDivFrame2. Open this folder and run the Main class. Once again experiment with supplying various integers and pressing the '=' button. What happens this time when:

- an input that is not an integer is supplied?
- we attempt to divide by 0?

□

```
public void performModDivision ( ) {
    try {
        int numValue = Integer.parseInt(numerator.getText());
        int denomValue =
                    Integer.parseInt(denominator.getText());
        int modValue = numValue%denomValue;
        result.setText(""+modValue);
        message.setText(task);
    } catch (Exception e) {
        message.setText("error: try again");
    }
}
```

Discussion

If an exception is thrown while the method performModDivision in the class ModDivFrame2 is being executed, the message 'error: try again' is displayed. Let us consider in detail how the code manages to catch and handle the thrown exceptions.

To catch and handle the exceptions in this example we use a *try-catch* statement with the following syntax:

```
try {
        // code that can throw the exceptions
        // we need to handle.
} catch ( exception_class e) {
        // code to handle this exception
}
```

This structure sits over the basic code we write adding another dimension to our programs. It is like the fire escape on our building. In the case of the method performModDivision, *exception_class* is the class Exception itself, but it could have been any subclass of Exception.

The try-block is executed first. If no exception is thrown, on completion of the execution of the block the code in the catch-block is ignored and the program continues execution in the usual way.

If, however, an exception is thrown during the execution of the try-block, this block immediately aborts execution and the catch-block is checked to see if the thrown exception is an object of the class *exception_class* or one of its subclasses. In the case of ModDivFrame2, *exception_class* is the class Exception, and as every exception object is an object of the class `Exception` or one of its subclasses, any thrown exception will be caught by the catch-block.

When the thrown exception object is an object of the class *exception_class* or one of its subclasses, the exception object is assigned to the parameter (`e` in the example code above) and the catch-block executed. In the `ModDivFrame2` class, the parameter `e` is effectively ignored as it is not referred to by the code in the catch-block. The thrown object `e` contains information about the exception that occurred and this information can be output by inserting a statement such as `System.out.println(e)` within the catch-block.

If the thrown exception object is not caught (i.e. the thrown exception is not an object of *exception_class* or one of its subclasses) the thrown exception is propagated just as if there had been no try-catch block in the first place.

When the catch-block is completed, execution continues in the usual way.

Catching specific exceptions

A problem with the way exceptions are handled in the class `ModDivFrame2` is that all exceptions are caught and handled in the one catch-block . To handle different exceptions in different ways we need to detect which type of exception has been thrown.

Consider the class `ModDivFrame3` which is identical to the class `ModDivFrame1` except that the method `performModDivision` is now:

```
public void performModDivision ( ) {
    try {
        int numValue = Integer.parseInt(numerator.getText());
        int denomValue =
                    Integer.parseInt(denominator.getText());
        int modValue = numValue%denomValue;
        result.setText(""+modValue);
        message.setText(task);
    } catch (NumberFormatException e) {
        message.setText
                ("numbers must both be integers: try again");
    } catch (ArithmeticException e) {
        message.setText("cannot divide by zero: try again");
    }
}
```

PROBLEM 3: catching specific exceptions

The folder *Modular Division 3* contains the class `ModDivFrame3`. Open this folder and run the `Main` class. Once again experiment with supplying various integers and pressing the '=' button. What happens this time when:

- an input that is not an integer is supplied?
- we attempt to divide by 0?

□

Discussion

In Problem 3, if non-integer data is contained in either of the first two text fields and the '=' button pressed, the message 'numbers must both be integers: try again' is displayed. On the other hand, if the first text field contains an integer and the second text field the integer 0, the message 'cannot divide by zero: try again' is displayed.

The *try-catch* statement used in the class `ModDivFrame3` differs from that used in the class `ModDivFrame2` in two respects.

First, there are two catch-blocks rather than just one.

Second, rather than using the class `Exception` in the catch-blocks, the subclasses `NumberFormatException` and `ArithmeticException` are used respectively instead.

In this case, if an exception is thrown during the execution of the try-block, this block immediately aborts execution and the first catch-block is checked to see if the thrown exception is an object of the class `NumberFormatException` or one of its subclasses.

- If so, the first catch-block is executed and the second-catch block is completely ignored.
- If not, the first catch-block is ignored and the second catch-block is checked to see if the thrown exception is an object of the `ArithmeticException` class or one of its subclasses.
  - If so, the second catch-block is executed.
  - In not, the exception is handled just as if there had been no try-catch block in the firstplace.

As we remarked earlier, the exception thrown when non-integer data is contained in the first two text fields is an object of the `NumberFormatException` class, while the exception thrown when we attempt to do integer division by 0 is an object of the class `ArithmeticException`. Consequently, if either of these exceptions occur while the method `performModDivision` is being executed, the appropriate catch-block will be invoked with the result that an appropriate message is displayed.

When we have more than one catch-block, as in the case above, it is important to place the more specific catch-block before the more general otherwise the general catch-block would catch the error best handled by a more specialised exception handler. For example, if the class `Exception` was associated with the first catch-block then this would catch all exceptions and subsequent catch-blocks would never be invoked. In fact, in such a case the compiler would detect that the subsequent catch-blocks cannot be reached. In our case, `NumberFormatException` is not a subclass of `ArithmeticException` or vise versa, so the order in which the catch-blocks are coded does not matter.

PROBLEM 4: more on specific exceptions

Construct a class `ModDivFrame4` which is identical to the class `ModDivFrame1` except that the method `performModDivision` is changed so that if the '=' button is pressed:

- when non-integer data is contained in the first text field, the message 'numerator must be an integer: try again' is displayed;
- when an integer is contained in the first text field but non-integer data is contained in the second text field, the message 'denominator must be an integer: try again' is displayed;
- when an integer is contained in the first text field and 0 is contained in the second text field, the message 'cannot divide by zero: try again' is displayed.

Create a folder *Modular Division 4* that contains the class `ModDivFrame4` and an appropriate `Main` class. Compile and run the `Main` class to test your code.

For help with this problem see Hints.

□

Passing back exceptions

In the examples so far we have caught and handled exceptions within the method where the exceptions are thrown. Sometimes however, rather than handling an exception within this method we prefer to pass the exception back to the invoking method.

To see how this works, consider the `ModDivFrame5` class that is identical to `ModDivFrame1` except that the `performModDivision` method is now

```
public void performModDivision ( )
        throws NumberFormatException, ArithmeticException {
    int numValue = Integer.parseInt(numerator.getText());
    int denomValue = Integer.parseInt(denominator.getText());
    int modValue = numValue%denomValue;
    result.setText(""+modValue);
    message.setText(task);
}
```

while the method `actionPerformed` in the anonymous inner class used to add the action listener to the `equalBut` action button is now:

```
public void actionPerformed(ActionEvent evt) {
    try {
        performModDivision();
    } catch (NumberFormatException e) {
        message.setText
                ("numbers must both be integers: try again");
    } catch (ArithmeticException e) {
        message.setText("cannot divide by zero: try again");
    }
}
```

PROBLEM 5: passing back exceptions

The folder *Modular Division 5* contains the class `ModDivFrame5`. Open this folder and run the `Main` class. Once again experiment with supplying various integers and pressing the '=' button. Be convinced that if

- an input that is not an integer is supplied, or
- we attempt to divide by 0

the application has behaviour which is identical to the application created by the class `ModDivFrame3` in Problem 3.

□

The throws-clause

The major distinction between the method `performModDivision` in the class `ModDivFrame5` compared with the class `ModDivFrame1` is that the signature of this method in the former is extended to include the *throws-clause*:

```
throws NumberFormatException, ArithmeticException
```

This clause is placed immediately after the declaration of the method's parameter list; it comes immediately before the left brace denoting the beginning of the method's code-block. The throws-clause in this case indicates that if an exception object of either of the classes `NumberFormatException` or `ArithmeticException` (or subclasses of these classes) is thrown in the method and not dealt with by an appropriate try-catch statement, the exception object will be passed back to the invoking method. The invoking method in its turn can either deal with the exception or throw it back to the method that invoked it, and so on.

In the class `ModDivFrame5`, the method `actionPerformed` invokes the method `performModDivision`, and so it is to the method `actionPerformed` that the thrown exceptions are passed. As we can see from the code for the method `actionPerformed`, the exceptions in this case are handled there rather than being passed back further.

In fact, if the throws-clause for the method `performModDivision` had been omitted the result would have been the same. When there is no code to direct otherwise, any object of `RunTimeException` or a subclass (e.g. a number-format or arithmetic exception) is handled by throwing it back to the invoking method. Despite this, it is wise not to rely upon the default behaviour but include a specific throws-clause as in the method `performModDivision`.

Indeed, if it is possible for an exception of the class `IOException` (or any subclass of this class) to be thrown within a method, Java insists we explicitly handle this exception in the method either by coding an appropriate try-catch statement or by inserting an appropriate throws-clause. Unlike run-time exceptions, Java does not allow us to simply ignore I/O exceptions in the hope that the system will supply some default mechanism to handle them. We shall have more to say about I/O exceptions in Section 11.2.

The throws-clause added to the `performModDivision` method has two associated exception classes. In general, any number of exception classes can be associated with a throws-clause. The only restriction is that if a method is redefined in a subclass, the redefined method cannot throw an exception back unless the original method in the superclass also does so. In other words, if an exception class is in a throws-clause in a redefined method, the original method in the superclass must have either that exception class or a superclass of that exception class included in its own throws-clause.

Some general issues

Before leaving the modular division GUI, there are a couple of general issues that need to be discussed.

First, in this example we have chosen to handle division by zero by using Java's exception handling mechanism. We could just as readily have handled this situation by writing code which checks the value of the numerator and gives a warning if this value is 0. Instead we chose to proceed with the division regardless and then catch the thrown exception if division by 0 is attempted. In general, using Java's exception mechanism to handle such arithmetic exceptions is not recommended. We should use standard code to ensure such situations don't occur, rather than catching the exceptions that arise if we let them occur.

In this case however, making use of Java's exception mechanism to detect attempted division by zero could be philosophically justified on the grounds that the exception is triggered by inappropriate input from the user. The suggestion is that the exception is similar in style to that which arises when the user supplies non-integer input. It could be argued that making use of the exception handling mechanism here unifies the approach to all inappropriate user input.

Second, in Problem 5 we added a throws-clause to the `performModDivision` method so as to illustrate the mechanism whereby exceptions can be passed back to the invoking method. For the modular division GUI there would be little point in actually doing this. In this case it is much better to handle the exceptions in the method where they occur.

In some situations, particularly those arising from I/O exceptions (see Section 11.2), the invoking method may often be better placed to deal with any thrown exceptions and it would be for that reason that we would make use of a throws-clause to pass back the thrown exceptions. As a general rule, the run-time exceptions we have encountered in this section should be dealt with where they occur and not passed back to the invoking method. A throws-clause also acts as a signal to the compiler that the given exception can possibly occur within the method.

Overview of some exception classes

Here is a brief overview of a few of the exception classes that are subclasses of the class `RunTimeException` (which is in turn a subclass of `Exception`). All these classes can be found in the *java.lang* package. For each class we give an informal description of the exception condition which leads to an object of the class being thrown. For more information browse the class `Exception` in the Java documentation.

- `ArithmeticException`

  invalid arithmetic condition, e.g. division by zero
- `ArrayStoreException`

  attempt to store an object in an array that is not of the array's type

- `ClassCastException`

  attempt to cast an object to an invalid type

- `IllegalArgumentException`

  the message's argument and the method's parameter are different types

- `ArrayIndexOutOfBoundsException`

  the index of an array is out of the array's declared bounds

- `NegativeArraySizeException`

  attempt to define an array with a negative dimension

- `NullPointerException`

  attempt to use a variable whose value is a null reference

To complete this section, consider once again the temperature conversion GUI we first met in Section 10.3.

PROBLEM 6: temperature conversion exceptions

Open the folder *Temperature Conversion*. Modify the class `ConversionFrame` so that if the 'deg F' (respectively 'deg C') text field contains text that cannot be converted into a floating point number, when the 'convert F to C' (respectively 'convert C to F') button is pressed, 'bad input' is printed in the 'deg F' (respectively 'deg C') text field.

For help with this problem see Hints.

□

11.2 File input and output

In this section, we look at reading from input and writing to output devices. An input device could be a disk, in which case the input is obtained from a file on the disk, or it could be the keyboard, in which case the input is obtained by pressing the keys in some sequence. An output device could also be a disk, in which case the output goes to some file on the disk, or it could be the screen, in which case the output will appear in some window on the screen.

Java supplies a huge package, *java.io*, to cater for almost every conceivable I/O situation. Our focus will be on only a small but representative part of Java's I/O capabilities. In particular, the main concern of this section will be on text file I/O. But we will also see how we can input text directly from the keyboard.

Restricting our focus to text I/O certainly limits our scope considerably, but text input and output is a major part of computing so it is an excellent place to start. Furthermore, text files are stored in a text-readable form so we will be able to use a standard text editor or word processor to see the results we produce.

We will consider only sequential processing of text files. This means that we can only process a file (whether reading or writing) in one pass. We will start at the beginning of a file and move in sequence to its end; we will not be able to move back or jump forward out of sequence.

Sending output to a text file

To begin, we will look at how to output information to a file created on a disk. Consider the class `TextFileOut` whose code is given below:

```
import java.io.*;

public class TextFileOut {

    public static void main (String [] args)
                                throws IOException {
        String fileName = "RandInt.txt";
        FileWriter fw = new FileWriter(fileName);
        PrintWriter pw = new PrintWriter(fw);
        pw.println("20 Random Integers between 0 and 99:");
        pw.println();
        for (int i=1; i<=20; i++)
            pw.println((int)(100*Math.random()));
        pw.close();
    }
}
```

Although some aspects to this code may seem strange, most of the statements to do with writing text to a file are intuitive and you should be able to guess what the program will produce when it executes. We will explain the detail of this code shortly, but first try the following problem.

PROBLEM 7: text file output

The class `TextFileOut` is in the folder *Text File Out*. Open this folder and run the class.

A file *RandInt.txt* is created in the same folder. Open this file using any available text editor and check if the file created corresponds to your expectations. Try to explain each line within the file by relating its presence to some code statement.

Modify the class `TextFileOut` so that the 20 random integers are printed on the same line with a space between each integer.

Experiment with outputting other information to a text file.

For help with this problem see Hints.

□

Discussion

Consider the code for the class `TextFileOut`. First, the package *java.io* is imported. This package contains the Java classes needed to perform I/O.

Next, the `main` method has the throws-clause:

```
throws IOException
```

Methods involving file I/O may throw an exception of the class `IOException` and Java insists that any such method either handle it with an appropriate try-catch statement or pass the exception back to the calling method. In this case the choice is to pass it back (to the underlying Java system).

Now consider the object `pw` of the class `PrintWriter`. This object can print strings, numbers, characters etc. in text format. However, to make use of the output produced by the object `pw` we need to combine this object with a destination object such as a file. This is done in three steps:

1. First, a `String` object is constructed naming the text file to receive the output:

   ```
   String fileName = "RandInt.txt";
   ```

   In our case the file *RandInt.txt* will be in the same folder as the class `TextFileOut`. If we want the file to be in some other place, we need to stipulate the path. For example, the string `"a:\\RandInt.txt"` will denote a file *RandInt.txt* on the A-drive, while the string `"stuff\\RandInt.txt"` will denote a file *RandInt.txt* in the folder *stuff* in the same folder as `TextFileOut`. (Remember that the character '\' is an escape character. To get the character '\' in a string we must include two such characters.)

2. Next a `FileWriter` object is constructed with the `String` object denoting the name of the text file (as constructed in the previous step) being passed as an argument to the constructor method:

```
FileWriter fw = new FileWriter(fileName);
```

This object is responsible for converting Java encoded information into a format that can be output to the given file. The details of how this works will not concern us. Methods of this class can throw I/O exceptions.

3. Finally a `PrintWriter` object is constructed with the `FileWriter` object constructed in the previous step being passed as an argument to the constructor method:

```
PrintWriter pw = new PrintWriter(fw);
```

An object of the class `PrintWriter` can invoke instance methods `print` and `println` which are similar to those invoked by the `System.out` object. These methods can be used to print primitive types (`int`, `double`, `char`, `boolean`, etc.), strings and objects in the usual way. Methods of this class never throw I/O exceptions.

Of course, the above three steps can be combined into one. That is, the three statements

```
String fileName = "RandInt.txt";
FileWriter fw = new FileWriter(fileName);
PrintWriter pw = new PrintWriter(fw);
```

in the class `TextFileOut` can be replaced by the single equivalent statement:

```
PrintWriter pw =
        new PrintWriter(new FileWriter("RandInt.txt"));
```

The process defined above to enable text to be written to a file is somewhat laborious. It is not necessary to understand all the details of the classes involved. The important thing is to know how to construct an object of the class `PrintWriter` and that such an object can be sent the usual `print` and `println` messages. The rest can be treated as annoying but necessary background noise.

The remainder of the class `TextFileOut` is as expected, except for the final statement

```
pw.close();
```

which signifies that the output is ended and the connection to the file can be closed. In practice, output is buffered (held temporarily in memory) which means that there may be a short delay before data sent to a file is actually placed in the file. This buffering is done to ensure hardware resources are handled efficiently. The method `close` first flushes the buffer to ensure all data is written to the file before the link to the file is closed.

Printing to the Output window

We already know how to print to the Output window using the `System.out` object. Here is an alternative method.

When declaring a print writer object as above, rather than invoking a constructor method `FileWriter` by passing a string as argument, invoke instead a constructor method `FileWriter` by passing the object `FileDescriptor.out` as argument. The output now goes to the Output window rather than a file.

The class `FileDescriptor` contains information about the underlying machine-specific hardware; the object `FileDescriptor.out` represents the standard output stream.

This demonstrates the elegant way I/O is handled in Java. Writing text to a file or to the screen can be seen as essentially similar processes.

PROBLEM 8: printing to the Output window

Using the object `FileDescriptor.out`, modify the class `TextFileOut` so that output goes to the Output window rather than to the file.

For help with this problem see Hints.

□

Appending output to a file

Every time we run the class `TextFileOut` we either create a new *RandInt.txt* file (when the file does not already exist) or (when the file already exists) the existing contents of the file are replaced by the new output. If we want the new output to be appended to the existing contents we instead invoke a `FileWriter` constructor method that has two parameters.

The first parameter, as before, is a string giving the name of the file. The second parameter is a Boolean. When we pass the value *true* as argument to the second parameter, if the class is run and the named file does not exist it will be created, while if the file already exists any new output will be appended to the existing contents.

PROBLEM 9: appending file output

Modify the class `TextFileOut` so that every time the class is run the output is appended to the file *RandInt.txt*. For help with this problem see Hints.

□

Here is one more problem to conclude this subsection on file output.

PROBLEM 10: the first 250 primes

Construct a class `Primes` which writes the first 250 primes to a file *primes.txt* at 10 numbers per line.

For help with this problem see Hints.

□

We now turn our attention to input. We will look at reading files we have previously created and also reading from the keyboard.

Reading input from a text file

Consider the class `TextFileIn`:

```
import java.io.*;

public class TextFileIn {

    public static void main (String [] args)
                                        throws IOException {
        String fileName = "RandInt.txt";
        FileReader fr = new FileReader(fileName);
        BufferedReader br = new BufferedReader(fr);
        br.readLine();
        br.readLine();
        int sum = 0;
        int count = 0;
        String line = br.readLine();
        while (line != null) {
            sum = sum + Integer.parseInt(line);
            count++;
            line = br.readLine();
        }
        System.out.println("Average = "+(double)sum/count);
        br.close();
    }
}
```

This class reads from the file *RandInt.txt* created by the class `TextFileOut` in Problem 7. We will explain the detail of this code shortly, but first try the following problem.

PROBLEM 11: text file input

The class `TextFileIn` is in the folder *Text File In*. Open this folder and run the class.

The random integers in the file *RandInt.txt* are input and their average is computed and printed in the Output window.

Modify the class `TextFileIn` so that the average of the random integers is appended to the file *RandInt.txt*. You will need to close the file for input before attempting to write to it.

For help with this problem see Hints.

□

Discussion

Consider the code for the `TextFileIn` class. Just as with the `TextFileOut` class, and for the same reasons, the package *java.io* is imported and the `main` method has the throws-clause:

```
throws IOException
```

Recall that when outputting data we constructed an object of the `PrintWriter` class. This object understood the messages `print` and `println` for writing numbers, characters, strings, etc. However, there is no equivalent class when we need to input data. Instead we use the class `BufferedReader` that has a method `readLine()` that reads the next line of a text file and inputs it as a string. Consequently, if we want to interpret an input string as a number we then need to do some conversion.

Apart from this, the process for constructing objects to handle file input is closely analogous to the process for constructing objects to handle file output that we met earlier. In particular, the object `br` of the class `BufferedReader` is constructed in three steps:

1. First, a `String` object is constructed naming the text file to be read:

   ```
   String fileName = "RandInt.txt";
   ```

   In our case the file *RandInt.txt* is in the same folder as the `TextFileIn` class. If the file is in some other place, we need to stipulate the path. If the file does not exist an I/O exception will be thrown when we attempt to open it at Step 2.

2. Next a `FileReader` object is constructed where the `String` object denoting the name of the text file (as constructed in the previous step) is passed as argument to the constructor method:

```
FileReader fr = new FileReader(fileName);
```

This object is responsible for converting the input from the file into an encoded format that Java can understand. As with the case of file output considered earlier, the details of how this works will not concern us. Methods of this class can throw I/O exceptions.

3. Finally a `BufferedReader` object is constructed where the `FileReader` object constructed in the previous step is passed as argument to the constructor method:

```
BufferedReader br = new BufferedReader(fr);
```

Once again of course, these three steps can be combined into one. The above three statements in the class `TextFileIn` can be replaced by the single statement:

```
BufferedReader br =
        new BufferedReader(new FileReader("RandInt.txt"));
```

To read from the text file *RandInt.txt* in the class `TextFileIn` we send the `BufferedReader` object `br` the message `readLine()`. This returns a string denoting the next line in the file. We start with the two statements

```
br.readLine();
br.readLine();
```

which read (and ignore) the first two lines of the file. (The first line is the string

```
"20 Random Integers between 0 and 99: "
```

while the second line is blank.) The remaining lines of the file *RandInt.txt* each denote an integer. We read the lines in one at a time and convert them from a string to an integer in the usual way:

```
int sum = 0;
int count = 0;
String line = br.readLine();
while (line != null) {
    sum = sum + Integer.parseInt(line);
    count++;
    line = br.readLine();
}
```

In the process we can sum these integers. If we read past the end of the file, the message `readLine()` returns `null`; we can use this to test for the file's end.

Finally, all we need to do is output the average of the numbers and close the file:

```
System.out.println("Average = "+sum/20.0);
br.close();
```

PROBLEM 12: copying a file

Construct a class `CopyFile` that when run opens a dialog box requesting the user supply the name of some existing text file. When this name is supplied, a second dialog box opens requesting the user supply a second file name. The program then creates a text file with the second name that is a copy of the first file. If a file with the second name already exists it is replaced.

For help with this problem see Hints.

□

Tokenizing text input

In the file *RandInt.txt* in Problem 11, the 20 random integers were very conveniently arranged on distinct lines. As a consequence, after ignoring the first two lines in this file the expression

```
Integer.parseInt(line);
```

is guaranteed to return an integer value without throwing a number-format exception.

Suppose however, that the 20 integers were stored in the file 5 numbers to a line. For example, the file *RandIntAgain.txt* contains the text:

```
20 Random Integers between 0 and 99:

43 47 50 68 9
84 91 8 48 59
35 18 65 43 32
45 50 10 18 17
```

In this case, the code fragment

```
BufferedReader br =
    new BufferedReader(new FileReader("RandIntAgain.txt"));
br.readLine();
br.readLine();
String line = br.readLine();
```

would result in the variable `line` becoming the string `"43 47 50 68 9"`. The expression `Integer.parseInt(line)` would then throw an exception of the class `NumberFormatException` as this string cannot be converted into one integer.

What we need to do is partition each line into sub-strings representing its constituent numbers. Fortunately, Java supplies a special class, `StringTokenizer`, to do just this. This class is in the *java.util* package.

To give some idea of how a string tokenizer can be used, here is the code for a class `TextFileInAgain` that reads the file *RandIntAgain.txt* and prints in the Output window the average of the integers:

```
import java.io.*;
import java.util.*;

public class TextFileInAgain {

    public static void main (String [] args)
                                    throws IOException {
        BufferedReader br = new BufferedReader
                    (new FileReader("RandIntAgain.txt"));
        br.readLine();
        br.readLine();
        int sum = 0;
        int count = 0;
        String line = br.readLine();
        while (line != null) {
            StringTokenizer st = new StringTokenizer(line);
            while (st.hasMoreTokens()) {
                sum = sum + Integer.parseInt(st.nextToken());
                count++
            }
            line = br.readLine();
        }
        System.out.println("Average = "+(double)sum/count);
        br.close();
    }
}
```

PROBLEM 13: using `StringTokenizer`

The class `TextFileInAgain` and the file *RandIntAgain.txt* are in the folder *Text File In Again*. Open this folder and run the class to confirm it does what is claimed.

Modify the class `TextFileInAgain` so that when it is run it prints in the Output window the smallest of the integers.

For help with this problem see Hints.

□

Tokens and delimiters

Consider how string tokenizers are used in the class `TextFileInAgain`. The relevant code is:

```
int sum = 0;
int count = 0;
String line = br.readLine();
while (line != null) {
    StringTokenizer st = new StringTokenizer(line);
    while (st.hasMoreTokens()) {
        sum = sum + Integer.parseInt(st.nextToken());
        count++;
    }
    line = br.readLine();
}
```

After each new line in the file has been read to give the string `line`, a new object of the class `StringTokenizer` is constructed:

```
StringTokenizer st = new StringTokenizer(line);
```

Notice that the string that we want to work with (i.e. `line`) is passed as the argument to the constructor method. The string tokenizer object `st` constructed in this way enables us to partition the string `line` into sub-strings called *tokens* that do not contain white-space characters (i.e. a space, tab or new-line) but rather are separated from each other by such characters. The white-space characters in this context are called *delimiters*.

Two particular instance methods of the class `StringTokenizer` are relevant:

- `hasMoreTokens()`

  returns a Boolean which has the value *true* if and only if there is one or more token remaining to be extracted from the string

- `nextToken()`

  returns the next token in the string

PROBLEM 14: primes between 900 and 1000

The file *primes.txt* was produced by Problem 10 and consists of the first 250 primes stored 10 primes to a line. This file can be found in the folder *Counting Primes.*

Construct a class `CountingPrimes` that reads the file *primes.txt*, counts the number of primes between 900 and 1000 and writes this number to the Output window.

For help with this problem see Hints.

□

PROBLEM 15: totaling a shopping list

The file *shopping.txt* is in the folder *Shopping List* and contains a list of items and their cost:

```
milk            2.35
soft drinks     5.15
bread           2.95
fruit and veg   9.54
```

Construct a class `ShoppingList` that reads this file and writes to the Output window the total cost of the items in the list. Your class should be quite general so that it will work for any shopping list similar to the above.

Hint: As we want to extract just the floating point numbers, we can test each token in each line to see if it can be converted into a floating point number. This can be done with a try-catch statement using the fact that the expression

```
Double.valueOf(st.nextToken()).doubleValue()
```

where `st` is a string tokenizer will throw an object of `NumberFormatException` if `st.nextToken()`cannot be converted into a floating point number.

An alternative approach is to search for the last token in each line as this token is the floating point number we want to extract.

For further help with this problem see Hints.

□

Keyboard input

We saw earlier that the object `FileDescriptor.out` represents standard output and enables us to write to the Output window. In a similar way, the object `FileDescriptor.in` represents standard input and enables us to input characters directly from the keyboard.

Here is the code for a class `KeyboardIn` which requests that integers are input using the keyboard:

```
import java.io.*;

public class KeyboardIn {

    public static void main (String [] args)
                                throws IOException {
        BufferedReader br = new BufferedReader
                    (new FileReader(FileDescriptor.in));
        String line;
        int sum = 0;
        System.out.println("Input integers:");
        while(true) {
            try {
                line = br.readLine();
                sum = sum + Integer.parseInt(line.trim());
            } catch (NumberFormatException e) {
                System.out.println("sum of numbers: "+sum);
                System.exit(0);
            }
        }
    }
}
```

Notice in this code that the object `FileDescriptor.in` is passed as argument to the constructor method invoked when creating an object of the class `FileReader`.

When the class `KeyboardIn` is run, a string is input by pressing the digit keys in sequence and then pressing the 'enter' key. First this string is *trimmed*, i.e. any leading or trailing spaces are removed. This is achieved by sending the message `trim()` to the string. Then the trimmed string returned is converted into an integer in the usual way.

If any string is entered that cannot be converted into an integer after trimming, the sum of all the integers input to this point is printed in the Output window and the application ceases execution.

PROBLEM 16: keyboard data input

The class `KeyboardIn` is in the folder *Keyboard In*. Open this folder and run the class to confirm it behaves as described above.

Modify this class to construct a class `KeyboardToFile` whereby any non-empty sequence of characters can be input from the keyboard and each time the 'enter' key is pressed the sequence just typed is printed as a line to the text file *keyboard.txt*. When the null line is entered the file *keyboard.txt* is closed and the program stops execution.

For help with this problem see Hints.

□

11.3 Case study: a telephone book

In this case study we will look at how we can build a simple telephone book to record names and telephone numbers. We want the data contained in the telephone book to be stored in a text file called *PhoneBook.txt*. We shall construct a GUI that enables us to add entries to and retrieve information from the telephone book.

The class `InitPhoneBookFrame` whose code is given on the next page constructs a GUI with

- 2 text fields in the centre of the window labelled 'name' and 'phone number';
- 4 action buttons at the bottom of the window labelled 'store', 'lookup', 'next' and 'quit';
- a label at the top of the window for displaying a message.

This class is very similar to classes we met in Chapter 10 so we won't give a detailed explanation of the code. Notice however, that for each action button the associated action listener does nothing; the statement block of the corresponding `actionPerformed` method is empty.

The class `InitPhoneBookFrame` simply establishes the GUI components and their layout in the window, nothing more. It is the purpose of this case study to construct code to implement the functionality of the GUI.

```
import genesis.*;
import javax.swing.*;
import java.awt.*;
import java.awt.event.*;

public class InitPhoneBookFrame extends ExitFrame {

    /*
    GUI to manage a file PhoneBook.txt of
    names and telephone numbers.
    */

    // instance variables
    private JTextField name, phoneNum;
    private JLabel message;

    // constructor
    public InitPhoneBookFrame ( ) {
        setTitle("Telephone  Book");
        setBounds(100, 100, 375, 175);
        message = new JLabel
            ("NAMES AND TELEPHONE NUMBERS", JLabel.CENTER);
        name = new JTextField("", 28);
        phoneNum = new JTextField("", 20);
        JLabel nameLabel =
                    new JLabel("name:", JLabel.RIGHT);
        JLabel phoneNumLabel =
                new JLabel("phone number:", JLabel.RIGHT);
        JButton storeBut = new JButton("store");
        JButton lookupBut = new JButton("lookup");
        JButton nextBut = new JButton("next");
        JButton quitBut = new JButton("quit");
        storeBut.addActionListener(new ActionListener() {
            public void actionPerformed(ActionEvent evt){
            }
        });
        lookupBut.addActionListener(new ActionListener() {
            public void actionPerformed(ActionEvent evt) {
            }
        });
        nextBut.addActionListener(new ActionListener() {
            public void actionPerformed(ActionEvent evt) {
            }
        });
```

```
        quitBut.addActionListener(new ActionListener() {
            public void actionPerformed(ActionEvent evt) {
            }
        });
        Container c = getContentPane();
        JPanel pNorth = new JPanel();
        pNorth.add(message);
        c.add(pNorth, "North");
        JPanel pCentre = new JPanel();
        pCentre.add(nameLabel);
        pCentre.add(name);
        pCentre.add(phoneNumLabel);
        pCentre.add(phoneNum);
        c.add(pCentre, "Center");
        JPanel pSouth = new JPanel();
        pSouth.add(storeBut);
        pSouth.add(lookupBut);
        pSouth.add(nextBut);
        pSouth.add(quitBut);
        c.add(pSouth, "South");
    }
}
```

PROBLEM 17: the telephone book GUI

The class `InitPhoneBookFrame` is in the folder *Initial Phone Book*. Open this folder and run the `Main` class.

Study the class `InitPhoneBookFrame` to identify those code statements responsible for constructing each component of the GUI.

□

Here is an informal description of the functionality we want to associate with the 4 action buttons:

- the 'store' button

  When this button is pressed we want the name and phone number currently in the respective text fields to be appended as a line to the file *PhoneBook.txt*.

- the 'lookup' button

  When this button is pressed we want the telephone number associated with the current entry in the 'name' text field to be displayed in the 'phone number' text field.

- the 'next' button

  When this button is pressed we want the next name and phone number entry in the telephone book to be displayed in the respective text fields.

- the 'quit' button

  When this button is pressed we want to close the application, saving the file *PhoneBook.txt* in its most up-to-date state.

We shall now add code to the class `InitPhoneBookFrame` to implement this functionality. First we need to add 3 extra instance variables:

```
private BufferedReader br;
private PrintWriter pw;
private boolean reading = false;
```

The first two variables, `br` and `pw`, will denote the objects responsible for respectively reading and writing data to and from the file *PhoneBook.txt*. The third variable, `reading`, is a Boolean that will tell us whether or not the file *PhoneBook.txt* is currently open for reading .

Storing data

The storing of data is invoked by pressing the 'store' action button. According to the informal description above, when the button 'store' is pressed we want the name and telephone number currently in the respective text fields to be appended as a line to the file *PhoneBook.txt*.

To achieve this we need to add appropriate code to the `actionPerformed` method in the anonymous inner class construct used to add an action listener to the button 'store'. Here is an informal scenario describing what we want to happen when this code is invoked:

- if the file *PhoneBook.txt* is currently being read, close the `BufferedReader` object `br` and set the Boolean `reading` to *false*;
- construct a new `PrintWriter` object `pw` to append data to *PhoneBook.txt*;
- append the displayed name and phone number as a line to the file;
- close the object `pw`.

Here is our code to implement this scenario:

```
storeBut.addActionListener(new ActionListener() {
    public void actionPerformed(ActionEvent evt){
        try {
            if (reading) {
                br.close();
                reading = false;
            }
            pw = new PrintWriter(new
                    FileWriter("PhoneBook.txt", true));
            pw.println
                (name.getText()+" \t "+phoneNum.getText());
            pw.close();
            message.setText("NEW ENTRY STORED");
        } catch (IOException e) {
            System.out.println("I/O error while storing");
            System.exit(0);
        }
    }
});
```

Discussion

We need to embed the code in a try-catch statement as an I/O exception may be thrown and Java insists that such exceptions are not ignored but are dealt with either explicitly as here or by having an appropriate throws-clause as part of the method's declaration.

The first argument passed to the `FileWriter` constructor method when constructing the `PrintWriter` object `pw` identifies by name the file to which we want to write, i.e. *PhoneBook.txt*. The second argument is the Boolean *true*, indicating that we want to append to this file, not recreate it (see Problem 9).

When writing the name and phone number to the file *PhoneBook.txt* we put both on one line and separate the two items of data by the string `" \t "`. As we shall soon see, the tab character will enable us to extract as single tokens names and phone numbers each of which may include the space character. Both names and telephone numbers are handled as strings. Notice that we add a space both before and after the tab. This ensures that no name or number entry is completely empty.

The `message` label at the top of the window is changed to display the string `"NEW ENTRY STORED"` indicating that the operation has succeeded.

Finally, if an I/O exception is thrown we simply print an appropriate message in the output window and close the application.

Retrieving data

The retrieval of data is invoked by pressing the 'lookup' action button. What we want is to display in the 'phone number' text field the number associated with the entry currently displayed in the 'name' text field.

This time we need to add code to the `actionPerformed` method in the anonymous inner class construct used to add an action listener to the 'lookup' button. Here is a scenario describing what we want to happen when this code is invoked:

- if the file *PhoneBook.txt* is currently being read, close the `BufferedReader` object `br`;
- construct a new `BufferedReader` object `br` to read from the beginning of the file *PhoneBook.txt*;
- set the Boolean `reading` to *true*;
- read in a line of the file *PhoneBook.txt*;
- check to see if the 'name' part of this line (trimmed to remove leading or trailing spaces) matches the (trimmed) entry currently in the 'name' text field;
  - if so, the match is found so display the 'number' part of this line trimmed in the 'phone number' text field;
  - if not, read in the next line;
- continue until a match is found or the end of the file is reached;
- if no match is found, close the object `br` and set the Boolean `reading` to *false*.

Our code to implement this scenario is at the top of the next page.

Discussion

Consider the code for the `lookupBut` on the next page. Just as with the implementation of the action listener for the 'store' button, we need to embed the code in a try-catch statement to deal with any I/O exception.

Two arguments are passed to the `StringTokenizer` constructor method when constructing the object `st`. The first argument passes the string whose tokens we want to extract. The second argument is a string whose characters are to be the delimiters for those tokens.

In the string tokenizer applications we met in Section 11.2 this second argument was omitted, with the result that the delimiters default to the white-space characters. In the case here, however, the second argument is the string `"\t"` so the tab character becomes the (only) delimiter. As a consequence, space characters can now appear within a token.

```
lookupBut.addActionListener(new ActionListener() {
    public void actionPerformed(ActionEvent evt) {
        try {
            if (reading) br.close();
            br = new BufferedReader
                        (new FileReader("PhoneBook.txt"));
            reading = true;
            boolean found = false;
            String line = br.readLine();
            while (!found && line != null) {
                StringTokenizer st =
                            new StringTokenizer(line,"\t");
                if (st.nextToken().trim().equals
                                (name.getText().trim())) {
                    found = true;
                    phoneNum.setText(st.nextToken().trim());
                    message.setText("TELEPHONE NUMBER FOUND");
                } else line = br.readLine();
            }
            if (!found) {
                message.setText("NO MATCHING ENTRY FOUND");
                br.close();
                reading = false;
            }
        } catch (IOException e) {
            System.out.println("I/O error doing lookup");
            System.exit(0);
        }
    }
});
```

This is precisely what we want, as both a name and a telephone number can include the space character. Each line of the file *PhoneBook.txt* will be partitioned into exactly two tokens: the name and the telephone number. (We shall assume that no name or phone number contains the tab character. In any case, we cannot insert a tab into a text field; when a tab is typed we automatically go to the next text field.)

Only if no match is found do we close the `BufferedReader` object `br` and set the Boolean `reader` to *false*. If a match is found we preserve the object `br` so that if the 'next' action button is pressed the entry immediately following the currently displayed entry in the file *PhoneBook.txt* will be the one displayed (see below for details).

Stepping through the data

We display in the text fields the name and phone number stored in the next line of the file *PhoneBook.txt* by pressing the 'next' action button. If we are at the file's end when 'next' is pressed the first line of the file is displayed. If the file is empty no data is displayed.

This time we need to add code to the `actionPerformed` method in the anonymous inner class construct used to add an action listener to the 'next' button. Here is a scenario describing what we want to happen:

- if the file *PhoneBook.txt* is not currently being read
  - construct a new `BufferedReader` object `br` (to read from the beginning of the file);
  - set the Boolean `reading` to *true*;
- read in the next line of the file;
- if the line is null (i.e. if at the end of the file *PhoneBook.txt*)
  - close the `BufferedReader` object `br`;
  - construct a new `BufferedReader` object `br` (to read from the beginning of the file);
  - read in the first line of the file (if any);
- display the (trimmed) first token of the line in the 'name' text field and the second token in the 'phone number' text field.

The code to implement this scenario is straightforward and follows the pattern established when implementing the previous two action buttons:

```
nextBut.addActionListener(new ActionListener() {
    public void actionPerformed(ActionEvent evt) {
        try {
            if (!reading) {
                br = new BufferedReader
                        (new FileReader("PhoneBook.txt"));
                reading = true;
            }
            String line = br.readLine();
            if (line == null) {
                br.close();
                br = new BufferedReader
                        (new FileReader("PhoneBook.txt"));
                line = br.readLine();
                if (line == null)
                    line = " \t ";  // if file is empty
            }
```

```
                StringTokenizer st =
                            new StringTokenizer(line, "\t");
                name.setText(st.nextToken().trim());
                phoneNum.setText(st.nextToken().trim());
                message.setText("NEXT ENTRY");
            } catch (IOException e) {
                System.out.println("I/O error doing next");
                System.exit(0);
            }
        }
    });
```

Notice that if the file *PhoneBook.txt* is able to be read when the 'next' button is pressed, the next line of data in the file (or the first line of data if we are currently at the end of the file) is displayed. If the file is empty no data is displayed.

Quitting the application

All that remains is to implement the 'quit' action button. This time we need to add code to the `actionPerformed` method in the anonymous inner class construct used to add an action listener to the 'quit' button. Here is what we want to happen when this button is pressed:

- if the file *PhoneBook.txt* is currently being read, close the `BufferedReader` object `br`;
- terminate the application.

Here is our code to implement this scenario:

```
    quitBut.addActionListener(new ActionListener() {
        public void actionPerformed(ActionEvent evt) {
            try {
                if (reading) br.close();
                System.exit(0);
            } catch (IOException e) {
                System.out.println("I/O error while quitting");
                System.exit(0);
            }
        }
    });
```

It is only necessary to test if the file *PhoneBook.txt* is currently being read before terminating the application. Testing if the file is currently being written is unnecessary as writing to the file takes place only if the ‘store’ action button is pressed. The code invoked in this case itself closes the `PrintWriter` object `pw`.

Notice that clicking with the mouse on the ‘X’ in the upper-right corner of the GUI window will terminate the application immediately without first closing the `BufferedReader` object `br`. To ensure a safe exit from the GUI, the application should be terminated by pressing the ‘quit’ button.

PROBLEM 18: preventing duplicate entries

The full code for the telephone book GUI is in the class `PhoneBookFrame`. This class can be found in the folder *Phone Book*. Open this folder and run the `Main` class.

A file *PhoneBook.txt* containing some data is in the same folder. To test the GUI try adding new entries, or looking up information, or stepping through the entries.

One problem with the class `PhoneBookFrame` is that it allows us to store more than one entry with the same name. Modify the code associated with the action button ‘store’ so that if the name associated with an entry is already in the book, when the ‘store’ button is pressed the message label at the top of the window warns us that the name already appears in the book. In this case the entry is not appended to the file *PhoneBook.txt*.

For help with this problem see Hints.

□

To complete this case study, here is a more challenging problem.

PROBLEM 19: removing entries

Add an action button ‘remove’ to the telephone book GUI which when pressed results in the removal from the book of all entries which have as their ‘name’ component the string currently being displayed in the first text field.

For help with this problem see Hints.

□

11.4 Case study: map making

To complete this chapter we present as a case study a simple GUI enabling us to map and record the coastline of an island.

PROBLEM 20: mapping the coastline

Open the folder *Map Making* and run the Main class.

Consider the window on the left labelled 'Create the Map'. We shall refer to this as the *create* window. Use the mouse to click a sequence of positions representing the coast of some island. The positions selected by the mouse clicks must be in sequence moving around the coastline either clockwise or anti-clockwise. When satisfied, enter a file name into the text field at the bottom of the create window and press the 'save' action button. The coordinates of the positions selected by the mouse clicks will be saved as text in the named file.

Consider now the window on the right labelled 'Display the Map'. We shall refer to this as the *display* window. Enter the same file name used in the create window into the text field at the bottom of the display window and press the 'display' action button. A map of the island just constructed is displayed.

Try constructing a map of your favourite island by clicking with the mouse on positions representing the island's coastline.

(We have done this ourselves for our favourite island, Australia, and saved the coordinates in the file oz.txt in the same folder. To look at our effort enter this file name into the text field at the bottom of the display window and press the 'display' button. Our attempt is somewhat unimaginative. Feel free to use your artistic flair when creating your map.)

□

Creating a map

Here is the code for the classes `CreateMapFrame` and `CreateMapPanel` that together implement the create window:

```
import genesis.*;
import javax.swing.*;
import java.awt.*;
import java.awt.event.*;

public class CreateMapFrame extends ExitFrame  {

    /* Create the map of an island */

    // instance variables
    private JTextField fileName;
    private CreateMapPanel map = new CreateMapPanel();
```

```
    public CreateMapFrame ( ) {
        setBounds(0, 50, 450, 450);
        setTitle("Create the Map");
        fileName = new JTextField("", 20);
        JButton save = new JButton("save");
        save.addActionListener(new ActionListener() {
            public void actionPerformed(ActionEvent evt){
                map.saveMap(fileName.getText());
            }
        });
        JButton quit = new JButton("quit");
        quit.addActionListener(new ActionListener() {
            public void actionPerformed(ActionEvent evt){
                map.closeMap();
                System.exit(0);
            }
        });
        Container c = getContentPane();
        JPanel p = new JPanel();
        p.add(save);
        p.add(fileName);
        p.add(quit);
        c.add(p, "South");
        c.add(map, "Center");
    }
}
```

```
import javax.swing.*;
import java.awt.*;
import java.awt.event.*;
import java.io.*;

public class CreateMapPanel extends JPanel {

    // instance variables
    private int [] xs = new int [500];
    private int [] ys = new int [500];
    private int size = 0;
    private PrintWriter pw;

    // constructor
    public CreateMapPanel ( ) {
        setBackground(Color.white);
```

```
        addMouseListener(new MouseAdapter( ) {
            public void mousePressed (MouseEvent e) {
                xs[size] = e.getX();
                ys[size] = e.getY();
                size++;
                repaint();
            }
        });
    }

    public void paintComponent (Graphics g) {
        // draw map
        super.paintComponent(g);
        if (size  > 0) {
            for (int i = 0; i< size-1; i++)
                g.drawLine(xs[i],ys[i],xs[i+1],ys[i+1]);
        }
    }

    public void saveMap (String fileName) {
        try {
            pw = new PrintWriter(new FileWriter(fileName));
            pw.println(size);
            for (int i = 0; i < size; i++)
                pw.println(xs[i]+" "+ys[i]);
            pw.close();
            size = 0;
            repaint();
        } catch (IOException e) {
            System.out.println("Error in saving map: "+e);
        System.exit(0);
        }
    }

    public void closeMap ( ) {
        if (pw != null) pw.close();
    }
}
```

Discussion

Consider first the class CreateMapPanel.

The instance variables xs and ys are arrays of integers to record the x- and y-coordinates of the coastline positions as selected by the mouse clicks. We have allowed up to 500 positions to be selected. (If the mouse is clicked more than 500 times when creating a map we throw an array-out-of-bound exception.)

The instance variable `size` denotes the current number of selected positions on the coastline. It denotes the number of times the mouse has been clicked.

A mouse listener is added so that whenever the mouse is clicked the x- and y-coordinates of the mouse's position are added to the arrays `xs` and `ys` respectively. With each new mouse click the coastline is repainted.

The `paintComponent` method invokes the instance method `drawLine` in the class `Graphics`. This method is similar to the other `Graphics` methods such as `drawRect` and `drawOval` that we met in Section 9.1. It has 4 integer parameters. The first two parameters denote respectively the x- and y-coordinates of a position p, say; the last two parameters denote respectively the x- and y-coordinates of a position q, say. When the `drawLine` method is invoked a straight line is drawn from p to q. In our case we get a straight line from the previously selected position to the newly selected position.

The code for the method `saveMap`:

- constructs a new `PrintWriter` object `pw` to write from the beginning of the text file whose name is passed as argument when the method is invoked;
- prints the number of selected positions (i.e. `size`) as the first line of the file;
- prints on each subsequent line the x- and y-coordinates of the next position selected, placing a space between them; this continues until all the selected positions have had their coordinates placed in the file;
- closes the print writer `pw`;
- resets `size` to 0 and repaints the panel (which consequently will now appear blank).

To confirm that the format of data stored on the given file is as described above, open the file *oz.txt* using any text reader and browse its contents.

The code for the method `closeMap` closes the `PrintWriter` object `pw` if it is not null (and as a consequence flushes the output stream ensuring the given file is up to date).

Consider now the class `CreateMapFrame`.

This class defines the window frame for the create window. It adds the two action buttons and the text field to a panel added to the bottom of the window pane, and instantiates an object of the class `CreateMapPanel` which it adds to the centre of the window pane.

When the button 'save' is pressed, the saveMap method is invoked in the class CreateMapPanel with the string appearing in the text field passed as argument. Hence the string names the file in which the map is stored.

When the button 'quit' is pressed, the closeMap method is invoked in the class CreateMapPanel, after which the program is terminated.

Displaying a map

Here is the code for the classes DisplayMapFrame and DisplayMapPanel which together implement the display window:

```
import genesis.*;
import javax.swing.*;
import java.awt.*;
import java.awt.event.*;

public  class DisplayMapFrame extends ExitFrame {
    /* Display the map stored in a file. */

    // instance variables
    private JTextField fileName;
    private DisplayMapPanel map = new DisplayMapPanel();

    public DisplayMapFrame ( ) {
        setBounds(450, 50, 450, 450);
        setTitle("Display the Map");
        Container c = getContentPane();
        fileName = new JTextField("", 20);
        JButton display = new JButton("display");
        display.addActionListener(new ActionListener() {
            public void actionPerformed(ActionEvent evt){
                map.displayMap(fileName.getText());
            }
        });
        JPanel p = new JPanel();
        p.setBackground(Color.white);
        p.add(display);
        p.add(fileName);
        c.add(p, "South");
        c.add(map, "Center");
    }
}
```

```
import javax.swing.*;
import java.awt.*;
import java.io.*;
import java.util.*;

public class DisplayMapPanel extends JPanel {
    // instance variables
    private int [] xs, ys;
    private int size = 0;
    private BufferedReader br;
    // constructor
    public DisplayMapPanel ( ) {
        setBackground(Color.blue);
    }
    public void paintComponent (Graphics g) {
        // draw map
        super.paintComponent(g);
        if (size > 0) {
            g.setColor(Color.yellow);
            g.fillPolygon(xs, ys, size);
        }
    }
    public void displayMap (String fileName) {
        try {
            br = new BufferedReader(new FileReader(fileName));
            size = Integer.parseInt(br.readLine());
            xs = new int [size];
            ys = new int [size];
            String line;
            for (int i = 0; i < size; i++) {
              line = br.readLine();
              StringTokenizer st = new StringTokenizer(line);
              xs[i] = Integer.parseInt(st.nextToken());
              ys[i] = Integer.parseInt(st.nextToken());
            }
            br.close();
            repaint();
        } catch (IOException e) {
            System.out.println("Error in displaying map: "+e);
            System.exit(0);
        }
    }
}
```

Discussion

Consider first the class DisplayMapPanel.

The code for the method displayMap:

- constructs a new BufferedReader object br to read from the beginning of the text file whose name is passed as argument when the method is invoked;
- reads the number of coordinate positions from the first line of the file and assigns the variable size to be this number;
- establishes the arrays xs and ys of length size; just as for the class CreateMapPanel these arrays record the x- and y-coordinates of the positions on the island's coastline;
- reads each subsequent line of the given file to extract the coordinates of the next position, and assigns these values to the arrays xs and ys respectively;
- closes the object br;
- repaints the panel.

The paintComponent method invokes the instance method fillPolygon in the class Graphics. This method is similar to the other Graphics methods such as fillRect and fillOval that we met in Section 9.1. It has 3 parameters. The first two parameters are integer arrays denoting respectively the x- and y-coordinates of positions in the plane; the last parameter denotes the number of such positions stored in these arrays.

When the fillPolygon method is invoked a solid polygon is drawn whose vertices have x- and y-coordinates given by the arrays xs and ys. In our case, the result is that a solid polygon is drawn whose vertices are the positions stored in the given file.

Consider now the class DisplayMapFrame. This class defines the window frame for the display window. It adds the action button and text field to a panel added to the bottom of the window pane, and instantiates an object of the DisplayMapPanel class which it adds to the centre of the window pane.

When the button 'display' is pressed, the displayMap method of the class DisplayMapPanel is invoked with the string appearing in the text field passed as argument. Hence this string denotes the name of the file storing the map to be displayed.

PROBLEM 21: improving map making

Once again open the folder *Map Making* and run the Main class.

Use the mouse to select positions in the create window and then press the 'save' button but without first entering a file name into the create window's text field. You will notice that a file-not-found exception is thrown and the application terminates.

Similarly, a file-not-found exception is thrown and the application terminates if the 'display' button is pressed without first entering a file name into the display window's text field.

Modify the code for the class `CreateMapPanel` so that if the 'save' button is pressed when there is no file name in the create window's text field, the string 'invalid file name' is displayed in the Output window.

Similarly modify the code for the class `DisplayMapPanel` so that if the 'display' button is pressed when there is no file name in the display window's text field, the string 'invalid file name' is displayed in the Output window.

Now add an action button 'undo' to the create window which when pressed results in the removal of the last position selected.

For help with this problem see Hints.

□

Chapter 11 self-check

Can you

- catch and handle an exception when it is created?
- throw an exception to be handled in the invoking method?
- create a text file and output text to that file?
- input text from a text file?
- partition a string into tokens?
- input text from the keyboard?

Do you understand

- the classes Java uses to throw exceptions?
- how exceptions can be caught and handled?
- the classes Java uses to perform text input and output?
- that I/O exceptions must be handled by any method in which such exceptions may occur?

Applets 12

Prerequisites

Chapter 12 applies many of the ideas we met in earlier chapters. In particular, it requires an understanding of:

- basic Java programming constructs;
- graphics and event handling as discussed in Chapter 9;
- GUI components as discussed in Chapter 10.

We also assume you are familiar with how to use a web browser such as Netscape Communicator or Internet Explorer.

Overview

As we have seen throughout *Java Genesis,* Java is a multi-purpose object-oriented programming language ideal for coding general applications. But this by itself only partly explains Java's popularity. A major reason for the popularity of the Java language lies in the fact that special Java applications known as *applets* can be embedded within web pages. When a web page is requested by a local computer and downloaded over the internet, any embedded Java applet is also downloaded and executed, provided the local computer has a Java-enabled web browser installed.

Applets can greatly enhance a web page, enabling information to be animated, games to be played, goods to be ordered, and so on. In this unit we investigate how applets can be constructed and embedded within a web page.

An applet is little more than a Java class that extends the class `JApplet`. The `JApplet` class is in the *javax.swing* package and has many (but not all) of the features that we associate with a window frame. In particular, an applet window has a content pane to contain panels and graphical components for display. A consequence of this is that an applet can create and make use of graphical and GUI components such as images, action buttons and text fields.

An applet is defined, just like any other Java class, within a file with a *.java* extension which when compiled produces a file with a *.class* extension. However, applets are instantiated in a completely different way. An applet must be referenced in an HTML document, i.e. a web page. (Usually an HTML document is stored as a file that has a *.html* or *.htm* extension.) The applet is executed when the web page is loaded into a Java-enabled web browser. Alternatively, an applet can be executed by running a special applet interpreter, the *applet viewer*, provided with Java's SDK.

In fact, using the applet viewer to run an applet is not exactly the same as running an applet from within a web browser. Because a web page can be downloaded over the internet, security must be a major concern. Consequently, an applet running in a web browser is usually unable to modify a file on the local computer or run any local executable program. These restrictions do not necessarily apply if the applet is run in the applet viewer.

12.1 Introducing applets

We look at some simple applets and discover how they were constructed. The general structure of applets is explored.

Problems:

1 drawing in an applet

2 an applet to toggle a square

3 an applet to steer a square

4 action buttons in applets

5 using the status bar

6 how an applet runs

12.2 Converting applications to applets

We investigate rewriting applications as applets and extract general rules for this conversion.

Problems:

7 toggle-neighbours puzzle as an applet

8 temperature-conversion as an applet

Learning outcomes

At the conclusion of Chapter 12 you will understand:

- the general structure of a Java applet and how that structure differs from Java applications;
- the methods within an applet and how they each contribute to the running of the applet;
- how to write a simple applet;
- how to create a simple HTML document in which to embed an applet;
- how to convert a Java application into an applet;
- how to run an applet in the applet viewer supplied with Java;
- how to run an applet in a Java-enabled web browser;

12.1 Introducing applets

To begin our exploration of applets, let's run some!

Running applets in the applet viewer

To run an applet we can use the *applet viewer* supplied with Java's SDK. This allows us to view applets without the necessity of opening a web browser.

PROBLEM 1: drawing in an applet

Open the folder *DisplayApplet*. This folder contains the classes `DisplayApplet` and `DisplayPanel` as well as the HTML file *DisplayApplet.html*.

To run this applet using Java's applet viewer we enter

```
appletviewer DisplayApplet.html
```

at the command line. (If you are using an IDE such as Kawa, selecting the HTML file and pressing the 'Run Java' button, or equivalent, will run the applet viewer.)

The applet viewer opens displaying various graphical objects.

Modify the code for the class `DisplayPanel` to display different graphical shapes and figures.

□

Discussion

If you think that the graphics displayed in this problem look familiar, you are right: they are the same graphics as displayed in Problem 3 of Chapter 9. It is illustrative to compare the code for the classes in the folder *Display Applet* above with the classes in the folder *Display Window* for Problem 3 of Chapter 9.

The first thing to observe is that the class `DisplayPanel` is in both folders and the code is identical. It is this class that contains the code to paint the images that we wish to display.

Compare now the class `DisplayApplet` in the *Display Applet* folder with the class `DisplayFrame` in the *Display Window* folder. Here is the code for the class `DisplayApplet`:

```
import javax.swing.*;
import java.awt.*;

public class DisplayApplet extends JApplet {
    /*
    Display various graphical objects in a window.
    */

    public void init ( ) {
        Container c = getContentPane();
        DisplayPanel dp = new DisplayPanel();
        c.add(dp);
    }
}
```

If you turn back to the code for the class `DisplayFrame` listed just before Problem 3 in Chapter 9, you will notice `DisplayApplet` is almost identical except that the class `DisplayApplet`:

- extends the class `JApplet` rather than the class `JFrame`;
- has no messages `setTitle` and `setBounds`; this is because the title and dimensions of an applet are fixed by the web page in which the applet is embedded and cannot be changed by the applet's code;
- has no specific constructor method; the code that was in the constructor method of `DisplayFrame` to add the panel to the associated content pane is now placed in an `init` method.

In addition, there is a `Main` class in the *Display Window* folder but no such class in the *Display Applet* folder. Instead there is an associated HTML document:

```
<HTML>
<HEAD>
<TITLE>Drawing in an Applet</TITLE>
</HEAD>
<BODY>
<H1>Displaying Graphics</H1>
<HR>
<APPLET CODE=DisplayApplet.class WIDTH=500 HEIGHT=500>
</APPLET>
<HR>
</BODY>
</HTML>
```

An HTML document is stored as a text file with a *.html* extension. For example, the above document is stored as the file *DisplayApplet.html*.

When running an applet the HTML file is not compiled. It is in the HTML document that the applet's title and size are set. The important line in this file is the one beginning with the tag '<APPLET'; here the *.class* file of the applet is identified and the dimension of the applet window is specified.

For this applet to work, the above HTML file, the identified *DisplayApplet.class* file and the file *DisplayPanel.class* need to be in the same folder. We could give any name to the HTML file, but generally we will give it the same name as the name of the class that extends `JApplet`, but with a *.html* extension.

In particular, notice that there is no `main` method required to run the applet, unlike an application which always requires a `main` method in order to run.

[*An aside*: The HTML language (**h**yper**t**ext **m**ark-up **l**anguage) is a subject worth studying for its own sake, but the above is as complicated as is required for our needs. Briefly, entities enclosed in angle brackets are tags or markers. A HTML document starts with the tag <HTML> and ends with the tag </HTML>. In general, a tag beginning with a slash is a closing tag to the corresponding start tag. A 'head' section precedes a 'body', and it is within the body that the applet is referenced and its dimensions are specified. You will observe that all the HTML documents needed to run the applets in this chapter have the same simple structure as the one above. *End aside*]

Running applets in a web browser

In Problem 1 we used the applet viewer to run the applet. If however, you have a Java-enabled browser such as Netscape Communicator installed on your computer, you can run the applet within the browser. First open the *Display*

Applet folder and then either double-click on the file *DisplayApplet.html*, or alternatively drag and drop this file into an open browser.

It is possible that your Netscape browser supports only Java 1.1 and is unable to run applets that make use of the Swing classes. In this case you may need to obtain the Swing add-on to Java 1.1 from the `java.sun.com` web page. Add the file *swing.jar* to the *Netscape\Communicator\Program\Java\Classes* folder.

If this still does not work you may need to down-load and install the full 'Java Plug-In' from the Sun web-site. This enables your browser to execute an applet on an external run-time environment supplied by Sun. You will also need to convert your HTML document into a format required to make use of this external environment. Sun supplies an HTML converter tool for this purpose (see the Sun web-site).

In the next problem we make use of the event handling mechanisms that the class `JApplet` inherits. In fact, these features are inherited from the same source as the class `JFrame`, and hence the sytax and semantics is the same.

PROBLEM 2: an applet to toggle a square

Open the folder *Toggle Square Applet* and run *ToggleSquareApplet.html* using the applet viewer. A red square appears in the applet viewer window; this square can be toggled between solid and hollow by positioning the mouse in the window and pressing the (left) mouse button.

Modify the code for the class `ToggleSquarePanel` so that other things happen when the mouse button is pressed. For example, the square toggles between red or blue, or the square is drawn in a new random position.

□

Discussion

This problem implements as an applet what was previously implemented as an application in Problem 9 of Chapter 9. Again it is illustrative to compare the code for the classes in the folder *Toggle Square Applet* above with the classes in the folder *Toggle Square* for Problem 9 of Chapter 9.

The first thing to observe is that, as with Problem 1, the panel classes in both folders are the same, i.e. the class `ToggleSquarePanel` is in both folders and the code is identical.

Compare now the class `ToggleSquareApplet` in the *Toggle Square Applet* folder with the class `ToggleSquareFrame` in the *Toggle Square* folder. Here is the code for the class `ToggleSquareApplet`:

```
import javax.swing.*;
import java.awt.*;

public class ToggleSquareApplet extends JApplet {

    public void init ( ) {
        Container c = getContentPane();
        ToggleSquarePanel p = new ToggleSquarePanel();
        c.add(p);
    }
}
```

If you turn back to the code for the class ToggleSquareFrame (listed just before Problem 9 in Chapter 9) you will notice ToggleSquareApplet is almost identical except that the class ToggleSquareApplet:

- imports the package *javax.swing* rather than the package *genesis*;
- extends the class JApplet rather than the class ExitFrame (the *genesis* package is needed in the class ToggleSquare to import the ExitFrame class; the *javax.swing* package is needed in the class ToggleSquareApplet to import the JApplet class);
- has no messages setTitle and setBounds;
- has the void method init rather than a constructor method to add the panel to the associated content pane.

In addition, there is no main method associated with ToggleSquareApplet. Instead this class has an associated HTML document:

```
<HTML>
<HEAD>
<TITLE>Toggle the Square</TITLE>
</HEAD>
<BODY>
<H1>Applet to Toggle a Square</H1>
<HR>
<APPLET CODE=ToggleSquareApplet.class WIDTH=400 HEIGHT=400>
</APPLET>
<HR>
</BODY>
</HTML>
```

which identifies the *.class* file of the applet and specifies the dimensions of the applet window.

The next problem shows how to associate a key listener with an applet.

PROBLEM 3: an applet to steer a square

Open the folder *Steer Square Applet* and run *SteerSquareApplet.html* using the applet viewer. A red square appears in the applet viewer window. This square can be moved by 10 pixels right, left up or down by pressing the corresponding arrow key.

Modify the code for the class `SteerSquareApplet` so that when an arrow key is pressed the square moves in the designated direction randomly between 5 and 50 pixels.

For help with this problem see Hints.

□

Discussion

This problem implements as an applet what was previously implemented as an application in Problem 18 of Chapter 9. Again it is illustrative to compare the code for the classes in the folder *Steer Square Applet* above with the classes in the folder *Steer Square* for Problem 18 of Chapter 9.

Once again observe that, as with Problems 1 and 2, the panel classes in both folders are the same, i.e. the class `SteerSquarePanel` is in both folders and the code is identical.

Compare now the class `SteerSquareApplet` in the *Steer Square Applet* folder with the class `SteerSquareFrame` in the *Steer Square* folder. Here is the code for the class `SteerSquareApplet`:

```
import javax.swing.*;
import java.awt.*;

public class SteerSquareApplet extends JApplet {

    public void init ( ) {
        Container c = getContentPane();
        SteerSquarePanel p = new SteerSquarePanel();
        c.add(p);
    }
}
```

If you turn back to the code for the class `SteerSquareFrame` (listed just before Problem 18 in Chapter 9) you will notice `SteerSquareApplet` differs in the same manner as discussed in Problems 1 and 2. That is, `SteerSquareApplet`:

- imports the package *javax.swing* rather than the package *genesis*;
- extends the class `JApplet` rather than the class `ExitFrame`;
- has no messages `setTitle` and `setBounds`;
- has the void method `init` rather than a constructor method to add the panel to the associated content pane.

Once again, there is no `main` method associated with `SteerSquareApplet`. Instead this class has an associated *SteerSquareApplet.html* file which identifies the *.class* file of the applet and specifies the dimensions of the applet window.

The next problem shows how to add action buttons (and by analogy other GUI components) to an applet.

PROBLEM 4: action buttons in applets

Open the folder *Button Toggle Applet* and run *ButtonToggleApplet.html* using the applet viewer. A solid red square and an action button appear in the applet viewer window. The square can be toggled between solid and hollow by pressing the button.

As in Problem 2, modify the code for the class `SqPanel` so that other things happen when the action button is pressed.

□

Discussion

This problem implements as an applet what was previously implemented as an application in Problem 7 of Chapter 10. Again it is illustrative to compare the code for the classes in the folder *Button Toggle Applet* above with the classes in the folder *Button Toggle* for Problem 7 of Chapter 10.

Once again observe that, as with Problems 1, 2 and 3, the panel classes in both folders are the same, i.e. the class `SqPanel` is in both folders and the code is identical.

Compare now the class `ButtonToggleApplet` in the *Button Toggle Applet* folder with the class `ButtonToggleFrame` in the *Button Toggle* folder. The code for the class `ButtonToggleApplet` is given at the top of the next page.

If you turn back to the code for the class `ButtonToggleFrame` (listed just before Problem 7 in Chapter 10) you will notice `SteerSquareApplet` differs in just the way we would expect from analogy with Problems 1, 2 and 3.

```
import javax.swing.*;
import java.awt.*;
import java.awt.event.*;

public class ButtonToggleApplet extends JApplet {
    /*
    A square that toggles when a button is pressed.
    */

    // instance variable
    private SqPanel square = new SqPanel();

    public void init ( ) {
        JButton togBut = new JButton("toggle square");
        togBut.addActionListener(new ActionListener() {
            public void actionPerformed (ActionEvent e) {
                square.toggle();
            }
        });
        Container c = getContentPane();
        JPanel butPanel = new JPanel();
        butPanel.add(togBut);
        butPanel.setBackground(Color.white);
        c.add(butPanel, "South");
        c.add(square, "Center");
    }
}
```

Once again, there is no `main` method associated with `ButtonToggleApplet`. Instead this class has an associated *ButtonToggleApplet.html* file which identifies the *.class* file of the applet and specifies the dimensions of the applet window.

You may have observed that at the bottom of the applet viewer the current status of the applet is displayed. The area where this information appears is known as the *status bar*. We can output text to this bar by invoking the `showStatus` method and passing as a string argument the text we want to display. This is illustrated in the next problem.

PROBLEM 5: using the status bar

Open the folder *Buttons Applet* and run *ButtonsApplet.html* using the applet viewer. The applet viewer opens with two buttons at its top. When the button 'count' is pressed a message is displayed in the status bar indicating the total number of times the button has been pressed. When the button 'colour' is pressed the background colour of the window changes.

Here is the code for the class ButtonsApplet:

```
import javax.swing.*;
import java.awt.*;
import java.awt.event.*;

public class ButtonsApplet extends JApplet {

    // instance variables
    private Color [] colours =
        {Color.red, Color.green, Color.blue, Color.cyan};
    private int colourNum = 0;
    private int count = 0;
    private Container c;

    public void init () {
        c = getContentPane();
        c.setBackground(colours[colourNum]);
        JButton countBut = new JButton("count");
        countBut.addActionListener( new ActionListener() {
            public void actionPerformed (ActionEvent e) {
                count++;
                showStatus
                    ("You have pressed button 'count' "
                                                +count+" times.");
            }
        });
        JButton colourBut = new JButton("colour");
        colourBut.addActionListener( new ActionListener() {
            public void actionPerformed (ActionEvent e) {
                colourNum = (colourNum+1) % colours.length;
                c.setBackground(colours[colourNum]);
            }
        });
        JPanel p = new JPanel();
        p.add(countBut);
        p.add(colourBut);
        c.add (p, "North");
    }
}
```

Modify the code for the class ButtonsApplet so that when the button 'colour' is pressed, the new colour of the window is displayed in the status bar.

For help with this problem see Hints.

□

Discussion

As we would expect from analogy with the earlier applet problems, the GUI components are constructed within the `init` method. As before there is no main method. The statement

```
showStatus
    ("You have pressed button 'count' " +count+" times.");
```

is used to display in the status bar the number of times the 'count' button has been pressed.

Notice that if this applet is run in a browser such as Netscape Communicator rather than the applet viewer, the status bar is located at the bottom of the browser rather than at the bottom of the applet.

How an applet runs

All Java applications have a class containing a `main` method. It is this method that the system automatically invokes when we run the application. An applet on the other hand does not require a `main` method. Instead the `init` method is automatically invoked when we run the applet.

The class `JApplet` has an `init` method that is either inherited or redefined by any subclass. Often we redefine this method in our applet subclass so as to implement whatever initialisations are required. For example, in Problems 1 to 5 we redefined the `init` method.

The `init` method works much like a constructor method. Typically, code to set the value of instance variables, to create GUI components such as action buttons and text fields and to add event listeners to these GUI components is placed in the `init` method. The `init` method has the declaration:

```
public void init ( ) { ... }
```

This method is invoked once only.

After the `init` method has been invoked, the `start` method is automatically invoked. Like the `init` method, the `start` method is either inherited from the class `JApplet` or redefined in the applet subclass. In each of Problems 1 to 5 we have simply inherited this method and not redefined it.

The `start` method is invoked whenever the applet viewer window is reopened (after being minimised) or, if the applet is within a web page and is being run within a browser, whenever that page is returned to after loading some other page. Consequently, unlike the `init` method, the `start` method can be invoked repeatedly.

Typically, we redefine the `start` method if we want to resume some suspended animation whenever the applet viewer is reopened or the web page containing the applet is revisited. In our applet examples we will not need to redefine this method as we will not be doing anything that needs to be suspended when the applet viewer is minimized or some other web page is loaded. The `start` method has the declaration:

```
public void start ( ) { ... }
```

The `paintComponent` method of any associated panel is automatically invoked when the applet's window is displayed, e.g. when the applet is started for the first time, or when the applet is reopened after being minimised, or when the applet window is redisplayed after being obscured either by another window or because the applet window has been moved partially off the screen.

There is one other method, `stop`, that is relevant to our discussion of how an applet runs. This method is also inherited from `JApplet` and is automatically invoked when the user moves off the applet (or the web page containing the applet). The `stop` method, like the method `start`, can be invoked repeatedly. It only needs to be redefined if the applet performs animation or some other resource-intensive activity. We shall not need to redefine this method in any of our examples.

The next problem illustrates how the `init`, `start` and `paintComponent` methods are invoked.

PROBLEM 6: how an applet runs

Open the folder *Run Applet* and run *RunApplet.html* using the applet viewer. The applet displays information about the number of times the methods `init`, `start` and `paintComponent` have been invoked.

Experiment with this applet to observe what happens when we

- minimise and then reopen the applet;
- move the applet window so that it is (partially) off the screen and then move it back;
- move some other window to (partially) obscure the applet and then remove the obscuring window.

Here is the code for the classes RunApplet and RunPanel:

```
import javax.swing.*;
import java.awt.*;

public class RunApplet extends JApplet {

    /* Testing how an applet runs */

    // instance variables
    RunPanel p = new RunPanel();

    public void init ( ) {
        Container c = getContentPane();
        p.incInitCount();
        c.add(p);
    }

    public void start ( ) {
        p.incStartCount();
    }
}
```

```
import javax.swing.*;
import java.awt.*;

public class RunPanel extends JPanel {

    // instance variables
    private int initCount = 0;
    private int startCount = 0;
    private int paintCount = 0;

    public RunPanel ( ) {
        setBackground(Color.white);
    }

    public void incInitCount ( ) {
        initCount++;
    }

    public void incStartCount ( ) {
        startCount++;
    }
```

```
        public void paintComponent (Graphics g) {
            super.paintComponent(g);
            paintCount++;
            g.drawString
                ("init invoked "+initCount+" times", 50, 50);
            g.drawString
                ("start invoked "+startCount+" times", 50, 100);
            g.drawString
                ("paintComponent invoked "
                                +paintCount+" times", 50, 150);
        }
    }
```

Notice in particular that although the paintComponent method is invoked when anything obscuring part of the applet is removed, only those parts of the applet that were obscured are actually repainted.

□

12.2 Converting applications to applets

In each of Problems 1 to 4 in the last section we compared the code to run the associated applet with the code to run an equivalent application. From these comparisons its not too hard to deduce the essential steps required in order to convert an application into an applet (or vice versa). In this section we extract these steps explicitly by looking in detail at how to convert into applets the toggle-neighbours puzzle application (see Section 10.2) and the temperature conversion GUI application (see Section 10.4).

The toggle-neighbours puzzle

To remind yourself of what the toggle-neighbours puzzle looks like, open the folder *Tog Neigh Puzzle* and run the Main class. The code in this application comes unchanged from Problem 3 in Chapter 10.

Our conversion of this application into an applet will be done in two stages. First we will convert the application into an applet to run the 5 by 5 toggle-neighbours puzzle. Then we will extend this applet so as to run a toggle-neighbours puzzle of any dimension.

The 5 by 5 toggle-neighbours puzzle as an applet

Create a new folder *Tog Neigh Applet* and copy into this folder the two files *TogNeighFrame.java* and *SquarePanel.java* from the *Tog Neigh Puzzle* folder. (The `Main` class in the *Tog Neigh Puzzle* folder can be ignored as it contains only the `main` method and this will not be needed by our applet.)

Consider first the class `TogNeighFrame`.

Step1: adjusting the import list

To the import list at the top of the class add the statement:

```
import javax.swing.*;
```

We can also remove the '`import genesis.*;`' statement from the import list. The *genesis* package was needed only to extend the class `ExitFrame`, but as we shall see, this class is not extended in the applet.

Step 2: extending the class `JApplet`

Change the class declaration by changing the class name to `TogNeighApplet` and replacing the class `ExitFrame` by the class `JApplet`. The class declaration now becomes:

```
public class TogNeighApplet extends JApplet {
```

Step 3: converting the constructor to the `init` method

The code that normally goes in an application's constructor is put into an applet's `init` method. So replace the constructor method by changing the declaration to:

```
public void init ( ) {
```

Step 4: modifying the code for the `init` method

In the application the values of the variables `numWide` and `numHigh` are set by the user via dialog boxes. These values are then used to set the dimensions of the window. Because the dimensions of the applet's window must be fixed in advance and specified in the associated HTML document (as we shall see in Step 9 below) we need to follow a different strategy.

For the present we shall fix the value of both of these variables to be 5 and consider later how we can pass other values as parameters to the applet. So the first two lines of the code in the `init` method become:

```
numwide = 5;
numHigh = 5;
```

We also need to completely remove the `setTitle` and `setBounds` statements. The title and dimension of the applet will be specified in the associated HTML document.

Step 5: setting the size of the squares

In the application, the puzzle is positioned in the centre of the window with a border of white space. For the applet it is easier if we set the size of the window to exactly fit the puzzle with no border of white space.

We shall set the applet window to be 250 pixels wide and high (see Step 9 below) and, so that they fit exactly into the window, we shall set each puzzle toggle-square to be 50 pixels wide and high. Consequently we need to set the bounds of the panels representing the squares of the puzzle so that panel `i` has position and size given by:

```
panels[i].setBounds(50*(i%numWide), 50*(i/numWide), 50, 50);
```

This completes the conversion of `TogNeighFrame` to the `TogNeighApplet` class. The code for the `togNeighOf` method remain unchanged as it does not perform any actions that applets don't understand.

Here is the complete code for the class `TogNeighApplet`:

```
import javax.swing.*;
import java.awt.*;

public class TogNeighApplet extends JApplet {

    /*
    Rectangular grid of squares that each toggle together
    with neighbours when the mouse is positioned in the
    square and the button pressed.
    */

    // instance variables
    private int numWide, numHigh, totNum;
    private SquarePanel [] panels;

    public void init ( ) {
        numWide = 5;
        numHigh = 5;
        totNum = numWide*numHigh;
        Container c = getContentPane();
        c.setLayout(null);
        panels = new SquarePanel [totNum];
```

```
        for (int i=0; i<totNum; i++) {
            panels[i] = new SquarePanel(i, this);
            panels[i].setBounds
                (50*(i%numWide), 50*(i/numWide), 50, 50);
            c.add(panels[i]);
        }
    }

    public void togNeighOf (int index) {
        // toggle the neighbours of tile with given index
        if (index%numWide != numWide-1)
                panels[index+1].toggle();
        if (index%numWide != 0)
                panels[index-1].toggle();
        if (index < totNum-numWide)
                panels[index+numWide].toggle();
        if (index > numWide-1)
                panels[index-numWide].toggle();
    }
}
```

Step 6: converting the SquarePanel class

The class SquarePanel is essentially unchanged. The code for this class does not perform any action that applets don't understand. However, we do need to change the two references to the TogNeighFrame class to reference the TogNeighApplet class instead. To be specific, the second instance variable in this class becomes

```
private TogNeighApplet mediator;
```

and the declaration of the constructor method becomes:

```
public SquarePanel (int index, TogNeighApplet med) {
```

Step 7: converting main to start

Applets do not have a main method and code that normally appears in an application's main method goes into the applet's start method. In this case, however, the main method is the only method in the class Main in the *Tog Neigh Puzzle* folder, and this method does nothing but instantiate an object of the class TogNeighFrame and set it to be visible. As both these tasks for the class TogNeighApplet are performed automatically in an applet we can ignore this method (and hence the class Main) entirely and simply accept without redefinition the start method inherited from the class JApplet.

Step 8: compilation

Now we have converted the classes `TogNeighFrame` (to `TogNeighApplet`) and `SquarePanel` we can compile them.

Step 9: creating a web page

To run the applet we need to create an HTML document that embeds the applet. Here is our document which we've placed in the file *TogNeighApplet.html*:

```
<HTML>
<HEAD>
<TITLE>Toggle-neighbours Puzzle</TITLE>
</HEAD>
<BODY>
<H1>Toggle-neighbours Puzzle</H1>
<HR>
<APPLET CODE=TogNeighApplet.class WIDTH=250 HEIGHT=250>
</APPLET>
<HR>
</BODY>
</HTML>
```

Notice that the dimensions of the applet are defined to be 250 pixels wide and 250 pixels high. As each toggle-square in the puzzle is 50 pixels by 50 pixels then the 25 squares in the 5 by 5 puzzle will exactly fit within the applet's window.

Step 10: running the applet

To run the applet, use the applet viewer to run *TogNeighApplet.html*. Alternatively, if you have a Java-enabled web browser installed, open the *Tog Neigh Applet* folder and double-click on this HTML file, or drag and drop the file into an open web browser.

(We have done the conversion exactly as described above. To run our applet open the folder *Tog 5 by 5 Applet*.)

The general toggle-neighbours puzzle as an applet

So far we have an applet for the 5 by 5 toggle-neighbours puzzle. But what about the general case where any number of columns and rows are allowed? In the original Java application the size of each square in the toggle-neighbours puzzle was fixed at 50 pixels by 50 pixels, but the dimensions of the window was then adjusted to fit the puzzle once the user had supplied the number of columns and rows.

For an applet, the dimensions of the window are fixed in advance and cannot be changed. So how can we generalise the 5 by 5 puzzle to allow for any number of rows and columns? Rather than adjusting the window's dimensions, we can leave them fixed at 250 pixels by 250 pixels and adjust instead the size of the squares in the puzzle so that the puzzle will fit within this window. Let us see how we can do this.

Step 11: declaring parameters

First modify the HTML document to become:

```
<HTML>
<HEAD>
<TITLE>Toggle-neighbours Puzzle</TITLE>
</HEAD>
<BODY>
<H1>Toggle-neighbours Puzzle</H1>
<HR>
<APPLET CODE=TogNeighApplet.class WIDTH=250 HEIGHT=250>
<PARAM NAME=across VALUE="5">
<PARAM NAME=down VALUE="5">
</APPLET>
<HR>
</BODY>
</HTML>
```

The only difference is that we have included the declaration of two parameters `across` and `down` and set the value of each to be the string `"5"`.

Notice the syntax for declaring parameters. In particular, notice that the value of a parameter is a string. The parameter declarations are placed before the tag </APPLET> that ends the 'APPLET' section. As we shall see in the next step, the values of these parameters can be passed to the applet.

Step 12: passing parameters to an applet

We want to set the values of the variables `numWide` and `numHigh` to be the values of the parameters `across` and `down` respectively, but in each case converted from a string into an integer. The values of these parameters are extracted by sending the `getParameter` message and passing as argument to this message a string representing the name of the parameter whose value we want. Hence in our current case we replace the first two lines of the code in the `init` method by:

```
numWide = Integer.parseInt(getParameter("across"));
numHigh = Integer.parseInt(getParameter("down"));
```

If we now recompile and run the applet we will get exactly what we had before because the value of both of the parameters is currently set to be the string "5".

Step 13: adjusting for arbitrary-valued parameters

In the case when the values of the parameters are arbitrary, we need to adjust the size of the puzzle's toggle-squares to fit the fixed-size applet window.

First, to the class `TogNeighApplet` add a new instance variable `size`:

```
private int size;
```

This variable will denote the common width and height of each puzzle square.

Next, to the method `init` insert the following statement as the third line of code:

```
size = 250/Math.max(numWide, numHigh);
```

This fixes the size of the puzzle's squares so that either the puzzle's width is the width of the window or the puzzle's height is the height of the window, whichever is the larger.

[*An aside*: Here we have used the value 250 as we know that the applet is 250 pixels wide and 250 pixels high. If we want to allow for an applet window of unknown dimensions we would code

```
Dimension d = getSize();
size = Math.min(d.width,d.height)/Math.max(numWide,numHigh);
```

replacing 250 by the minimum of the applet's width and height. *End aside*]

Next, change the declaration of `panels[i]` for each `i` in the for-loop at the end of the `init` method to become:

```
panels[i] = new SquarePanel(i, this, size);
```

That is, pass `size` as a third argument when constructing the panels for the squares so that the `SquarePanel` class knows how big to make the puzzle's squares. (Of course, we will therefore need to modify the class `SquarePanel` to accommodate this change; see the details below.)

Next, to allow for the squares' size, set the bounds of each panel so that button `i` has position and size given by:

```
panels[i].setBounds
        (size*(i%numWide), size*(i/numWide), size, size);
```

That is, the value '50' has been replaced throughout by 'size'.

Finally, update the code for the class SquarePanel. First, to this class add the instance variable size:

```
private int size;
```

As in the class TogNeighApplet, this variable will denote the common width and height of each puzzle square.

Next, change the declaration of the constructor method to become:

```
public SquarePanel
            (int index, TogNeighApplet med, int sqSize) {
```

That is, add one more parameter of type int. Now insert in this constructor method as the third line of code:

```
size = sqSize;
```

to set the variable size to the value passed as the third argument to the constructor method.

Finally, the '48' in the paintComponent method of the class SquarePanel is replaced by 'size-2'. Here is the complete code for this modified method:

```
public void paintComponent (Graphics g) {
    // paint square in the window
    super.paintComponent(g);
    g.setColor (Color.red);
    if (filled) g.fillRect(1, 1, size-2, size-2);
    else g.drawRect(1, 1, size-2, size-2);
}
```

PROBLEM 7: toggle-neighbours puzzle as an applet

Construct the file *TogNeighApplet.html* and create the classes TogNeighApplet and SquarePanel as described above, compile the classes and run the applet.

Try inserting other values for the parameters across and down in the file *TogNeighPuzzle.html* to check that the size of the puzzle's squares are automatically adjusted to fit into the applet's window.

For help with this problem see Hints.

□

Temperature conversion

What we shall do is go throught the steps required to convert the Fahrenheit/Centigrade temperature GUI application discussed in Section 10.4 into an applet.

To remind yourself of what the Fahrenheit/Centigrade temperature conversion application looks like, open the folder *Temperature Conversion* and run the `Main` class. The code in this application comes unchanged from Problem 6 of Chapter 10. Our conversion of this application into an applet will closely follow the steps we used to convert the toggle-neighbours puzzle application.

Create a new folder *Convert Temp Applet* and copy into this folder the file *ConversionFrame.java* from the *Temperature Conversion* folder. (The `Main` class in the *Temperature Conversion* folder can be ignored as it contains only the `main` method and this will not be needed by our applet.) We are now ready to convert the application into an applet.

Step1: adjusting the import list

We can remove the '`import genesis.*;`' statement from the import list. The *genesis* package was needed only to extend the class `ExitFrame` but this class is not extended in the applet.

Step 2: extending the class `Japplet`

Change the class declaration by changing its name to `ConversionApplet` and replacing the class `ExitFrame` by the class `JApplet`. The class declaration now becomes:

```
public class ConversionApplet extends JApplet {
```

Step 3: converting the constructor to the `init` method

Replace the constructor method by changing the declaration to:

```
public void init ( ) {
```

Step 4: modifying the code for the `init` method

As usual we remove the `setTitle` and `setBounds` statements. The dimension of the application window is 350 pixels by 250 pixels. The same dimensions will be specified for the applet in the associated HTML document, as we shall see later.

Step 5: adding the GUI components

The code for adding the GUI components is placed in the `init` method and is unchanged from the code previously in the constructor method.

Step 6: converting `main` to `start`

Once again the `main` method is the only method in the class `Main` in the *Temperature Conversion* folder, and this method does nothing but instantiate an object of the class `ConversionFrame` and set it to be visible. As both these tasks for the class `ConversionApplet` are performed automatically in an applet we can ignore this method (and hence the class `Main`) entirely and simply accept without redefinition the `start` method inherited from the class `JApplet`.

Step 7: compilation

The modifications are completed and we can compile the `ConversionApplet` class.

Step 8: creating a web page

To run the applet we need to create an HTML document that embeds the applet. Here is our document which is stored in the file *ConversionApplet.html*:

```
<HTML>
<HEAD>
<TITLE>Fahrenheit/Centigrade Conversion</TITLE>
</HEAD>
<BODY>
<H1>Fahrenheit/Centigrade Conversion</H1>
<HR>
<APPLET CODE=ConversionApplet.class WIDTH=350 HEIGHT=250>
</APPLET>
<HR>
</BODY>
</HTML>
```

PROBLEM 8: temperature conversion as an applet

Construct the file *ConversionApplet.html* and create the `ConversionApplet` class as described above, compile the class and run the applet.

Verify that the applet has the same functionality as the original application by inserting various temperatures into the text fields and converting them.

For help with this problem see Hints.

□

Chapter 12 self-check

Can you

- construct a simple applet?
- convert a Java application into an applet?
- embed an applet within a simple HTML document?
- use the applet viewer to run an applet?
- run an applet within a Java-enabled web browser?

Do you understand

- the difference between a Java application and an applet?
- which methods are needed to run an applet?
- the role played by the methods `init` and `start` in an applet?

Index